Perspectives on the History of Higher Education

ROGER L. GEIGER, EDITOR
THE PENNSYLVANIA STATE UNIVERSITY

EDITORIAL BOARD

Joan N. Burstyn, *Syracuse University*
Katherine Reynolds Chaddock, *University of South Carolina*
Lester F. Goodchild, *University of Massachusetts—Boston*
Lynn D. Gordon, *University of Rochester*
Peter D. Hall, *Harvard University*
Hugh Hawkins, *Amherst College*
Jurgen Herbst, *University of Wisconsin—Madison*
Philo Hutcheson, *Georgia State University*
Helen Lefkowitz Horowitz, *Smith College*
David R. Jones, *Daylesford,* Victoria, Australia
W. Bruce Leslie, *State University of New York, College at Brockport*
James McLachlan, *Princeton,* New Jersey
Walter P. Metzger, *Columbia University*
Patricia A. Palmieri, *CUNY,* Staten Island
Harold J. Perkin, *London,* England
David B. Potts, *Tacoma,* Washington
Harold S. Wechsler, Former Editor, *University of Rochester*
Roger L. Williams, *The Pennsylvania State University*

EDITORIAL ASSISTANTS

Christian K. Anderson, *The Pennsylvania State University*
Trudi T. Haupt, *The Pennsylvania State University*

On the Cover:
The faculty, friends, and coeducational student body of St. Olaf's School in 1879 (courtesy, Shaw-Olson Center for College History, St. Olaf College).

Perspectives on the History of Higher Education

History of Higher Education Annual

Volume Twenty-Four, 2005

Roger L. Geiger
EDITOR

LONDON AND NEW YORK

First published 2005 by Transaction Publishers

Published 2017 by Routledge
2 Park Square, Milton Park, Abingdon, Oxon OX14 4RN
711 Third Avenue, New York, NY 10017, USA

Routledge is an imprint of the Taylor & Francis Group, an informa business

Copyright © 2005 by Taylor & Francis.

All rights reserved. No part of this book may be reprinted or reproduced or utilised in any form or by any electronic, mechanical, or other means, now known or hereafter invented, including photocopying and recording, or in any information storage or retrieval system, without permission in writing from the publishers.

Notice:
Product or corporate names may be trademarks or registered trademarks, and are used only for identification and explanation without intent to infringe.

ISSN: 0737-2698
ISBN 13: 978-1-4128-0517-9 (pbk)

Contents

Editor's Note	vi
Piggy Goes to Harvard: Mass Magazines, the Middle Class, and the Re-Conceptualization of College for a Corporate Age, 1895–1910 *Daniel A. Clark*	1
"What Gender Is Lex?" Women, Men, and Power Relations in Colleges of the Nineteenth Century *Michael David Cohen*	41
The "Problem of the Gifted Student": National Research Council Efforts to Identify and Cultivate Undergraduate Talent in a New Era of Mass Education, 1919–1929 *Jane Robbins*	91
Reds, Race, and Research: Homer P. Rainey and the Grand Texas Tradition of Political Interference, 1939–1944 *Susan R. Richardson*	125
A Not-So-Systematic Effort to Study Art: Albert Barnes and Lincoln University *Edward Epstein and Marybeth Gasman*	173
Selected Recent Dissertations in the History of Higher Education	191
Contributors	211

Editor's Note

Perspectives on the History of Higher Education continues under this new title the *History of Higher Education Annual*. Since 1981 the *Annual* has been the principal academic journal in the United States for scholarship on the history of higher education. The new title signifies no alteration of that role, but rather a title that reflects content rather than periodicity. In addition to publishing high-quality, refereed historical scholarship, the journal has always sought synthetic and interpretive writings and broad review essays. It has also sought to serve the community of scholars engaged in this field through services such as "Selected Recent Dissertations in the History of Higher Education." In sum, the *Annual* has traditionally provided multiple perspectives on the history of higher education, and *Perspectives* is dedicated to continuing that role.

Roger L. Geiger
Editor

Piggy Goes to Harvard: Mass Magazines, the Middle Class, and the Re-Conceptualization of College for a Corporate Age, 1895–1910

Daniel A. Clark

For too long historians of higher education and American culture have taken for granted the swift embrace of college education by Americans. Choosing to focus more on the changes within academia and professions as the source of expansion for American higher education, scholars have viewed the rising popularity of college as a natural byproduct of modernization or of an expanding status-conscious middle class. Consequently, historians have overlooked how popular expectations of college may have shaped higher education and how the evolving conceptions of the benefits of a college education factored heavily into the emerging notions of class and masculinity around 1900.

This study seeks to examine some of the formative representations and visions of American colleges and universities in mass periodicals that helped to shape the broader public perception of the place of college in Americans' visions of success and identity (here male, middle-class identity). Essentially the nation's first truly national media, the mass magazines explored in this article (*Saturday Evening Post*, *Munsey's*, *Cosmopolitan*, *Collier's*, and *American Magazine*) functioned as a popular forum where editors, writers, contributors, and advertisers collectively redefined the ideal college education in ways that reflected the peculiar anxieties and longings of an emerging corporate middle class. In these magazines, the imagined benefits of a college education for a corporate businessman (posited as the American norm) coalesced around a vision of a hybrid curriculum that could at once instill the traditional liberal culture of a gentleman as well as the practical scientific mindset of the modern businessman. Ultimately this popular vision of the curricular benefits of college as filtered through and widely disseminated by the mass media informed American expectations of and demand for higher education at least as much as any reforms within higher education or any demands of industrialists for personnel.

As early as 1895, when *Munsey's Magazine* asked "Should Your Boy Go to College?" the article presented the subject not for the benefit of the elite but for the "practical men of action." The author

---

Perspectives on the History of Higher Education 24 (2005): 1-40.
©2005. ISBN: 1-4128-0517-1

had in mind the people who read *Munsey's*, people whose sons looked toward business careers and whose families had limited means and thus asked, justifiably, "whether or not those four years might have been better spent."[1] These magazines knew their readership. Their readers were not the wealthy upper class who took the old literary monthlies, but a new aspiring group, primarily engaged in business, looking both to the past and the future for guidance and inspiration.[2] George Horace Lorimer, editor of the *Saturday Evening Post*, had these very folks in mind when he asked the president of Princeton to pointedly address "Should a Business Man Have a College Education?" Such articles peppered these new mass periodicals (*Munsey's*, the *Post*, *Collier's Weekly*, and *Cosmopolitan*).[3]

Despite strong reservations about the curriculum at colleges, despite lingering doubts about the college graduate's fitness to start at the bottom, and despite the reluctance to give up on the self-made man, the answer that these magazines gave their readers to the question "should your son go to college?" was a resounding yes. Businessmen, railroad men—these were the rising professional-managerial class (a new middle class of white-collar, corporate oriented businessmen) that the magazines arose alongside and they had never considered college necessary, but times were changing fast.[4] In almost every instance where these magazines asked, "should your boy go to college?" the issue revolved around the new responsibilities of the businessman as a leader, business' need for good men, and (implicitly) concerns about the new paths to success. The "crying need at the top of the ladder," proclaimed a *Cosmopolitan* writer in 1901, "is for men with resourcefulness, executive ability and courage to assume responsibilities"; or "men who can act as lieutenants," as an industrialist quoted in *Collier's* noted.[5] Those self-made critics of education, according to former President Grover Cleveland in a featured *Post* article on the value of college education, failed to recognize "the extent of the revolution in the conditions of success." Enterprises were no longer small, stressed Cleveland; they operated on a vast scale.[6] A new order had dawned and the magazines would designate college men as the lieutenants-in-training— men who would, "solve the riddles of nature and push forward the electric chariot of the world's commerce."[7]

But just what exactly did these editors and contributors have in mind when they posited the college graduate as the new business leader for the modern age, and thus collectively trumpeted college as the new route to business success and upward mobility? Exactly what kind of leader and what kind of college? No magazine articles answered these questions or captured the profound generational angst (how to prepare young men for a changing business world) better than the *Post*'s series "Letters from a Self-Made Merchant to His Son" and its successor "Old Gorgon Graham," which together ran from 1901 through 1904. Written anonymously by *Post* editor George Horace Lorimer himself, the articles took the form of letters written by John "Old Gorgon" Graham to his son. Graham was the fictitious head of his own Chicago pork-packing firm that he built up from scratch, a quintessential self-made man. With the rushing tide of changes sweeping a rapidly industrializing America, Lorimer could have used such a voice as Graham's to address any number of pressing social issues. But, significantly, the overarching issue Lorimer wished to confront was the passing of the torch, so to speak, from the self-made men to their more privileged sons, and through this issue, the greater problem of fashioning leadership for a new corporate and commercial age.[8]

Responding to this growing concern, Lorimer's "Letters from a Self-Made Merchant" and the "Old Gorgon Graham" series tackled the issue of the ideal training for the next generation of commercial and industrial leaders. And the very first letter indicated the radical element of this proposed new training, as John Graham addressed his son Pierpont (affectionately known as "Piggy") preparing for his final year at Harvard.[9] Why a college education for a future meat packer? "Like most fellows who haven't any too much of it," wrote John, "I've a great deal of respect for education." For John Graham (Lorimer), this meant an education rooted in Matthew Arnold-style liberal culture, acquainting oneself with the best that has been thought and done, and thus satisfying one honored component of Victorian manhood.[10]

But, significantly, culture hardly constituted the sole reason Old Gorgon Graham sent Piggy to Harvard. Times had changed and the college man, according to Graham, could prove a valuable asset. To demonstrate, Graham recounted the tale of the first college man he ever hired—the son of a friend fallen on hard times. Putting the fellow to work on a loading gang, Graham expected the boy to break only to find later that the college man had been promoted. And he continued to progress up through the ranks by thinking of ways to make the work easier—an overhead railway system for the loading gang, a time clock to keep track of men, ordering typewriters rather than having a personal secretary copy the letters. College had trained his mind to consider the big picture, to look beyond his narrow job and to use the newest scientific technology to solve problems. Finally, Graham's college man excelled at advertising, the new frontier of scientific commercial conquest that also required creativity and breadth.[11] Graham (Lorimer) depicted the college man as possessing the ideal education for the future executive—liberal education endowing the proper culture of a gentleman yet also bestowing the mental precision and breadth to bring scientific order and creativity into the business world.

In essence, Lorimer formulated a blueprint for all who aspired to be the lieutenants and captains, the managers and executives of the emerging corporate world. The "Letters" series represented how the magazines, in their efforts to address the concerns and aspirations of their readers, posited the American college as an experience uniquely suited to fulfill the emerging notions of success and masculinity. Piggy went to Harvard to become cultured and a gentleman. And this liberal breadth seemed particularly important for a future leader, but so did the problem-solving skills a liberal education simultaneously imparted, reflecting higher education's new association with modern science. Hard work in the stockyards and working up through the ranks purged the unmanly elements still associated with college, as did the advent of college athletics.[12] The series, then, exemplified the magazine's attempt to both resonate with and guide its readers, actively participating not only in a reconfiguration of the channels to success in a new age, but also re-conceptualizing the benefits of college to fit these new demands.

Historians have long taken the emergence of college as a new rung on the ladder of American success as an obvious byproduct of modernization.[13] Collectively, these studies illuminated the major currents of change in academia and the emerging corporate world that indeed brought the heretofore-antagonistic worlds together.[14] Most of these histories explore only pieces of either curricular or business transformation. They shed little light on exactly how Americans integrated college into their cultural identifications and expectations. The correlation between college and success blossomed out of altered cultural perceptions as much as direct practical utility since, as David Brown has pointed out, around the turn of the century when enrollments began to rise at colleges and more graduates entered into business, specialized courses accounted for only a small percentage of coursework. Most graduates, even those going into business, received a liberal education.[15] Historians have missed the role of the media and specifically the new middle-class magazines in defining, shaping, and developing the ideal of the college-educated businessman.[16] And "The Plain Business Man" (as the *Post* put it), to the editors of these new mass periodicals, represented the quintessential American man, their typical male reader.[17] These magazines acted as forums that attempted to resonate with and help shape the identifications and expectations of an emerging group of Americans (the corporate, professional middle class), proud of their part in modern changes but anxious about these same changes and often longing for traditional signs of status and authority.[18]

A careful examination of these magazines uncovers a wide and searching discourse on the potential benefits of a college education in articles and editorials. And this discourse was intertwined with the magazines' efforts to address their readers' concerns over an evolving corporate world that called for the adaptation of cherished notions of advancement and manhood. The aspiring middle-class American man of the late nineteenth century clung to prevailing notion of success that stressed male autonomy, independence, and that through work, one acquired many of the key elements of character. Middle-class men, hired as corporate managers or white-collar employees, even when well compensated, faced the reality that their working lives failed to live up to the traditional conceptions of self-made manhood. How would one forge character and toughness as an accountant in an office? As scholars of American masculinity have articulated, American men (the middle class in particular) created new avenues to cope with this "crisis of masculinity," such as the rise of sports, fraternal orders, the reinvigoration of martial virtues, and in general the cult of the strenuous life.[19] And the larger study of which this article is a part explores in depth how the mass magazines spearheaded a refashioning of the popular image of college to assuage the conflicting and often contradictory elements that made up emerging conceptions of masculine identity in a corporate world. Through athletic competition in college one could still form the prized character traits of the self-made man, the grit and toughness, that one could no longer acquire working in a modern office performing menial tasks. Yet through sport one could also envision indulging in the passionate new rites of passage to manhood, a component of modern masculinity. Through the study of science (even the science of business), one also could lay claim to modern professionalism, a future executive. And, through a college education, one could acquire at least the symbol of traditionally valued cultural polish. Quite subtly but profoundly in this unprecedented national forum, the image of college was transformed in particular ways that satisfied the conflicting pressures bearing upon models of masculine success.

But the most critical reformulation of college in popular culture, the one upon which the other elements rested, was the positing of college as an ideal training for success in the new world of business. The resulting vision of a college education's advantages championed by the magazines constituted an educational hybrid. Overall, the magazines endorsed curricular reforms, particularly scientific, proto-professional, and presumably practical courses that fed the professional consciousness of those engaged in commerce and industry. But many of those writing for the magazine, quite often the same ones calling for reforms in the curriculum, also drew upon traditional arguments for college education when describing the ideal American businessman. The new leaders of America would require the cultured breadth of traditional professionals, especially if a new sense of regard for the public weal was to be infused into the industrial age.

One cannot dismiss the vision of college education's curricular benefits that took shape within the cultural forum of these magazines either as the creation of academics bent on increasing enrollments or as the workings of a hegemonic capitalism intent upon molding pliant employees. The process was more nuanced and complex. The conception of the ideal education for the future businessman that formed in these periodicals reflected a cultural negotiation that in many ways only the magazines could have accommodated. Magazines had to reflect their audience and the needs of capital, while also offering ideal visions of American business and society to strive toward.

In seeking to confront issues facing their archetypal readership, these magazines fashioned a new vision of the college-educated businessman that clearly merged and drew from traditional *and* modern conceptions close to the hearts of their middle-class readership. With the thrust of curricular changes in colleges as inspiration and the developing need for broadminded, public-spirited leaders of great corporations as a guiding progressive principle, a new route to ideal business manhood took shape in the pages of these new and critical national middle-class forums. Shifting economic imperatives and curricular changes may have fueled this new ideal, but only the magazine editors and writers fully articulated this vision and disseminated it far and wide. Consequently, the new conception of college education and the college-educated businessman fashioned in the magazines helped to shape American expectations of manhood, success, and college, by intimately interconnecting them in a coherent vision for the first time and on an unprecedented national scale.

Making the Liberal Arts Manly

While paeans to the self-educated clerk who rose on his own co-existed in these magazines with anxieties that such opportunities waned, the magazine editors spearheaded a mass rethinking of Americans' visions of business success involving college education beginning in the mid-1890s. *Cosmopolitan* magazine under the editorship of John Brisben Walker launched the earliest salvo aimed at transforming higher education to fit the demands of his readers adjusting to a new age. As one of the first magazines to revolutionize the industry, *Cosmopolitan* under Walker's leadership achieved an early feel for the pulse of changes in American life. Walker championed advertising, science, and technological advancement, and the greater efficiency of the trust or corporation. And while *Munsey's*, the *Post*, and *Collier's* certainly ran articles exploring and encouraging changing attitudes toward college education, Walker's *Cosmopolitan* initially led the way.[20]

In the spring of 1897 Walker penned the first article in a series he planned to pursue called "Modern College Education." In this inaugural piece, Walker bluntly fired a broadside at the defenders of the classical curriculum, "men who are steeped in tradition" residing "within cloistral walls." Walker considered Greek and Latin as mere ornamental knowledge sustained in the curriculum out of blind adherence to tradition. He likened the typical American college's classical training to sending out a raw recruit for battle "minus sword or gun."[21] The educational establishment needed "to step aside from beaten paths" and consider the education suited for the modern world.[22] These were typical, indeed somewhat sedate, indictments of the classical curriculum and its impracticality for the active man, and it indicates the scale or re-crafting necessary for the liberal arts college to become accepted by the average American, especially the businessman.

Walker invited leading college presidents and professors to respond, and respond they did, with defenders of the classics and liberal culture offering some of the most eloquent (and telling) articulations of the benefits of the traditional liberal arts. College should not be the "sum of all things," but rather through culture it would impart "a knowledge of the best things."[23] "Large of intellect, noble in affections, sound in ethics," these were the results of a liberal education according to college president Charles F. Thwing, and he and other apologists also took pains to highlight that such an education bred "no stinted ascetic," but strong leaders of men.[24] Yale president Arthur Hadley defined his students (still taking a largely prescribed curriculum) as being "among the best examples of manly culture and cultured manhood to be found anywhere in the world."[25]

Certainly these contributors to *Cosmopolitan*'s debate cast a liberal education in elite ways, but they purposefully used language and concepts that invited readers in this new medium to identify themselves as worthy of such an education. They described it in masculine terms, yet also tinged with an appealing genteel image, seductively allowing readers to use their own judgments and imaginations regarding whether they (or their children) might fit this mold.[26] Other articles in the *Cosmopolitan* such as "What is a Gentleman?" and "What Men Like in Men" utilized language very similar to that wielded by Hadley, Thwing, and the other defenders of the classical curriculum.[27] Despite the criticisms of its editor toward the classics, then, *Cosmopolitan* did not shrink from encouraging their readers to identify with culture and learning, as Walker's interest in the arts and education further demonstrated.[28] The impassioned and seductive characterization of the liberal arts graduate that emerged in *Cosmopolitan* was not radically new. In fact, it reflected an evolution within academia and American culture unfolding for some time.[29] But it did indicate a new trajectory for liberal culture's appeal among the expanding middle class the magazines reached, and similar characterizations poured across the pages of the other mass magazines, as well, aiming with increasing precision at the generic businessman.

How did a liberal education foster business success? College disciplined the mind. Again, the 1895 *Munsey's* article probing the question of sending sons to college was the first in such a magazine to articulate the advantages of the college man in detail. According to the mayor of New York quoted in the article, not specific knowledge but "rather his instruction in the art of the best and quickest way of attaining knowledge," and the developed capacity for "original thought and investigation" proved the college man's greatest assets. "His increasing broadness of vision, the greater extent of the resources at his command," the mayor continued, "will equip him [the college man] to contend with the exigencies of life, and to grasp the business problems that will confront him with a sure hand, a clearer head, and more ready determination than his brother," who had left school for business.[30] The *Saturday Evening Post* regularly addressed the subject. The *Post* editorial "Culture and Success" observed that "colleges are not primarily designed to teach a man to make money, but they teach him to measure his mental powers and make the most of them." When the college graduate then turned his "disciplined faculties" to business, he was likely to succeed.[31] Naturally, the college man would seem to be at a great disadvantage, having lost years to the lad who started as an office boy, reasoned President Patton of Princeton in "Should the Business Man Have a College Education?" Nevertheless, "[t]he Power which comes as the result of a liberal education will soon show itself," asserted Patton, "and some day the opportunity will arrive for the university man to reveal the advantage which he has over the man who left school to go into the office" due to his "trained powers." Liberal education, in other words, equipped the aspiring businessman not only with keener mental powers but also "ready determination," attributes formerly monopolized by the self-educated, self-made man.[32]

Advocates linked liberal education firmly to the building of manly character as well, an attribute long held as the most critical indicator of future success. As one *Post* writer argued, "a college man wins in life not by virtue of the special knowledge he has acquired so much as by the habits he has formed," such as work, punctuality, a sense of duty, and, most importantly, will power.[33] Using martial language, Roswell P. Fowler in *Munsey's* argued that "as the struggle of life sharpened, nothing will more thoroughly fit a boy for the battle of life" than the power of mind and frugal habits learned at college.[34] Another Lorimer favorite at the *Post*, Senator Albert Beveridge, also utilized martial images to characterize the benefits of the liberally educated. A liberal education, for Beveridge, developed the mind to its highest "efficiency…as highly disciplined as are the wrist and eye of a swordsman." In one *Post* editorial, Lorimer too used the term "efficient manhood" to rate the value of a liberal education. It made one "self-reliant," a "thinking toiler," or as President Patton argued, college bestowed the "franchise of manhood."[35] Such characterizations of the college man directly countered the common stereotypes of the elite, effeminate, and idle college boy and freely mingled modern ideals of masculinity such as efficiency with more traditional self-made habits of character. Magazine writers and editorialists articulated a new vision of the liberally educated man as one worthy and capable of winning in the sharpening struggle of life, a significant step in the redefinition of both college education's benefits and of the businessman.

Finally, these articles and editorials left little doubt that a college education fostered the ideal business leader. In one *Post* article asking, "Should Railroad Men Be College Men?" Thwing interviewed or corresponded with over a score of railroad officers and presidents. Though many of the correspondents cautioned that the college man must work his way up to leadership positions, college seemed indispensable in their opinion.[36] The railroads needed administrators capable of overseeing unprecedented problems connected to the "public weal," as Thwing himself intoned. For such tasks, the great need was for "the properly and nobly trained mind."[37] Other high railroad officials concurred in this opinion, perhaps reflecting an ideal image of themselves in the process.[38] As another *Post* writer portrayed the issue, "for the successful prosecution of the highest forms of business pursuits a liberal education is indispensable," since the magnitude and complexity of modern business demanded men of breadth.[39]

American business in its new scale needed leaders who saw beyond their narrow business pursuits and understood the relation of business to the "public weal." This required a liberal education. The most practical education, Lorimer preached in one editorial, was "civilized character," which Lorimer translated as "a comprehension of his relations to the world about him and his duties to it."[40] Such a comprehension blossomed through traditional liberal education that taught, according to Lorimer, "other kinds of success infinitely higher than moneymaking."[41]

In short, a liberal education groomed gentlemen to their duties. It imparted a "grace of manner, refined taste, the ability to appear at ease with cultivated people and to appreciate the best that has been said and done," as Patton summarized it, paraphrasing Matthew Arnold.[42] "Contemplation of the sublime," Thwing argued, bred adherence to "only the highest principles." One did not teach Ulysses to make the bow but "to rear men of strength, of self-restraint, who can bend the bow."[43] Perhaps there was a reason Thwing contributed so prolifically to these middle-class periodicals, since his statements simultaneously fed the anxieties and vanities of America's businessmen searching for competent lieutenants (and opportunities for their own sons). For Thwing and for many others, only a liberal education that fashioned cultured intellect and forged character "for the sake of the manhood of [the] man himself," rather than simply training in a skill, could inculcate a love of truth and beauty and instill a sense of conscience and duty.[44]

Defenders of liberal education in these magazines appealed to and helped to foster a new ideal image of the American businessman and the college simultaneously. Advocates of the liberally educated business leader certainly flattered the middle-class businessmen reading these magazines. In no uncertain terms businessmen were told that they were the new leaders of America and that they (or more likely their sons) merited the education of traditional genteel leadership. Such defenders encouraged a re-conceptualization of the businessman as a cultured, learned, and socially responsible gentleman, a leader who required a liberal education in order to handle his responsibilities. No doubt, some who made this argument nurtured hopes of reversing the rampant materialism of the business world and harbored progressive ideals of promoting the college-educated businessman as an efficient, service-minded executive. No less significant than this re-conceptualization of the businessman, however, was the infusion of martial language and traditional self-made ideals that masculinized the liberal arts. For the defenders of liberal education, a cultural training did not create the dilettante but forged disciplined manhood and "civilized character," thus qualifying one as a broadly educated yet manly gentleman capable of bearing the responsibilities of leadership while adhering to "sublime" higher principles. Forging genteel leadership had long been the avowed goal of a liberal education in the United States, but now magazine editors and contributors altered their language and pointedly launched their appeals at a new audience.

Champions of Modernity in the Curriculum

The earliest criticisms of a college education printed in the magazines reflected the typical dismissive characterizations of the college man registered by the self-made businessman. These early complaints revolved around two problems—the length of time spent at college (delaying one's all-important start in business) and the useless curriculum. For instance, one *Munsey's* article noted the comment of a famous banker that three-fourths of a college man's brain was "filled with classical knowledge, dead languages and high sounding unpractical ideals."[45] Similarly, for all its support of the college-educated businessman, the *Post* also ran strong denunciations of the time wasted at college.[46] The aspiring businessman who went to college devoting four of his most active years to college study would have to "unlearn" this useless knowledge "when he goes into the practical world."[47] One 1903 *Post* editorial attacked collegiate "educational frills," charging that the pursuit of Latin and Greek represented a desire for superiority and "ornamentation." Only the "lusty, alive hustler" maintained a foothold, and the colleges had to recognize this and drop "their beloved, moth-eaten trappings of mediavalism [sic]."[48] In the 1906 editorial "The Dead A.B.," Lorimer argued that the "archaic bachelors degree" should be replaced by a certificate that stated plainly the work performed by the student and what "actual value" it provided for particular jobs.[49]

Part of Lorimer's evident concerns stemmed from the oft-repeated indictment that the idleness of college life bred bad luxurious habits, rather than frugality.[50] Lorimer frequently published editorials and articles lambasting the Eastern colleges as bastions of elite snobbery and luxury, while praising what were termed the "freshwater colleges" of the Midwest, where real men and women of character could still be found laboring for a true education.[51] Lorimer and the *Post* also found in the Midwest another form of educational institution, the state university, which provided a model of collegiate curricular reform that dovetailed with that magazine's and the other middle-class periodicals' notions of what a modern college program should be like.[52]

Quite often in magazine articles, editorials, and fiction, writers recognized little distinction between a technical college graduate and a liberal arts college graduate. A college man was a college man was a college man, with the same haughty demeanor or charms depending on one's perspective. Articles that touched upon the newly complex demands of industry and commerce, however, increasingly mentioned the benefits of technical or "practical" collegiate courses, introduced with a quickening pace in the nation's Midwest and land grant colleges.[53] An 1899 *Munsey's* article on the profession of railroading, for instance, highlighted the benefits of a "first class engineering school." The writer emphasized the advantages of scientific training, but considered such studies no less effective in forming character and self-reliance, which he considered the main goals of a college education.[54] After 1900 the *Post* in particular championed the new technical and scientific courses of study as educational training in step with the changing times. One editorial in the college man's number of October 1900 proclaimed the dawning century, "The Golden Age of the Engineer."[55] Exploring a similar theme a month later, the article "Dividends Paid on College Parchments" informed readers how whole graduating classes from technical schools were finding immediate employment in the railroad shops and great new industries across the land. The article predicted that "the next generation will see the whole industrial system of the United States...directed by men of higher education, technically and professionally trained."[56]

Indeed, one of the *Post*'s 1901 College Man's numbers triumphantly celebrated the rise of professional and technical programs at the nation's colleges and universities and connected this phenomenon with the great economic forces shaping the United States. The five articles on college programs in this single issue each focused on new professional or scientific subjects. "The Young Man and the New Force" looked at electrical engineering. The director of the Case School of Applied Science in "The Value of Technical Education" remarked on the incredible demand for its graduates and insisted that, consistent with the dictates of liberal education, the Case School educated broadly to fit men to adjust to and to rise in their "new professions." Another key article in this issue described the new School of Commerce at the University of Wisconsin, which proposed to teach business just as an engineering school prepared the future engineer.[57] Articles such as these reinforced the perception, as an earlier *Post* article had declared, that a "New Era in Commercial Education" had dawned. The modern corporation needed men "in these modern days...sharpened by knowledge and strengthened by specialization...drilled, skilled, and educated."[58] Such articles helped to establish that new scientific university programs would provide the educated men to meet this need. As one writer in the technological college man's number noted, in the development of the new scheme of business (the corporation), "technological knowledge is beginning to be more and more to the advantage of the men who seek the great positions in these corporations."[59]

The magazines went a step further, however. They urged their businessmen-readers to associate a university education with the status of being a modern trained professional and linked such identifications squarely with corporate organization and modern business practice. The magazines collectively rejoiced in higher education's new scientific curriculum as evidence of the modern era and prompted their middle-class readership to connect developing notions of professional pride and expert status with modern, scientific college education. In articulating the new associations of higher education and science on one hand, and university training and modern professions on the other, these magazines played important and largely unappreciated roles in helping to guide developing conceptions of professionalism in America.

One example indicated the full development of the concept. Writing for the *Post* in 1911, business expert and writer Roger Babson's "A New Profession for the Young Man" outlined the need for a new university curriculum that he termed "Economic Engineering." This novel program would, he believed, fulfill the need for "practical men," who could be called upon to lead the great corporations and who combined scientific principles and the problem-solving technique of engineering with knowledge of economics and how the world functioned. Hardly alone, such an article not only took for granted that higher education had grown more technical and practical, it fused the image of the modern professional businessman with this reformed notion of the university as an agent of scientific authority.[60]

Forging a Hybrid Curricular Ideal

Even such calls for university-trained professionals in business, however, linked their vision with the university's long identification with leadership, an image the magazines forwarded regularly as well, and one connected implicitly with the broadening powers of the liberal arts. Babson's ideal courses mingled, for instance, the physical sciences, mathematics, and special business courses such as bookkeeping and banking with history, modern languages, and economics, cautioning that from his experience and talks with executives, a strictly technical engineering preparation, while valuable, proved far too narrow. Such men typically remained employees rather than administrators.[61] The simple fact that these magazines simultaneously offered their readers two very different and opposed visions of college's utility (liberal culture v. science and practicality) to choose from for their evolving identities proved quite significant. Yet as Babson's ideal program demonstrated, the magazines, in fact, performed a far more significant and unheralded cultural task in that they promoted a vision of college that combined the two extremes with the middle-class businessman firmly in mind.

Walker's series on modern education, for example, in addition to the eloquent defenders of the classics included many collegiate reformers as well (David Starr Jordan of Stanford and Daniel Coit Gilman of Johns Hopkins), men who supported the legitimacy of science in the curriculum. In essence, such reformers simply reworked the notion of liberal education, expanding the definition by dropping Greek and Latin and adding the sciences, modern humanities (recent literature and history along with modern languages), and social sciences.[62] They differed from the classical defenders in their conception of what should be included in a liberal education. Both Gilman and Henry Morton (the president of Stevens Institute) advocated a split curriculum, a combination of old and new subjects. Morton depicted the split curriculum at Stevens, what he termed a "liberal technical course," as the ideal liberal education uniting an "efficient technical training" and "liberal culture."[63] Neither would discard entirely, however, with the traditional belief that a liberal education was critical for character and morals. Their intellectual co-mingling of the modern and the traditional in a new liberal arts formula perfectly captured the current of the times and the temper of the popular magazine that straddled the line between the modern and the Victorian age.

A ubiquitous frame of reference in many articles that one might term "the businessman's lament"—old businessmen pondering missed opportunities or their own insecurities—also demonstrated that this hybrid mixing of educational ideals was not confined to educators. Laments often commented on the wish for scientific training with the ever-increasing pace of technical change in a rapidly industrializing America.[64] Still more laments expressed a longing on the part of self-made men for the broad knowledge that a liberal education supposedly imparted.[65] Most typically, though, writers and commentators recognized the benefits of both scientific and liberal training. As one New York manufacturer interviewed for a *Collier's* piece put it, not able to attend college himself, he envied "the men who had been able to gain their technical mastery while at the same time qualifying themselves as members of a community in which literary accomplishments accounts for something."[66] And nearly all laments linked such broad college training with the necessity of visionary leadership in a new age, so that they combined an ideal self-image (scientifically trained and traditionally cultured) with the issue of professional leadership and mobility. These laments, in essence, portended the definition of a new ideal man, a new model for success and manhood in a changing world, with college playing the essential role.

Just how the magazines actively endeavored more directly to shape higher education in the image of their readers may be viewed with the launching of Cosmopolitan University (a free correspondence school) in 1897. Conceived by *Cosmo* editor John Brisben Walker, Cosmopolitan University not only pushed a democratic re-envisioning of higher education—bringing college-level instruction to the "many who have the aspiration, but are deprived of the opportunity"—it championed a reworked idea of modern liberal education. As the school's president wrote, the present college curriculum tended to produce a "classically educated prig," a "gentleman of leisure."[67] "The substitute [education]," he cautioned, "must not be a school of technology," but a "seminary for liberal learning;" or a "broad and liberalizing education rather than one for earning a livelihood," according to Walker himself.[68]

Cosmopolitan University courses included several areas of vocational study. The breakdown of "departments" and courses reflected mostly conventional academic subjects—Wisdom, Science, English, Modern Foreign Languages, Citizenship, Arts, Pedagogy (the unconventional were Life and Accomplishments), but Walker also threw in a department of Business Preparation with courses in organization and accounting.[69] Though a single student would spend years taking all these courses, this curriculum reflected what Walker and his associates believed a modern liberal education should include. Courses that prepared for a vocation while acquainting one with the modern world were offered in conjunction with more traditional courses in the humanities (art, literature, history, and philosophy), intended to form character and ethics. All this ideally would be accented by courses in "voice culture" and manners designed, one would assume, to instruct middle-class aspirants in the ways of genteel society. Periodicals like *Cosmopolitan* essentially had been instructing their readers in a similar fashion through their articles and fiction from their inception.[70] Like the other middle-class magazines, *Cosmopolitan* attempted to encapsulate the ideals and tastes of the new middle class. The magazine encouraged the arts and literature. They ran features on culture. But they also proved enamored of science and progress, the modern corporation, and technology.[71] Now, an ideal college curriculum crystallized the overall educational project of the magazine—to uplift readers culturally and intellectually as well as to help them negotiate the modern world.

Walker's vision, in fact, proved too popular. Overwhelmed by over twenty thousand applicants in 1898, Cosmopolitan University succumbed in December of that year.[72] Walker sustained *Cosmopolitan*'s interest in reforming college education, however, by continuing the modern education series.[73] Throughout his editorship, then, Walker and *Cosmopolitan*'s criticisms of higher education revolved more around a re-conceptualization of the average American, whom to Walker was the middle-class man who read *Cosmopolitan*. Through the medium of his magazine, Walker endeavored to guide his readers toward an ideal vision of themselves— simultaneously revolutionary in that this vision included a college education and in that this popular vision of college education did not resemble most colleges. After 1900, the mantle of leadership in this endeavor transferred to Lorimer at the *Saturday Evening Post*.

As with *Cosmopolitan*, Lorimer's enthusiasm for college education was predicated both on the rise of new potential students and a reforming curriculum. Year after year and despite the occasional reform-minded criticism, the *Post* continued to celebrate the changes sweeping America's colleges—new students and new courses. The *Post* commented each year on the rising enrollments and trumpeted the improving caliber of the freshmen (no longer the effete snobs of the past).[74] For instance, the *Post* ran a gushing editorial saluting the graduates of Harvard and Yale who intended to go into the business world, their numbers for the first time outstripping those planning to enter the traditional professions.[75] Lorimer's *Post* trumpeted "The Broadening of the Colleges" and "The Modern College Man." These new students enrolled in the "special departments," and were taught to be experts, but "the idea of all-around training was not abandoned" and the "Modern College Man" was still imbued not only with a "capacity for work" but with an "interest in the better things of life."[76] Lorimer applauded and cheered the new students and the mixed curriculum that seemed to signify his conception of what the ideal education should be.

The editor did not carry the torch of educational reform alone. The *Post* recruited some of the same academics as other magazines—David Starr Jordan, Charles Thwing, Henry Morton of Stevens Institute—to voice support both for curricular change and the vision of the college educated businessman. In his "The College Man's Advantages in the Coming Century," Jordan argued that college should train for a specific end and instill scientific method, but that it should also allow the graduate "to see things which lie beyond his trade."[77] Non-academics, too, penned articles on this subject as well, targeting the businessman specifically. Russell Crittenden's "The Practical College Course for Young Men" concurred with Jordan's arguments. College should train for some definite end, but should also "afford...a broad foundation." "Narrow specialization in the education of the young man," wrote the author, "while perhaps fitting them early in life for moderately remunerative positions, is to be deprecated as lacking those essential qualities that produce broad mental development, of the kind repeatedly reported to be desired by businessmen." Too narrow a training was not truly practical. The best preparation arose from a combination that included "a broad and liberal education."[78] Some might not have realized their participation in helping to shape a new curricular and business ideal, but nevertheless a steady barrage of writers in the *Post* championed the benefits of a reformed college curriculum while firmly connecting this new idea of college with the ideal, modern executive.

No group of articles in the *Post*, however, represented that magazine's hardy promotion of a combined liberal and modern curriculum better than John Corbin's series "Which College for the Boy?" which ran over most of 1907. The series reviewed some of the nation's top colleges and universities. By itself the series reflected the *Post*'s increased attention to the supposed demands of readers for knowledge on the burning question of where to send their sons, an indication of the changing views of education in relation to potential success, but also of the self-perception of readers promoted by the magazine. And, significantly, the series came down squarely for a mixed curriculum that avoided the two extremes of either too much culture or too much science or utilitarian studies. Cornell perfectly captured the mix of traditional and modern values. Corbin noted that "the ideal at Cornell [was] to turn out specialists who were also men of liberal culture—able thinkers, writers and speakers, efficient men among men." "Breadth of character and depth of culture go hand in hand with utilitarian training," highlighted Corbin. He reveled not only in this ideal curricular mix but also in the astounding beauty of the campus, and, more impressively to Corbin, the simple living displayed by the devoted students, many of whom he noted received financial aid—a truly democratic university.[79]

The universities of Michigan and Wisconsin received similar if less detailed praise, though Wisconsin's excessive utilitarian bent seemed to bother Corbin. Moreover, Corbin judged Harvard too "German" with its free elective system and the University of Chicago still somewhat unstable.[80] The one university that rivaled Cornell in his estimation (and for similar reasons) was Princeton. Whereas Cornell perhaps tilted more to the side of science and the practical, Princeton leaned toward the liberal arts. Princeton had resisted the worst excesses of the elective system and adhered to a prescribed liberal arts curriculum for the first two years to "discipline the mind and enlarge sympathetic imagination." Juniors and seniors were allowed to specialize, but Corbin intoned, "first and last the college cultivates not science but the man." Moreover, Corbin preached that due to its liberal education Princeton and colleges like it across the nation needed to effect a spiritual uplift through their students, who constituted the future leaders, so that the nation as it grew did not lose its soul.[81] Princeton and Cornell received glowing praise as institutions that offered the ideal education for readers of the *Post*. They both combined a democratic ethos that included modern, specialized offerings with elite surroundings and traditional, genteel ideals of education such as forming character, intellect, and cultural breadth.[82]

Still, the *Post*'s stance on college education always must circle back to the editor's seemingly vacillating position and what it represented. His editorials were capable of working up a misty-eyed veneration of true culture or liberal education, which he thought cultivated "civilized character."[83] Or he could blast caustic barbs at collegiate snobbery and the impracticality of the classical curriculum (recall the aforementioned "Dead A.B."). One could best characterize Lorimer's most consistent thought on the subject, however, as a hybrid educational ideal that united a reworked and updated liberal education with modern "scientific" subjects in order to live an active life. His editorial, "A Liberal Education," for example, in charting his own list of possible areas of study harkened back to Walker's Cosmopolitan University breakdown. He listed four pillars upon which twentieth-century college education could be reconstructed in order to attract "sensible Americans," who believed that modern subjects equaled those of "the fifth century BC." He included an ability to think and write in English; "knowledge of the history of democracy and the emancipation of man"; knowledge of mechanisms of business, or "how commodities [were] produced, distributed and consumed"; and a knowledge of taxation. He considered "a man with such an education would be both competent and cultured."[84]

Lorimer even defended higher education from the attacks of the hypothetical "practical man," who still scoffed at colleges "as a kind of parlor institution where rich men's sons play football, wear fraternity pins and discuss Ibsen and sociology." Lorimer derided the overzealous practical man for thinking so and overlooking the science one used in business that colleges and universities advanced. Only the college graduate possessed the patience and knowledge of "investigation and experiment" to push science forward and help business.[85] He centered his endorsement on three elements: the balanced curriculum, the increasing democratic and meritocratic trends of higher education, and its benefit to American business. Lorimer's support hinged, though, on the transformation of the curriculum. In the 1904 editorial "Silk Purses and Sows' Ears," he commented on the vast changes in the curriculum, and its new utility in fashioning businessmen. He observed that "a generation ago the so-called liberal education was regarded as a mere ornament of life," its classical culture and "unapplied mathematics" useless to "the business man." The university, though, had since become broad enough "to include preparation for useful life in every sphere."[86] And Lorimer would continue to defend higher education as the new route to business advancement and opportunity.[87]

Lorimer's intellectual odyssey regarding the benefits of a college education touched upon common longings, reservations, and demands voiced by many Americans during those years, and perhaps best reflected the multidimensional lens through which many Americans looked at college hoping to define themselves. They could see college education as snobbish, elite, and frivolous and thereby glory in their own self-education and advancement. Or, conversely, they could harbor longings for the supposed cultivation and breadth they wished for and hoped to give their children, seeing in college identifications a way to become cultured. And they could look in the pages of *Cosmopolitan* or the *Post* and demand education fit the needs of the modernizing, "scientific" world in which they took pride. Consequently, they might revel, as Lorimer did, in the modern democratic development of American colleges and universities so different from European models and a growing source of genuine national strength. But one cannot ignore that all these characterizations coexisted and blended together, principally in the *Post* and *Cosmopolitan*, but to some degree in all of the magazines.

Imagining the Education of the Ideal Business Man in Advertising and Fiction

Naturally the attitudes of editors and contributors toward education and its increasing relevance to readers emerged most potently in magazine articles and editorials. These magazines, however, were conceived as a total package, instructive as well as entertaining organs, with advertising and fiction as integral features of this endeavor. While editors did not guide the contents of their magazine's fictional offerings as strongly as they did the article content, the flavor of mass magazine fiction followed the demands of Walker and Munsey, for example, that fiction reflect the modern times.[88] In many ways advertising performed much the same task. Both Lorimer and Munsey defended advertising as an educational force, a teacher of commerce and civilization, to paraphrase Lorimer.[89] Advertisers intended to sell products, but the most successful products were those that resonated with the lifestyle, anxieties, and longings of the new middle-class readers.[90] Though in slightly different ways, then, advertising and fiction attempted to both reflect and guide readers, offering lessons on how to live and to construct their lives. And, not surprisingly, certain evolving assumptions regarding the place of college education in readers' lives entered forcefully into both fiction and advertising.

The largest, most numerous and most potent ads that pertained to education and success remained those related to correspondence and business schools. And these ads definitely advanced the association between trained, expert knowledge and success on the job even as they often pointedly disavowed the necessity of formal higher education.[91] Beginning around 1902, however, some correspondence schools began to purposefully cultivate collegiate associations by either directly claiming their programs were college level or by creating ads with key words or images that at least conjured such an association.[92] The International Correspondence University, the most conspicuous example, not only appropriated the term "university," it launched an impressive ad campaign in 1904–05 utilizing many images of academia in support of a "higher" business training. In actuality, the university supplied no bachelor's degrees. All of their courses, in fact, were vocationally oriented—accounting, banking, commercial arithmetic, foreign commerce, and U.S. economic history.[93] Proprietary business colleges (schools that normally taught bookkeeping, etc.) also began tailoring their programs to the increasingly accepted dictates of modern corporate success. By 1908 and 1909, the Peirce School (a business college) ads emphasized Peirce grads being leaders owing to the school's combined "general education [and] technical training in commercial subjects."[94] Though clearly not pushing the notion of a college-educated business man in such ads, correspondence and business schools nonetheless altered their language to fall in line with the idea that the manager/administrator needed a broader training, all while they continued to link education generally to scientific authority and quasi-expert status.

Colleges and universities made forays onto the advertising pages of these magazines as well, with the most impressive ads from expanding universities (such as NYU, the University of Pittsburgh, and Valparaiso) pushing professional and business programs.[95] As early as 1902 the School of Commerce, Accounts and Finance of New York University ran advertisements with the large caption, "University Training for Business," "Higher Education for Business," and "Training for Business Management," claiming the school "equips men to succeed in business."[96]

No programs or institutions that advertised in the middle-class periodicals, however, represented the endeavor to distill a liberal education for the busy American better than Dr. Eliot's Five-Foot Shelf of Books or the Harvard Classics. Collier and Son Publishers sought and received Eliot's (and Harvard's) participation.[97] Enthusiastically marketed and quite popular, the Harvard Classics have been recognized by scholars as a watershed in the project of disseminating culture to the masses, part of the transition to a consumer-oriented, middlebrow culture.[98] But the program's significance in the transforming meaning of college has been less appreciated. Certainly, the Harvard Classics were offered as an alternative to college attendance. Fifteen minutes a day and one could acquire "the essentials of a liberal education." This was hardly the first collection of books or program of reading offered as a route for readers to acquire culture. Nor was it the first to use the term "liberal education." Nonetheless, it was the first to utilize a marketing strategy that traded on the prestige of an institution and its famous president to legitimize its cultural program.[99] Even a few years prior to the Collier's venture, it was hardly necessary to bolster a cultural product's authority through association with an institution. This said as much about the rising acceptance and prestige of college as it did about the increasing desire for culture generally by the American public. Touting colleges as the new ideal location for Americans to receive the benefit of liberal culture was a relatively recent development and one intertwined with the magazine's role in popularizing this shift in perception for the businessman.

Nonetheless, the fact that Harvard and especially Charles W. Eliot were exalted as icons of liberal education must be considered even more significant. Certainly Harvard was the oldest and most well known of American colleges. But under Eliot, Harvard had also become renowned for its reforms, the most critical of which was the elective system. Eliot believed in a student's free will to choose the studies that would benefit him most and prepare him for his life's vocation. He accelerated the introduction of scientific and specialized courses at Harvard, while discarding the prescribed Latin and Greek. Charles Eliot loomed as the high priest of modern higher education, celebrated as the champion of practical utility over classical learning.[100]

Eliot was far from a radical with regard to the curriculum, though. In fact, his vision fell in step with the rather vague and all-encompassing ideal of a liberal college education that took shape later in the middle-class magazines. At Harvard Eliot had in effect redefined liberal education to include the sciences and specialized subjects. And this included "something of what has been done and thought in the world"—a weak nod to Matthew Arnold.[101] Eliot disavowed narrow vocational pragmatism as well as classical learnedness at the undergraduate level and advocated a combination that prepared one for usefulness while also imparting a learned breadth.[102] The new middle-class magazines had endorsed educational reformers like Eliot. It seems quite natural, then, that a magazine publisher and an educational reformer should join forces to launch a commercial product offering the promise of becoming liberally educated. Each in their own way had pioneered a new definition of liberal education to fit shifting times.

The ad copy and the editorial promotion of the Harvard Classics hit the same themes—the same mixture of respect for Arnoldian liberal culture and for broad knowledge as a base for useful action. A *Collier's Weekly* editorial announcing the new project, for instance, contained several references to the value of liberal culture. But this set was for "sensible men and women" and not for "pedants," who remained devoted to ideas "built upon Greek and Latin." Only what Eliot deemed "most useful" made the cut.[103] And the ads followed suit. "The Five-Foot Shelf" was for the millions "busy doing the nation's work—professional men, office men, farmers, salesmen, mechanics." The volumes would provide classics of literature "essential for a liberal education" that formed the foundation for one's intellect, "the foundation of the world's thought and achievement."[104] These would not be just old classics, then, but also works on modern subjects. It appealed to the longing for an acquaintance with liberal culture and to the modern sense that such an education still needed to be useful, calibrated for active Americans. Eliot's vision of a liberal education, then, dovetailed with the vision that took shape in middle-class magazines and now the two worlds merged in a common commercial promotion advertised in the pages of middle-class periodicals.

Though the first to neatly market the growing prestige of a college education to magazine readers, Collier and Son publishing was hardly alone.[105] While the direct association to a college was not present, the Mentor Association intensified the play upon hidden anxieties regarding a lack of culture and liberal education. Spread usually over an entire page, their ads asked, "Have you ever envied the culture, the wide familiar knowledge" of those who have traveled or who possessed a "liberal education?"[106] The Mentor Association claimed to have sprung from a meeting of businessmen at a club, each lamenting his lack of time to acquire a broad cultural knowledge. The ads that expanded on these founders' concerns noted that the businessmen had realized that knowledge meant power and they desired to "know about the important things of the world—foreign lands, famous books, great men and women, the great achievements of history." They supposedly pooled their money to hire an editor to prepare periodic lessons delivered twenty-four times per year that contained (according to their ads) six essays from authorities on art, literature, history, and geography, along with reprints of famous paintings.[107] Now they invited others to join the "better class of Americans [who] have been growing more interesting, more cultivated and more refined."[108]

The emergence of Eliot's Five-Foot Shelf and the Mentor Association signaled the wide currency of the new educated businessman ideal. They also indicated how deep the imagined benefits of a college education had been implanted in the American matrix of both masculine identity and business success. These enterprises owed a great deal of their success to the fact that they hit a nerve, they tapped into the anxiety of not living up to a new ideal, one cultivated in the pages of the national periodicals. Being a cultured man had long been honored, but now the examples bombarded readers weekly and monthly from these magazines, and were tied more powerfully than before to a college education. Together these ads reinforced the redefinition of the businessman as a highly trained, scientific professional, but also broad-gauged and cultured enough to fulfill high executive positions. And the ads drew a closer association between the qualities of a redefined businessman and the imagined benefits of a modern college education endorsed elsewhere in the magazines.

Magazine fiction, too, increasingly utilized college-educated characters, and in such fiction one may see the full development of the college-man amalgam—the evolving set of assumptions surrounding the connections between ideal male attributes and college education. The earliest magazine stories involving college characters in a positive light focused on college life or sports. Most stories that intertwined college and business settings or characters neglected the issue of curricular change. It simply was not a driving force for plots.[109] But the subject did surface often enough to reinforce the developing consensus surrounding the benefits of college worked out in other elements of the magazines—emphasizing a character's broad, liberal education, his culture, or what might be termed a generic intellectual prowess that college education imparted.

When authors specifically explored the issue of how the college man's education potentially affected business, they focused on his creativity and rational, efficient, and "scientific" solutions to problems. H. K. Webster's "The Matter with Carpenter" offered one of the earliest treatments of the subject. One problem with the college man often cited by employers was the graduate's impatience with menial tasks that led to inattention to details and poor work habits. College boys expected to rise too fast. Webster addressed this issue with Carpenter. The story opened with Carpenter daydreaming of past college gridiron glory, unhappy with his job as a draftsman. Enduring the knowing snickers of non-college draftsmen when late from lunch again, Carpenter was called into the boss's office. But the boss moved Carpenter out of the monotonous job of drafting and into research and development, where he excelled (he also won the girl).[110] Carpenter's tale highlighted the connection between college education and modern thinking that was both creative and efficient.

Two prominent *Post* serials fleshed out characters who fully exemplified the new college educated leader in the business world—liberal education's role in grooming gentleman leaders. Hampden Scarborough in David Graham Phillip's "The Cost" (1903), hailed from wholesome, self-made, all-American farm stock in the Midwest. Nevertheless, he yearned for a college education and worked his way through college after his father forbade him from going.[111] At "Battlefield College" Scarborough championed democratic independents against the Greeks in school government, excelled as a student, and proved a champion debater.[112] And, after a brief descent into the debauched life of a college sport, he achieved financial success selling books during the summer break and then again after graduation, even becoming manager of other salesmen before deciding to go into law and reform politics.[113] Similarly, Wister in John Corbin's 1907 serial "The Cave Man," though a Harvard man and the owner-operator of an auto-manufacturing business, was described as an "academic," who devoted himself to the business and particularly to research and development.[114]

Distinction between what type of college curriculum a particular character attained before arriving in business was almost nonexistent. In fiction, when business-related characters had been to college, what seemed to matter was that college had prepared them for leadership. This proved true even when stories specifically mentioned a business character's technical or engineering background. Most often such a background marked him as middle-class (as opposed to a wealthy background), perhaps as technically competent, but most importantly, as a manager of some variety.[115] When authors increasingly utilized collegiate references, even in passing, for their business-related characters, the characters were not clerks, but salesmen, managers, or men on the rise—a new professional, managerial class with advanced educated skills and a broad vision.[116] The portrayal of college's benefits in magazine fiction, then, paralleled in descriptive form the arguments forwarded elsewhere in the magazines, though with less clarity. In fact, fiction authors seemed to boil down the benefits of college into the most agreed upon elements—a combination of liberal culture, intellectual sharpness, creativity, and leadership.

Conclusion

Did the magazine treatment of college education start a stampede to college campuses? Can it explain why corporations would increasingly begin to hire college graduates and promote them into management? Were editors like Walker and Lorimer responsible for curricular reforms on the college campuses? Not completely. People chose to go to college or decided not to go due to a variety of influences. Owners, corporate boards, and managers made decisions on hiring without consulting a magazine, and many college administrators and faculty pushed curricular reforms without having read debates in the magazines. But the mass magazines brought the concerns of the middle-class, the big-businessman, and curricular reformers together in an unprecedented national forum and focused all of these voices toward a vital issue for all—how to achieve success in a changing world. The power of this medium eludes direct measurement. Unquestionably, though, it possessed a power to set agendas, to conjure and promote ideals and values its editors and contributors deemed important, and did so on a vast new scale. And one cannot comprehend the explosion of collegiate expectations in America during the twentieth century without understanding how the magazines encouraged a rethinking of the college curriculum in conjunction with a reworked vision of the businessman and his route to success.[117]

On a broad level the mass magazines forwarded a new conception of America remade to suit the middle class. Their readers were the ones coping with the new demands of a corporate and consumer world requiring quite different skills and attitudes. The magazines helped make sense of these changes and chart new identities, and this was especially true of the middle-class businessman. The self-made, Victorian ideals of the waning century, though still prized, seemed ill suited to the subordinate, white-collar functions of the corporate businessman. In attempting to address the concerns of the generic businessman (whether the iconic "Big Man" or striving employee) regarding how success would be achieved in the new age, the magazines constructed a suitable conception of the college curriculum to align with the mixture of traditional and modern identities that informed the cultural values of the emerging corporate middle class.

These middle-class magazines promoted curricular reforms in the nation's colleges, but the overall reformed vision of the college curriculum (and its benefits) that developed in these magazines represented a unique hybrid. This hybrid vision blurred the extremes of American higher education, neither utilitarian nor wholly devoted to liberal culture. The vision that evolved in the magazines sought to combine utility and science with liberal culture, and this vision seemed more inspired by the needs, demands, and wishes of the middle class (as perceived by the magazines) than from academic reformers. The issue of fashioning a new type of businessman for a new age permeated and informed the entire discourse on curricular reform, so that the American embrace of higher education as part of the formula for success in no small part took shape largely filtered through the pages of these magazines.

On a cultural level, the reformed vision of a college education and the ideal of the college-educated corporate businessman were informed by and in turn helped articulate the values of the emerging middle class. Through a revamped, manly liberal arts, the aspiring businessman could forge Victorian virtues and lay claim to genteel leadership qualities—breadth of vision and character—that rendered him a worthy heir to the self-made man and yet also a promising new captain to chart business' more socially responsible course. Through higher education's increasing linkage with science, however, the new corporate lieutenants could establish themselves as modern men, proud of their association with the forces of change, the promises of efficiency and abundance. The new vision of college education united the potentially discordant streams of masculinity and business success. Through a college pedigree, one could now simultaneously cultivate Victorian virtues, aspire to genteel culture and leadership, as well as a modern identity, thus perfectly capturing the hybrid identity of the middle class itself—longing both for traditional and modern images of self.

The college curriculum was undergoing reform. Businessmen and manufacturers were discovering the value of educated and technically skilled individuals. And many Americans increasingly wished to improve or safeguard their family status by sending their sons to college. But these developments cannot explain the voluminous discourse touching upon higher education and business in the middle-class periodicals. In fact, the discourse itself helped to articulate and disseminate these changing impressions, informing popular attitudes. These magazines functioned as integral forums of negotiation where evolving meanings and identities were hammered out in the process of cultural transformation alongside other parallel discourses. The twentieth-century view of higher education was formed out of that process as much as by college presidents or corporate policies. In other words, the magazine discourse on college education and business success did not only reflect or rationalize a changing reality. It was an active part of constructing new ideals, erecting a new hero to replace the self-made businessman. The magazine editors and contributors held up an idealized mirror to their readership, one in which they could envision the best of the past and the future.

Notes

1. "Should Your Boy Go to College?" *Munsey's Magazine* 13 (August 1895): 461. The article pointedly addressed the question of business success, asking, "Is a college course the best training for a boy designed for a business career?"
2. This was the nation's first truly national mass media. Advertising revenue facilitated a drastic reduction in price after 1893. *Munsey's* and *McClure's* led the way and soon had circulations above 300,000, whereas the old genteel monthlies, such as *Harper's*, were rarely over 100,000 (usually quite a bit lower) and, thus, were very expensive. *Munsey's* hovered between 500,000 and 700,000 from 1900–1910, while *Cosmopolitan* gradually rose to 750,000 by 1911 (in 1905 Walker sold it to William Randolph Hearst). The weekly *Collier's* made huge strides from a meager 170,000 in 1900 to a consistent circulation above 500,000 after 1905. Matthew Schneirov, *The Dream of a New Social Order: Popular Magazines in America, 1893–1914* (New York: Columbia University Press, 1994), 11. Statistics taken from Schneirov, *The Dream of a New Social Order*, Appendix 1. The new industry leader, however, became the *Saturday Evening Post*. Purchased by Cyris Curtis in 1897 and edited by George Horace Lorimer, the *Post* started as a magazine for men (the husbands and sons of Curtis' *Ladies Home Journal* readers), led the industry in 1904 with 725,000 readers, and reached an incredible 1,000,000 by 1909. Helen

30 Perspectives on the History of Higher Education

Damon-Moore, *Magazines for the Millions: Gender and Commerce in the Ladies Home Journal and the Saturday Evening Post, 1880–1910* (New York: SUNY Press, 1994), 109; and Schneirov, *The Dream of a New Social Order*, Appendix 1.

3. Francis L. Patton, "Should a Business Man Have a College Education?" *Saturday Evening Post*, 26 May 1900, p. 1094; Charles F. Thwing, "Should Railroad Men Be College Men?" *Saturday Evening Post*, 11 January 1902, pp. 11–12. A small sampling of articles that directly raised the issue of college education for the businessman and advocated such a path include Benjamin Ida Wheeler, "Is Scholarship a Promise of Success in Life?" *Saturday Evening Post*, 26 May 1900, p. 1095; James B. Dill, "The College Man and the Corporate Position," *Munsey's Magazine* 24 (October 1900): 148–152; Thwing, "Making a Choice of Profession—Insurance," *Cosmopolitan* 34 (March 1903): 575–78; and Senator Albert J. Beveridge, "The Young Man and College Life," *Saturday Evening Post*, 10 June 1905, pp. 1–2.

4. Statistics cannot reveal the whole story, but the numbers with regard to the changing business scene point to staggering change. Clerical workers as a percentage of the workforce rose 784 percent between 1870 and 1900 compared to blue-collar work, which rose only 125 percent, an indication of the rise of "big business" or corporations and thus also technical and managerial positions. Janice Weiss, "Educating for Clerical Work: The Nineteenth-Century Private Commercial School," *Journal of Social History* 14 (Spring 1981): 407. She computed her statistics from Alba M. Edwards, *Comparative Occupational Statistics for the United States, 1870–1940, 16th Census of the United Stated: 1940*, IV (Washington, 1943). The number of managers, executives, and non-farm proprietors grew 45 percent between 1900 and 1910 and 14 percent between 1910 and 1920. The number of professional and technical workers saw an even larger increase—42 percent from 1900–1910 and 33 percent from 1910–1920. Jurgen Kocka, *White Collar Workers in America, 1890–1940: A Social-Political History in International Perspective* (Beverly Hills: Sage Publications, 1980), 19. This while the number of self-employed Americans decline markedly from 67 percent in 1870 to 37 percent in 1910. Gail Bederman, *Manliness and Civilization: A Cultural History of Gender and Race in the United States, 1880–1917* (Illinois: The University of Chicago Press, 1995), 12.

5. William J. Wilgus, "Making a Choice of a Profession," *Cosmopolitan* 35 (August 1903): 462–63; Poultney Bigelow, "Can a University Help Me to Earn a Living?" *Collier's Weekly*, 18 October 1902, p. 8; "Wanted: A Master," *Saturday Evening Post*, 28 February 1903, p. 15. Another *Post* editorial quoted Harvard president Charles Eliot's speech to a trade congress where he claimed that the successful merchant had to know more than ever. "New Era in Commercial Education," *Saturday Evening Post*, 11 November 1899, p. 378. Two other articles celebrating a dawning new age of business leadership were Frank A. Munsey, "The Reign of the Business Man," *Munsey's Magazine* 15 (June 1896): 383; and Munsey, "Impressions by the Way," *Munsey's Magazine* 24 (November 1900): 308–9.

6. Grover Cleveland, "Does a College Education Pay?" *Saturday Evening Post*, 26 May 1900, p. 1089.

7. Bigelow, "Can a University Help Me to Earn a Living?" 8. Other articles that highlighted the increasing opportunities for college men as leaders for the new age were Russell H. Crittenden, "The Practical Course for Young Men," *Saturday Evening Post*, 27 October 1900, p. 6; Francis B. Crocker, "The Young Man and the New Force," *Saturday Evening Post*, 22 June 1901, pp. 1–2; and "Dividends Paid on College Parchments," *Saturday Evening Post*, 24 November 1901, p. 6.

8. This topic of generational transition deeply troubled Lorimer. Other examples from the *Post* attacking this issue are, "Sudden Wealth, Snobs, and Smart Sets," *Saturday*

Evening Post, 11 October 1902, p. 12; and Mary K. Warwick, "Little Children of the Rich," *Saturday Evening Post*, 11 April 1908, pp. 3–5 and 27–28.

9. "Letters from a Self-Made Merchant to His Son," *Saturday Evening Post*, 3 August 1901, p. 11. It is no coincidence that Lorimer chose meatpacking as the industry setting for this issue. When Lorimer dropped out of Yale, he left to work for Armour in Chicago. Helen Damon-Moore, *Magazines for the Millions*, 109.
10. "Old Gorgon Graham," *Saturday Evening Post*, 3 September 1904, p. 89.
11. "Letters from a Self-Made Merchant to His Son," *Saturday Evening Post*, 17 August 1901, p. 11. Graham explained that he had no sympathy "for these old fellows who go around bragging of their ignorance and saying that boys don't need to know anything except addition."
12. In one letter, Graham exhorted Piggy to more strenuous efforts by using the example of a small but fiery red-haired fullback they had both witnessed in action against Columbia, an early reference connecting college football and business that would grow over time. "Letters from a Self-Made Merchant to His Son," *Saturday Evening Post*, 22 March 1902, p. 5.
13. Scholars writing on changes in higher education who emphasized the influence of the increasing scientific and professional curriculum as a cause of expansion include Burton J. Bledstein, *The Culture of Professionalism: The Middle Class and the Development of Higher Education in America* (New York: W. W. Norton, 1976); Roger L. Geiger, *To Advance Knowledge: The Growth of American Research Universities, 1900–1940* (New York: Oxford University Press, 1986); Robert Wiebe, *The Search for Order, 1877–1920* (New York: Hill and Wang, 1967); and Clyde Barrow, *Universities and the Capitalist State: Corporate Liberalism and the Reconstruction of Higher Education, 1894–1928* (Madison: University of Wisconsin Press, 1990). Scholars writing on the expansion of higher education who conversely emphasized the increasing wealth of many Americans (especially the business classes), their desire for signs of status or prestige as a primary cause for rising enrollments include Laurence Veysey, *The Emergence of the American University* (Chicago: University of Chicago Press, 1965); Joseph Kett, *Rites of Passage: Adolescence in America, 1790 to the Present* (New York: Basic Books, 1977); David O. Levine, *The American College and the Culture of Aspiration, 1915–1940* (Ithaca, N.Y.: Cornell University Press, 1986); Helen Lefkowitz Horowitz, *Campus Life: Undergraduate Culture from the End of the Eighteenth Century to the Present* (New York: Alfred A. Knopf, 1987); and W. Bruce Leslie, *Gentlemen and Scholars: College and Community in the "Age of the University," 1865–1917* (University Park: Pennsylvania State University Press, 1992). Business historians touching on the increased hiring of college graduates include Alfred D. Chandler, *The Visible Hand: The Managerial Revolution in American Business* (Cambridge, Mass.: Harvard University Press, 1977); David Noble, *America by Design: Science, Technology and the Rise of Corporate Capitalism* (New York: Knopf, 1977); Quentin Schultze, "'An Honorable Place': The Quest for Professional Advertising Education," *Business History Review* 56 (Spring 1982): 16–32; Olivier Zunz, *Making America Corporate, 1870–1920* (Illinois: University of Chicago Press, 1990); and Alan R. Raucher, "Dime Store Chains: The Making of Organization Men, 1880–1940," *Business History Review* 65 (Spring 1991): 130–63.
14. Additionally, many of these studies work from the premise that the rising popularity of college, the growth of a practical curriculum in college, and the increased hiring of college graduates stemmed from the spreading ideological hegemony of corporate capitalism. Most conspicuously, Noble, *America by Design*; Barrow, *Universities and the Capitalist State*; Joel Spring, *Images of American Life: A History of*

Ideological Management in Schools, Movies and Television (New York: SUNY Press, 1992).

15. David K. Brown, *Degrees of Control: A Sociology of Educational Expansion and Occupational Credentialism* (New York: Teachers College Press, 1995). Brown's data and conclusions hinted at the necessity of a shift in cultural perceptions, while his methodology precluded exploring such evidence. Brown falls in the functionalist camp, however, as he concludes that college grads, even with a liberal arts curriculum, likely still proved their value as managers of men, a speculation I agree with but that still demands some evidence of cultural shifts in perceptions regarding higher education.

16. Historians who have identified the new middle-class magazines as important avenues for exploring the developing cultural ideals of the corporate, professional-managerial middle class, neglected to delve into the increased importance of college education. Examples are Jan Cohn, *Creating America: George Horace Lorimer and the Saturday Evening Post* (Pennsylvania: University of Pittsburgh Press, 1989); Helen Damon-Moore, *Magazines for the Millions*; Matthew Schneirov, *The Dream of a New Social Order*; and Richard Ohmann, *Selling Culture: Magazines, Markets and Class at the Turn of the Century* (New York: Verso Press, 1996).

17. Alexander H. Revell, "The Plain Business Man," *Saturday Evening Post*, 1 September 1900, pp. 16–17. No surveys of readers existed until much later and the editors (in good middle-class fashion) steadfastly refused to define their readers by class—they were Americans. Two editors of related magazines, however, Edward Bok of the *Ladies Home Journal* and S.S. McClure of *McClure's*, described their readers as the "broad Middle Class" and the "literate middle class," respectively. The readers were considered to be primarily men, fairly well educated, and of the new middle class, which included traditional professionals and business proprietors as well as the urban, white-collar employees of the emerging corporate world—managers, salesmen, researchers, and accountants. This study emphasized the male readership as businessmen with good reason. Although the very definition of the businessman was undergoing a transformation (as this article helps to illuminate), these magazines identified the businessman as their typical male readers, but conceived of business quite broadly: "the world of affairs." When the magazines discussed the changing conditions for success in America for their male readers, they discussed the rise of the corporation in the world of business. Articles addressing the traditional professions occurred, but the overwhelming discourse concerning their male readers assumed that most were engaged in the world of business. For more see Cohn, 10–11; Damon-Moore, 129–30; and Ohmann, 25. The quotes of Bok and McClure appear in Schneirov, 97.

18. The authors who have principally informed my vision are Schneirov, *The Dream of a New Social Order*; Ohmann, *Selling Culture*; and Damon-Moore, *Magazines for the Millions*. The new order envisioned in these magazines formed part of the process of economic-cultural transformation. It was in and through these magazine forums (among other places) that economic changes were worked out or understood on a cultural plane and given meaning. To paraphrase Stuart Hall, it was through such national media that "social knowledge," a "social imagery through which we perceive the 'worlds,' the lived realities of others and imaginarily reconstruct their lives and our own into some intelligible 'world-of-the-whole,' some lived totality." Stuart Hall, "Culture, the Media and the 'Ideological Effect,'" in *Mass Communication and Society*, eds. James Curran, Michael Gurevitch, and James Woolacott (Beverley Hills: Sage Publications, 1979), 340–46. In other words, the magazines formed a cultural arena from which identities and values were influenced. With the creation of the college-educated, businessman ideal, I believe, one is

19. witnessing not an after-the-fact rationalization of accomplished fact, but the hopeful creation of a new model for emulation, and one that reflected the hopes, fears, and aspirations of the new middle-class particularly well.
19. Most scholars working on the cultural construction of masculinity during this period argue that while not a "crisis," it was a period of deep anxiety and shifting definitions of how gender was constructed. My assumptions on modern, "passionate" masculinity have been most shaped by Anthony Rotundo, *American Manhood: Transformations in Masculinity from the Revolution to the Modern Era* (New York: Basic Books, 1993). Additionally, though, I particularly liked Gail Bederman's interpretation of the restructuring of masculinity in this period. She stressed that different strategies emerged. Middle-class men stressed both virility and physical vigor or strength (Rotundo's passionate man) on the one hand with Theodore Roosevelt's cult of strenuosity and the glorification of sport (the match of any uncivilized man, such as blacks or new immigrants flooding America), while also asserting the civilized superiority of the white man. Gail Bederman, *Manliness and Civilization: A Cultural History of Gender and Race in the United States, 1880–1917* (Illinois: University of Chicago Press, 1995), 11–23. Excellent works on transforming concepts of masculinity include, Joe L. Dubbert, *A Man's Place: Masculinity in Transition* (Englewood Cliffs, N.J.: 1979); Peter G. Filene, *Him/Her/Self: Sex Roles in Modern America* (Baltimore: Johns Hopkins University Press, 1986); J. A. Mangan and James Walvin, eds., *Manliness and Morality: Middle-Class Masculinity in Britain and America, 1800–1940* (New York: St. Martin's Press, 1987); Mark C. Carnes and Clyde Griffen, eds., *Meanings for Manhood: Constructions of Masculinity in Victorian America* (Illinois: University of Chicago Press, 199).
20. In his study of the ideal vision of society fostered by the middle-class magazines around the turn of the century, Matthew Schneirov focused particularly on Walker's *Cosmopolitan*. He viewed it as typical in that it mixed many of the traditional cultural and political projects of the genteel literary monthlies (such as *Harper's*) with an embrace of modern changes such as advertising, advancing science and technology, and even viewing the trust or modern corporation as a force for efficiency in business. Matthew Schneirov, *The Dream of a New Social Order*, 80–94 and 110–11, especially.
21. John Brisben Walker, "Modern College Education," *Cosmopolitan* 22 (April 1897): 685.
22. Ibid., 681.
23. Timothy Dwight, "Modern Education," *Cosmopolitan* 23 (August 1897): 438–39. Charles F. Thwing, "Modern Education," *Cosmopolitan* 24 (April 1898): 665.
24. Thwing, "Modern Education," 665.
25. Arthur T. Hadley, "Modern Education," *Cosmopolitan* 28 (November 1899): 104–5.
26. President of Yale, Arthur T. Hadley, argued that "liberal education in the proper meaning of the word is the education which rightly belongs to the free man…[and] fits a member of the ruling class…for the duties and enjoyments of his position." "Higher education of this sort," Hadley believed, "must train gentlemen," and a liberal education that developed character was fundamental. Hadley, "Modern Education," 104–5.
27. Adam Singleton, "What is a Gentleman?—A Lady?" *Cosmopolitan* 29 (August 1900): 398–400; Rafford Pyke, "What Men Like in Men," *Cosmopolitan* 33 (August 1902): 402–6.
28. Schneirov, *The Dream of a New Social Order*, 92–5. An example of *Cosmopolitan*'s effort to supply uplifting cultural edification is (the regular department) "In the World of Arts and Letters," *Cosmopolitan* 23 (May 1897): 99–104.

29. During the nineteenth century, acquiring the proper literary and artistic tastes became an increasingly important aspect of achieving the inner character traits idealized by most Americans. Veysey, *The Emergence of the American University*, 180–251. Many liberal culture partisans, especially at Harvard and Yale, would also cast the benefits of such a liberal education in far more masculine terms during the last decades of the century. Kim Townsend, *Manhood at Harvard: William James and Others* (New York: W. W. Norton and Company, 1996), 80–131; and Robert J. Higgs, "Yale and the Heroic Ideal, Gotterdammerung and Palingenesis, 1865–1914," in Mangan and Walvin, eds., *Manliness and Morality*, 160–75.
30. "Should Your Boy Go to College?" 461.
31. "Culture and Success," *Saturday Evening Post*, 12 October 1901, p. 12.
32. Patton, "Should a Business Man Have a College Education?" 1094.
33. Wheeler, "Is Scholarship a Promise of Success in Life?" 1095.
34. "Should Your Boy Go to College?" 461–62.
35. Albert J. Beveridge, "The Young Man and College Life," *Saturday Evening Post*, 10 June 1905, pp. 1–2; and "What Makes the Wheels Go Round," *Saturday Evening Post*, 20 September 1902, p. 12.
36. Most agreed that the college graduate's "well-trained mind" proved advantageous. Thwing, "Should Railroad Men Be College Men?" 11.
37. Thwing, "Should Railroad Men Be College Men?" 12.
38. Ibid.
39. Russell H. Crittenden, "The Practical Course for Young Men," *Saturday Evening Post*, 27 October 1900, p. 6.
40. "Practical Education as Applied," *Saturday Evening Post*, 18 April 1908, p. 18.
41. "Culture and Success," *Saturday Evening Post*, 12 October 1901, p. 12.
42. Patton, "Should a Business Man Have a College Education?" 1094.
43. Charles F. Thwing, "The Chief Worth of a College Education," *Saturday Evening Post*, 30 January 1909, p. 5.
44. Ibid.
45. "Should Your Boy Go to College?" 463.
46. From 1900 through the end of the decade, the *Post* printed numerous articles and editorials calling for a shorter college course to enable the young man to get his start in life sooner. William Matthews, "The Age for Entering College," *Saturday Evening Post*, 22 December 1900, p. 10; "Saving Valuable Years," *Saturday Evening Post*, 1 August 1903, p. 14; and "Three Years or Five at College?" *Saturday Evening Post*, 7 April 1906, p. 14. As one can see, this subject was a consistent theme in *Post* editorials and it was predicated on Lorimer's belief in the benefits of college for the businessman.
47. Bird S. Coler, "The Man Who Can't Go to College," *Saturday Evening Post*, 29 June 1901, p. 8. See also David Gray, "Do Mental Gymnastics Make Strong Men?" *Saturday Evening Post*, 2 February 1901, p. 12.
48. "Cut Out Educational Frills," *Saturday Evening Post*, 6 June 1903, p. 14; Lorimer made this point again in "Why Greek and Latin," *Saturday Evening Post*, 13 January 1906, p. 12.
49. "The Dead A.B." *Saturday Evening Post*, 17 March 1906, p. 12.
50. "The Boy at College," *Saturday Evening Post*, 7 September 1907, p. 14.
51. D. K. Pearsons, "Freshwater Colleges," *Saturday Evening Post*, 26 May 1900, p. 1110; John Corbin, "High Life and Higher Education," *Saturday Evening Post*, 14 November 1903, pp. 10–11 and 20; "Our Freshwater Colleges," *Saturday Evening Post*, 13 May 1905, p. 12; and, "Gentlemen in Hard Luck," *Saturday Evening Post*, 20 March 1909, p. 18.

52. "Education Becoming Democratic," *Saturday Evening Post*, 11 February 1911, p. 22; and "Democracy and Education," *Saturday Evening Post*, 11 March 1911, p. 24.
53. Still the best discussion of the rise of the "utility" or practical ideal in American higher education is Veysey, *The Emergence of the American University*, 57–120.
54. H. G. Prout, "Railroading as a Profession," *Munsey's Magazine* 22 (March 1900): 876–77.
55. "The Golden Age of the Engineer," *Saturday Evening Post*, 27 October 1900, p. 14.
56. "Dividends Paid on College Parchments," *Saturday Evening Post*, 24 November 1900, p. 6.
57. Crocker, "The Young Man and the New Force; Electrical Engineering," 1–2; Arthur S. Wright, "The Value of Technical Training," *Saturday Evening Post*, 22 June 1901, p. 7; and William A. Scott, "The School of Commerce," *Saturday Evening Post*, 22 June 1901, p. 2. Similar articles in this number were N. S. Shaler, "Science as a Profession," *Saturday Evening Post*, 22 June 1901, p. 6; and W. H. Schuerman, "College-Trained Engineer," *Saturday Evening Post*, 22 June 1901, p. 6.
58. "The New Era in Commercial Education," *Saturday Evening Post*, 11 November 1899, p. 378.
59. Crocker, "The Young Man and the New Force," pp. 1–2.
60. Roger Babson, "A New Profession for the Young Man," *Saturday Evening Post*, 27 May 1911, pp. 37–38. One *Post* editorial from 1905 called for a university of business to "train men to finance as a profession" in order that they could be directors of organizations with purely "detached" professional interests. "Business as a Profession," *Saturday Evening Post*, 29 July 1905, p. 12.
61. Ibid.
62. Daniel Coit Gilman, "Modern Education," *Cosmopolitan* 23 (May 1897): 36.
63. Henry Morton, "Modern Education," *Cosmopolitan* 23 (June 1897): 186.
64. In one such "lament" from a 1903 *Cosmopolitan* article, the general manager of the Erie Railroad regretted not going to college because he found that no branch of modern business did not require scientific knowledge. Daniel Willard, "Making a Choice of a Profession: Civil Engineering," *Cosmopolitan* 35 (October 1903): 659.
65. As *Munsey's* put it in 1895, most "of those who have gained success without a college course look back upon their early days with a sense of having missed something that would have helped them all through life." "Should Your Boy Go to College?" 461. This article captured a classic lament from one of the self-made men consulted for the article, who stated frankly, "I cannot help wishing sometimes that in my youth I had had a better opportunity for developing my natural abilities." "Should Your Boy Go to College?" 462.
66. Bigelow, "Can a University Help Me to Earn a Living?" 8. One U.S. Bureau of Education report quoted an observer from the University of Berlin in 1905, who noted that American businessmen seemed to desire more than technical training for their college trained employees. They seemed to want a training that enabled a person in business "to participate in intellectual activities previously monopolized by the aristocratic classes." Irvin G. Wyllie, *The Self-Made Man in America: The Myth of Rags to Riches* (New Brunswick, N.J.: Rutgers University Press, 1954), 113–14.
67. Elisha Benjamin Andrews, "Two New Educational Ideals," *Cosmopolitan* 23 (September 1897): 573.
68. Ibid., 574.
69. "The Cosmopolitan University," *Cosmopolitan* 24 (January 1898): 335–40.
70. Walker had pronounced that the university targeted a new group, and the only statistics compiled on enrollments fit the profile of the new middle class perfectly. A

sampling of roughly 2500 applicants found the vast majority to be either businessmen (795) or clerks (471), with mechanics (298) and teachers (256) the next highest. Unfortunately, nothing is recorded regarding their choice of courses. Walker, "The Cosmopolitan University," *Cosmopolitan* 24 (November 1897): 101–2. The upper middle class of the old literary monthlies would not have needed voice culture and manners instruction. The new middle-class men, who were struggling to rise yet also wished for the stamp of legitimacy, longed for such culture and also the broad liberal knowledge that magazines and books told them marked a gentleman.

71. Some conspicuous examples from *Cosmopolitan* include "Some Examples of Recent Art," *Cosmopolitan* 24 (April 1898): 669–72; Harry Thurston Peck, "Balzac and His Work," *Cosmopolitan* 27 (July 1899): 238–45; George E. Waring Jr., "Great Business Operations: The Utilization of City Garbage," *Cosmopolitan* 24 (February 1898): 405–12; and John H. Bridge, "The Story of the World's Largest Corporation," *Cosmopolitan* 35 (October 1903): 657–59.
72. A general historical overview of Cosmopolitan University is found in Susan Waugh McDonald, "From Kipling to Kitsch, Two Popular Editors of the Gilded Age: Mass Culture, Magazines and Correspondence Universities," *Journal of Popular Culture* 15 (Fall 1981): 50–61.
73. For example, David Starr Jordan, "A Consideration of Herbert Spencer's Essay on Education," *Cosmopolitan* 29 (July 1900): 266–76.
74. For instance, "A Great College Year," *Saturday Evening Post*, 27 October 1900, p. 15; and "Better Looking Students," *Saturday Evening Post*, 27 October 1900, p. 15. Other short articles or editorials reporting positively on the growth of colleges or the more democratic and enthusiastic student body include "The Colleges and College Folk," *Saturday Evening Post*, 28 October 1899, p. 330; James Melvin Lee, "How to be Self-Supporting at College," *Saturday Evening Post*, 27 October 1900, pp. 26–27; "Education Becoming Democratic," *Saturday Evening Post*, 11 February 1911, p. 22.
75. "The New Kind of Graduates," *Saturday Evening Post*, 18 July 1903, p. 14.
76. "The Broadening of the Colleges," *Saturday Evening Post*, 27 October 1900, p. 15; and "The Modern College Man," *Saturday Evening Post*, 27 October 1900, p. 15.
77. David Starr Jordan, "The College Man's Advantage in the Coming Century," *Saturday Evening Post*, 26 May 1900, p. 1090.
78. Russell H. Crittenden, "The Practical College Course for Young Men," *Saturday Evening Post*, 27 October 1900, p. 6.
79. John Corbin, "Which College for the Boy?" *Saturday Evening Post*, 7 September 1907, pp. 8–9. The characterization of Cornell as "democratic" may seem a stretch, but we are dealing with perception. Many praised even Yale and Princeton for their democracy in that once a student was in, he could rise on his merits (usually through athletics) and be admitted into the "right" clubs.
80. The University of Michigan was described as a democratic Yale, where the sons of farmers, mechanics, shopkeepers, and clerks intermixed and where the curriculum combined the liberal aspects of Yale and the German-research aspects of Harvard. John Corbin, "Which College for the Boy?" *Saturday Evening Post*, 19 October 1907, pp. 9–11. Wisconsin is covered in Corbin, "Which College for the Boy?" *Saturday Evening Post*, 22 June 1907, pp. 3–5. The University of Chicago was described by Corbin in "Which College for the Boy?" *Saturday Evening Post*, 20 July 1907, pp. 14–15 and 18.
81. Corbin, "Which College for the Boy?" *Saturday Evening Post*, 17 August 1907, p. 6. He noted that even in Princeton's graduate schools, "science has not quite exorcised the humanities," Corbin, p. 7.

82. Cornell's democratic nature has already been noted. For Princeton, Corbin described the nature of that campus's democracy as "organized," as opposed to the unorganized and natural democracy of the West. Corbin, "Which College," 17 August 1907, p. 7.
83. "Practical Education as Applied," *Saturday Evening Post*, 18 April 1908, p. 18. For instance, he praised the outcome of true liberal education—character—in an editorial eulogy of esteemed Harvard professor Nathaniel Shaler (a committed teacher of men rather than a lonely scholar). "The Making of a Man," *Saturday Evening Post*, 26 May 1906, p. 14; and "Culture and Success," 12 October 1901, p. 12.
84. "A Liberal Education," *Saturday Evening Post*, 3 December 1904, p. 18.
85. "Too Much Common Sense," *Saturday Evening Post*, 11 August 1906, p. 16.
86. "Silk Purses and Sows Ears," *Saturday Evening Post*, 4 November 1905, p. 14.
87. For example, "The Educational Stepladder," *Saturday Evening Post*, 11 August 1906, p. 16; "Education That Pays," *Saturday Evening Post*, 28 July 1906, p. 16. "Education Becoming Democratic," *Saturday Evening Post*, 11 February 1911, p. 22, rejoiced in the rise of the great state universities that had put classical literature in its proper place: only one aspect of the humanities, not the end in itself.
88. In her look at the interconnectedness of middle-class magazine advertising and fiction, Ellen Gruber Garvey characterized the magazines using the older definition of a magazine as a "repository of goods and merchandise." She argued that the magazines "joined in one package, or booklet, the commercial world of goods and sales with the world of private musing and fantasy." Ellen Gruber Garvey, *The Adman in the Parlor: Magazines and the Gendering of Culture, 1880s to 1910s* (New York: Oxford University Press, 1996), 3–4. I would extend that total package concept beyond ads and fiction, to include articles and editorials. I think my research especially reveals how readers were encouraged to indulge and identify with a developing ideal image of college and the college-educated businessman that was promoted throughout every element of the magazine in remarkably similar ways.
89. For instance, "The Dignity of Advertising," *Munsey's Magazine* 13 (June 1895), 319; and "Educational Advertising," *Saturday Evening Post*, 20 May 1905, p. 14. Gruber Garvey and Matthew Schneirov also comment on this for other magazines, as well. Gruber Garvey, *Adman in the Parlor*, 11–15; and Schneirov, *Dream of a New Social Order*, 87–91.
90. Ohmann, *Selling Culture*, 89–117.
91. For example, ICS, *Saturday Evening Post*, 21 March 1908, p. 29. In half- and full-page ads, the text screamed "The trained man wins" or asked, "You don't want to remain in the time-clock and dinner pail class all your life?" International Correspondence School [ICS], *Saturday Evening Post*, 21 March 1908, p. 29; and American School of Correspondence, *Saturday Evening Post*, 20 March 1909, p. 39.
92. As early as 1902, the Home Correspondence School advertised legitimate college courses in the ancient and modern languages, literature, history, mathematics, and the sciences offered under the "direct personal charge" of professors from Cornell, Harvard, and Yale. Another school ran the slogan "college in your cottage." They would bring real college-level courses, including commercial subjects, to the people. The Home Correspondence School, *Saturday Evening Post*, 13 December 1902, p. 17; and National Correspondence Schools, *Collier's Weekly*, 25 May 1901, p. 28. Home Correspondence School, *Saturday Evening Post*, 28 July 1900, p. 22, also mentioned instructors from Brown and Harvard, and the fact that their courses could lead to an A.B. The Home Correspondence School, in fact, did offer a bachelor's degree. Most such schools did not.
93. Intercontinental Correspondence University, *Saturday Evening Post*, 22 October 1902, p. 21; and Intercontinental Correspondence University, *Saturday Evening*

Post, 25 February 1905, p. 31. The 1905 ad listed twenty courses, and all except Consular Service and World Politics dealt with commerce, but more from a broad academic perspective. Banking, Business Law, and Commercial Geography were the most practical. Others were informative, such as History of Commerce, International Commerce, Maritime Economics, and Economics of Industry. The American School of Correspondence actually did offer a B.S. in engineering through the Armour Institute, but in 1909 announced that due to "the call of business" and the need for men trained in the "bigger phases" of their work, they opened new courses in commerce, accounting, and business administration. American School of Correspondence, *Saturday Evening Post*, 18 September 1909, p. 37.

94. Peirce School, *Saturday Evening Post*, 31 July 1909, p. 29. By the second decade of the century, the Alexander Hamilton Institute, a new and quite successful correspondence school, catered not to entry-level clerks but to men aspiring to administrative positions. Aspiring young businessmen today required "broad business training" rather than specialization. Alexander Hamilton Institute, *American Magazine* 82 (October 1916): 88.

95. Valparaiso listed a classical department, but emphasized their specialized, professional study like pharmacy, dental, medical, engineering, and commercial training. They promised to prepare one for "practical life" in the shortest time at the least expense. Valparaiso University, *Saturday Evening Post*, 31 July 1909, p. 29. The ad was two columns wide and a full page in length. At the time it claimed to be the second largest university in the United States. University of Pittsburgh, *Saturday Evening Post*, 13 August 1910, p. 47. A few lesser-known colleges and universities had placed small ads in the magazines—women's colleges or music schools—since around 1900. By the middle years of the first decade, Harvard and the University of Michigan ran ads as well. Harvard University, *Saturday Evening Post*, 13 April 1907, p. 24; and University of Michigan, *Saturday Evening Post*, 13 April 1907, p. 24.

96. The quotes come respectively from the following advertisements: New York University, *Saturday Evening Post*, 9 August 1902, p. 16; New York University, *Saturday Evening Post*, 11 August 1906, p. 23; and New York University, *Saturday Evening Post*, 18 August 1906, p. 24. The final quote came from the text of the August 11 advertisement.

97. Hugh Hawkins, *Between Harvard and America*, 292. Eliot was contracted to compile three to four volumes per month and enlisted the help of faculty members. Hawkins, 294.

98. Rubin, *The Making of Middlebrow Culture*, 27–29.

99. P. F. Collier and Son Publishers, advertisement for Harvard Classics, *Collier's Weekly*, 12 June 1909, back cover.

100. Hawkins, *Between Harvard and America*, 200–202; and Veysey, *The Emergence of the American University*, 90–98.

101. Hawkins, *Between Harvard and America*, 200–203. The quote is from an Eliot speech noted by Hawkins (203).

102. Ibid., 204; and Veysey, *The Emergence of the American University*, 90.

103. "Reading for Americans," *Collier's Weekly*, 5 June 1909, p. 9. This was the first announcement of the project.

104. P. F. Collier and Son Incorporated, *Saturday Evening Post*, 24 August 1912, p. 45. Hawkins pointed out in his look at this subject that the Harvard Classics was not a collection of the Great Books as someone like Hutchins would have defined them. Eliot saw it rather as a record of human thought and achievement, including the sciences. Moreover, Eliot envisioned the Five-Foot Shelf much as the smorgasbord of Harvard electives. One could choose to focus on certain areas and acquire guides

for more information to suit one's taste—a far cry from the liberal culture ideal of absorbing the Great Books and a point that emphasizes again the changing definition of a liberal arts education that had become operative. Hawkins, *Between Harvard and America*, 294–95.

105. The Review of Reviews Company, for example, quickly attempted to outflank the Harvard Classics. The Review of Review's "Masterpiece Library" had narrowed the books "a cultured person must read" down to a three-foot shelf. Hawkins, *Between Harvard and America*, 294.

106. The quotes appear respectively in, The Mentor Association, *American Magazine* 81 (March 1916): 109; and The Mentor Association, *American Magazine* 81 (January 1916): 69.

107. The Mentor Association, *American Magazine* 81 (February 1916): 100.

108. The Mentor Association, *American Magazine* 82 (November, 1916): 121.

109. One might surmise that the first positive mentions of the college curriculum would reflect the introduction of more scientific and practical courses. The earliest appeared in late 1901 with "The Wedge." The college boy's engineering training merited only a brief mention, however. The story focused instead on his football and leadership skills as he formed a group of immigrant scabs into a well-oiled team in order to break through the line of strikers at the end of the day. Henry K. Webster, "The Wedge," *Saturday Evening Post*, 28 December 1901, pp. 7–8. References to a technical or engineering background began to appear with regular frequency only toward the latter years of the first decade, much later than one would expect. The college characters who boasted technical training in these stories, though, were all in a business or industrial setting. And, more significantly, nearly all were characterized as self-supporting students, rising up the corporate ladder to management, and often with middle-class backgrounds (few sons of the wealthy). I deal with this topic more fully in a chapter of my book manuscript, "Creating the College Man: Mass Magazines and the Transformation of Middle-Class Masculinity in America, 1890-1915," now under consideration.

110. H. K. Webster, "The Matter with Carpenter," *Saturday Evening Post*, 26 March 1904, pp. 6–7 and 28. Another story, "The Efficient Salamander," revolved around a college graduate working as an assistant manager in an immigrant textile shop, a job procured for him by his father. While seemingly concerned more with how a "scientific manager" should dress than with the requirements of the job, the son shocked all when he quickly diagnosed several inefficiencies in the operation. He apparently attained this ingrained managerial outlook from a few classes at college. Montague Glass, "The Efficient Salamander," *Saturday Evening Post*, 26 August 1911, pp. 13–16 and 40.

111. David Graham Phillips, "The Cost," *Saturday Evening Post*, 21 November 1903, pp. 11–13.

112. Phillips, "The Cost," *Saturday Evening Post*, 28 November 1903, pp. 10–11 and 31–32.

113. Phillips, "The Cost," *Saturday Evening Post*, 5 December 1903, pp. 15–17 and 53; and Phillips, "The Cost," 12 December 1903, pp. 10–11 and 24.

114. John Corbin, "The Cave Man," *Saturday Evening Post*, 2 February 1907, pp. 15–17.

115. For instance, "The Triumph of Billy" (1906) featured Billy Helmerston, a tech grad of '02, employed by an electrical company. The story revolved around Helmerston's love for the daughter of the owner of the company and the problems of class that accompanied the attraction. Herbert Quick, "The Triumph of Billy," *Saturday Evening Post*, 8 December 1906, pp. 5–7.

116. A good general example is a comic tale by George Fitch from 1911, "Sic Transit Gloria All-America." The story revolved around the humbling difficulty for college

grads to find gainful employment in the big city. Nevertheless, the two main characters eventually become low-level managers, who hire an out-of-work ex-football hero out of pity. The point being, for this discussion, they were not clerks but managers. George Fitch, "Sic Transit Gloria All-America," *Saturday Evening Post*, 15 April 1911, pp. 15–17.

117. In particular, I believe that my scholarship renders the fine work of scholars like David O. Levine and Paula Fass, who explore the popularity of college in the 1920s, much more understandable. The inclusion of college into the "culture of aspiration," to quote Levine, did not just arise in the 1920s. This phenomenon reflected new cultural perceptions, the formation of which took several years. One cannot comprehend the seemingly sudden emergence of college within America's culture of aspiration and the booming enrollments of the 1920s without the cultural foundation for altered perceptions of college that this article explores. David O. Levine, *The American College and the Culture of Aspiration, 1915–1940* (Ithaca, N.Y.: Cornell University Press, 1987) and Paula Fass, *The Damned and the Beautiful: American Youth in the 1920s* (New York: Oxford University Press, 1977).

"What Gender Is Lex?" Women, Men, and Power Relations in Colleges of the Nineteenth Century

Michael David Cohen

This study reexamines the extracurricular experiences of young women and men at Midwestern colleges between the 1870s and 1890s. The decades after the Civil War saw the rise of coeducation as the dominant form of higher education in the Midwestern and Far Western United States. Historians have commonly stressed the social segregation and extracurricular inequality by gender that prevailed at some colleges in spite of integration in the classroom. This study, however, draws on students' experiences at the two colleges in Northfield, Minnesota, to propose an alternative model. In particular, it argues that male and female students at Carleton and St. Olaf Colleges sought each other's romantic companionship, enjoyed many formal and informal extracurricular activities together, and shared similar opportunities for involvement in electoral politics. It suggests that, while some colleges may have fully adopted the homosocial organization and gender inequality characteristic of the Victorian era, others offered young women opportunities for heterosocial interaction and relative gender equality unattainable in American society at large.

> Prof. "What gender is lex?" Freshman. "Masculine." Prof. "Oh no, it is feminine." Freshman. "If I had known that I should not have obeyed it."
> —*St. Olaf College* Manitou Messenger, *March 1887*[1]

In a famous essay, Joan Wallach Scott discusses the several meanings of the word *gender*. Historically, it began as a grammatical term; linguistic conservatives continue to resist its use in any other fashion. Here *gender* functions as "a way of classifying phenomena, a socially agreed upon system of distinctions rather than an objective description of inherent traits." In this usage, the gender of a word, object, or person carries no meaning beyond its grammatical classification. More recently, however, historians and other scholars have adapted the term to describe cultural understandings of women and

---

Perspectives on the History of Higher Education 24 (2005): 41-90.
©2005. ISBN: 1-4128-0517-1

men in the past and present. In Scott's carefully formulated bipartite definition, "gender is a constitutive element of social relationships based on perceived differences between the sexes, and gender is a primary way of signifying relationships of power."[2] Not only does gender carry meaning about men and women: Gender is a major locus through which people create political meaning.

Both definitions factored in the above joke printed in the student newspaper of coeducational St. Olaf College in Northfield, Minnesota. On the one hand, the freshman mistook the grammatical gender of the Latin word for "law." But the punch line depended on his (presumably this fictional student identified as masculine, not feminine) understanding of gender as more than grammar. *Lex*, law, power belonged to the masculine, not the feminine. Illustrating both parts of Scott's definition, the student constructed power through the language of gender and imagined appropriate power relationships as based in dominant masculine and submissive, or at least not dominant, feminine identities. At the same time, though, he acknowledged the real or potential appearance of feminine authority. If *lex* were feminine, he would choose to defy that law. For the newspaper's readers to get the joke, they must, even if they scorned the idea, have been able to conceive of women in power.

* * *

Historians have not traditionally seen nineteenth-century coeducational colleges as strongholds of political or social opportunities for women. Most of the few scholars who have examined gender relations in those schools identify hostile environments for female students. They acknowledge the greater liberality of Midwestern educators, which produced a commitment to gender egalitarianism that combined with economic pressures to encourage the formation of coeducational colleges. Thus in the late nineteenth century, colleges throughout the United States, but especially in the Midwest (and Far West), became coeducational.[3] With few exceptions, however, scholars deny that Midwestern liberality produced socially integrated environments. Researchers argue that throughout the country, both male professors and male students resented women's presence. The former had no choice but to teach all students, but the latter could and did choose to distance themselves from women socially. Though an occasional man and woman became friends, as a rule men offered women only insults. Scholars focusing on the Midwest, who tend to study the period after 1890, observe that in contrast to both Eastern and Far Western schools, male students there welcomed women to campus, but the latter chose to isolate themselves. Either way, women and men created separate extracurricular lives.[4] Meanwhile, the women's and coordinate colleges that appeared in Eastern states beginning in the 1860s offered their students entry into such traditionally masculine fields as athletics and campus politics. But these opportunities arose precisely from men's absence.[5] When young women and men came together, women's involvement in men's activities, let alone empowerment through mixed organizational leadership or political participation, vanished.

The newspapers, yearbooks, and other surviving documents from the two colleges in the small Minnesotan town of Northfield tell a very different story. Carleton and St. Olaf Colleges, both coeducational from their beginnings in 1867 and 1875, respectively, by the 1880s offered women and men remarkably similar opportunities.[6] Carleton advertised proudly, "ALL DEPARTMENTS OPEN TO STUDENTS OF EITHER SEX."[7] St. Olaf, too, except possibly in its divinity school, did not restrict female students' curricular options.[8] But historians of higher education note that the student-designed extracurriculum, not the faculty-mandated curriculum, dominated college students' lives in the nineteenth century. College men and women's activities outside of class most strongly influenced their overall college experience.[9] And here, students created a sexually integrated environment. On both informal and formal levels, St. Olaf and Carleton students of the late 1870s through the early 1890s, when most studies of Midwestern college life begin, came together across gender lines to create a single student life. When faculty stepped in to check their mixing, students resisted. Though women's opportunities did not equal men's, their participation in the single extracurriculum made them partners, not subordinates or exiles, on Northfield's campuses. They even shared leadership positions and political roles. These post-Reconstruction colleges, while by no means egalitarian utopias, offered women interaction with men that produced far greater opportunities for power than American society at large.

* * *

Townspeople founded Northfield College in 1866 under the auspices of the Congregational Church; it opened a year later, and in

1871 the name changed to honor benefactor William Carleton. From the beginning, the College welcomed both men and women and, despite the formal church affiliation, Christians of all denominations. These decisions reflected not only the the Midwest's relative sympathy to women's higher education and the economic necessity of admitting both women and non-Congregationalists, but that church's tradition of establishing colleges without demanding control over their policies. Local citizens, rather than Eastern church leaders, chose Carleton's constituency and purpose. They sought to educate young women and men morally and intellectually, imparting a broadly Christian message. A preparatory department readied younger students for the college course, and an English department offered secondary education to students who did not plan to pursue further study. The collegiate department, in fact, did not open until 1870, after the first students finished their preparatory years. The first graduating class, that of 1874, consisted of one man and one woman, who later married.[10]

The curriculum grew more varied as the student body expanded. Beginning in 1877, the College offered three four-year bachelor's programs, with preparatory programs tailored to each, emphasizing the classics, modern literature, and science. Carleton introduced courses in music in 1872, art in 1889, and stenography in 1891, all of which were open both to students enrolled in the academic courses and to those interested only in learning these skills. The College established a program leading to the master of arts degree in 1885, and trained students for the doctorate of philosophy beginning in 1891.[11] Meanwhile, the College's enrollment grew from eighty-one students attending part or all of the 1867–68 academic year, to 254 a decade later, and 337 in 1892–93. Although both male and female students could and did study in all courses, men tended to gravitate toward the classical and scientific tracks, and women toward the literary; the music and art departments attracted a mostly female enrollment. Men outnumbered women overall, however, until the early 1880s, and in the collegiate department until the late 1880s. Thereafter, women consistently comprised the majority of the student body (see Table 1).[12]

Carleton had barely graduated its first class when it lost its monopoly over higher education in Northfield. In 1874, Norwegian Lutherans founded (and in winter 1875 opened) St. Olaf's School on the same street corner as one of Carleton's buildings; it moved to

Table 1
Carleton College Enrollments

	English		Preparatory		Colleg	Total**	
	Boys	Girls	Boys	Girls	Men	Boys/Men	Girls/Women
1867–68	38	26	9	8	–	47	34
1868–69	43	18	35	3	–	78	21
1869–70	39	19	24	6	–	63	25
1870–71	41	23	30	10	4	75	35
1871–72	60	33	39	12	6	105	48
1872–73	57	33	36	12	4	97–108	48–67
1873–74	73	54	29	8	5	107–118	64–86
1874–75	81	40	53	29	12	146–159	70–90
1875–76	87	49	58	26	15	162	94
1876–77	50	39	71	23	18	142	84
1877–78	50	45	69	28	22***	149	105
1878–79	44	34	50	23	23	123	80
1879–80	47	55	51	27	27	141	119
1880–81	54	58	54	46	32	157	147
1881–82	50	49	45	43	27	137	154
1882–83	55	51	79	51	22	175	155
1883–84	55	68	50	65	20	154	206
1884–85	33	68	36	52	22	127	202
1885–86	15	52	56	39	18	117	174
1886–87	25	58	55	45	23	133	181
1887–88	38	51	57	50	18	131	183
1888–89	30	49	53	52	20	123	178
1889–90	28	46	52	51	14	117	180
1890–91	33	37	46	38	12	123	198
1891–92	–	–	77	84	20	126–185	141–200
1892–93	–	–	33	39	26	133	204

* Single numbers appear where graduate students' genders are unknown

** Includes students enrolled only in the music, art, or stenography courses; ranges appear where those students' numbers and genders are uncertain

*** Includes two students pursuing both the classical and scientific courses

**** Graduate students' genders are unknown between 1882 and 1885

Dash indicates course did not exist in a year or no data is known; Carleton eliminated the English course in 1891 the other side of the Cannon River in 1878. Like Carleton, St. Olaf's included a preparatory department; here the collegiate department opened in 1886, and the institution became known as St. Olaf College three years later. In addition to the collegiate and preparatory courses of study, an English course educated young people with no plans to enter college. Elementary classes enrolled younger girls and boys. Finally, a divinity school, which seems to have admitted only men, opened the same year as the collegiate department. Excluding the divinity school, for which enrollment numbers have not survived, St. Olaf counted fewer students than Carleton. But it grew. In its first academic year, which consisted of only the winter and spring trimesters of 1875, it enrolled fifty students; a decade later, that number had risen to eighty-two, and in 1887–88 it lept to 135. In 1892–93, the College counted 147 students (see Table 2).

Unlike Carleton's, St. Olaf's more narrowly denominational preparatory and collegiate curricula taught Lutheran theology alongside Latin and algebra.[13] Non-Norwegians attended at least as early as the 1880s, but the student population was much more nationally and religiously homogenous than Carleton's. Despite a faculty member's (or possibly a student's) telling some students in 1879 that "[o]ur relation to snow-capped Norway must be forgotten," and that they must "try to inculcate in our minds, that we are Americans and nothing else," the institution's ethnic and religious identity endured. In 1890, a student described St. Olaf as a school for the Norwegian race designed to preserve the Lutheran faith.

The Norwegian Lutheran Synod, however, opposed church-sponsored education, and especially coeducation. Bernt Julius Muus broke with the Church leadership when he founded this school for young men and women, and thus had to obtain funding from a private donor. St. Olaf became on its founding the first Norwegian-American Lutheran school or college to admit students of both genders (see Figure 1). Men nonetheless outnumbered women there into the twentieth century. By 1906, the College had awarded only six of its 138 bachelor of arts degrees to women. Still, female students formed an important part of the school, especially in the English and preparatory departments. St. Olaf's School's first two graduating classes, those of 1877 and 1878, consisted only of girls. And even in the collegiate department, far more women attended than graduated. Overall, girls and women hovered throughout the period I discuss at around one fourth of the student body (see Table 2).[14]

Table 2
St. Olaf College Enrollments

	Elementary, English, and Preparatory*		Collegiate		Total
	Boys	Girls	Men	Wo	
1875	38	12	-		
1875–76	34	10	-		
1876–77	48	14	-		
1877–78	74	25	-		
1878–79	51	13	-		
1879–80	57	17	-		
1880–81	68	24	-		
1881–82	70	27	-		
1882–83	72	20	-		
1883–84	79	30	-		
1884–85	64	18	-		
1885–86	64	18	-		
1886–87	63	18	5		
1887–88	92	28	14		
1888–89	66	24	18		
1889–90	84	25	24		
1890–91	89	38	20		
1891–92	102	46	30		
1892–93	78	36	30		

* May include students enrolled only in music classes
Dash indicates course did not exist in a year

Figure 1

The faculty, friends, and coeducational student body of St. Olaf's School posed in 1879 between the American and Norwegian flags. Male students, members of St. Olaf's Guard, wore military caps (courtesy, Shaw-Olson Center for College History, St. Olaf College).

The difference from Carleton, where female students outnumbered their male classmates after the early 1880s, is notable. Religion surely contributed to the discrepancy. Founder Muus held an unpopular view in the Norwegian Lutheran Synod; most denominational leaders opposed coeducation, and many or most parents of the rank-and-file presumably agreed with them and withheld their daughters from St. Olaf. Even those who believed higher education appropriate for young women must have questioned the value of theological training for a segment of the population excluded from the ministry. Yet those girls and women who did attend St. Olaf found similar opportunities to those experienced by their counterparts at Carleton. Many of the same opportunities for coeducational extracurricular life and female leadership appeared on both campuses. These remarkable differences from the broader society did not depend on the proportion of female students or denomonational affiliation, but rather accompanied coeducation in some colleges regardless of girls' and women's numbers and religion.

* * *

In June 1877, students published the first issue of the *Carletonian*, an annual newspaper that lasted through 1880. The *Carletonia* replaced it in June 1881, and beginning the following academic year appeared monthly. In April 1891, its frequency increased to about one issue every three weeks.[15] Several student newspapers appeared and failed in St. Olaf's early years: the weekly, handwritten *St. Olaf's Essayist* lasted a few months in early 1879; the *Cricket*, at least part of 1879–80; the weekly *St. Olaf's Echo*, several months in 1880–81; and the *Student's Reporter*, at least one issue in February 1884. No issue of the *Cricket* survives, and few issues of the others do. In 1887, however, students founded the permanent, monthly, and well-preserved *Manitou Messenger*.[16] In this article, I also draw on Carleton's yearbook (St. Olaf had none in my period), and student literary society records, student diaries, and other documents offer an additional window into student life at Northfield's two colleges. But the newspapers provide the bulk of my evidence. My period thus begins with the 1876–77 academic year, when the first newspaper appeared. It ends in 1892–93, both because other historians have focused on the period beginning in the 1890s and because presidential election years generated especially revealing newspaper coverage of gendered power relations.

Gender constituted the central attribute along which Northfield's students divided themselves. Of course, they identified themselves in numerous ways. I will argue that sexuality occupied many students' thoughts. But, although Michel Foucault points out that both the heterosexual/homosexual binary, and extensive discussion of nonprocreative sexualities, appeared in the late nineteenth century, student records from Northfield revealed only masculine-feminine romantic interest.[17] If sexuality divided college students, they kept quiet about all but its hegemonic incarnation. At St. Olaf, race and nationality converged as students prided themselves on their Norwegian "race," but their homogeneity eliminated this as a partitioning factor within the campus community.[18] Race in the sense we use it today hardly surfaced. One African American boy entered Carleton's preparatory department in 1874, but if any other nonwhite students attended either college in the early years, the sources showed no sign of an impact on student life.[19]

Students did not describe economic class as a fracturing element. Many Carletonians, the newspaper noted in 1880, intended to become farmers, not professionals. A student speaker at St. Olaf's thirteenth anniversary celebration referred to the economic diversity among that college's student body.[20] But students did not divide socially along economic lines. The large proportion of students who joined literary societies and other organizations (see below) revealed that organized social life on these two campuses involved the mass of working- and farming-class young people, not just the small Northfield elite. Nor did geography divide students: until the twentieth century, few came to either college from outside the Upper Midwest.[21] They did nonetheless describe themselves as "from all parts of the country," but only rarely invoked this type of diversity.[22] Students' academic tracks played little or no role in life outside the classroom; the newspapers made only rare and brief mentions of these.[23] Age did divide students. One article described typical female and male college graduates as twenty-two and twenty-five, respectively, while children at least as young as fifteen attended the preparatory departments.[24] Indeed, age-based social strife produced extended violence between two classes at Carleton in the 1870s.[25] But at St. Olaf class-year conflict was minimal.[26] In any event, age appeared in students' writings far less often than gender.

I use gender as a binary, though the usage is somewhat problematic. Gendered identities among Carleton and St. Olaf students were not entirely immutable. Students understood that they could manipulate their physical appearance to temporarily shift their gender. A man could grow his hair "like a woman."[27] Or, if a game required an extra woman, a man with white hair could "'pass for a girl.'"[28] But these admissions were the exception. Students rarely referred to the troublesome nature of the gender binary.[29] Most of the time, students saw their world as made up of men who were men and women who were women. In this essay, I accept this categorization so that I may best understand *how they understood* gender relations and roles on campus. Gender differences, in their eyes, did not imply the separation of men and women, either at distinct colleges or in distinct social worlds within St. Olaf and Carleton. Both women and men enjoyed and sought each other's company. In some situations, this open atmosphere even permitted women to pursue traditionally masculine avenues to power. On the college campus, *lex* could be feminine.

A Successful Experiment

The newspapers expressed clear support for coeducation. Of course, these sources are biased. Except possibly St. Olaf's earliest newspapers, which had nothing to say on the subject, Carleton's and St. Olaf's papers were coeducational organizations themselves: both men and women served on their editorial boards. Students who believed young men and women should not sit in the same classroom would not likely join an organization that would increase their contact with the opposite gender. Still, the near absence of debate over coeducation suggests that the issue was not one of contention in the campus communities. Though neither paper often printed letters to the editor, they did discuss issues of campus interest. The *Carletonia* aimed to be "a true exponent of college sentiment," not "the organ of the editorial board."[30] Both schools' papers accomplished this, in that they acknowledged opinions popular among students, for example in politics, with which the editors disagreed. Such instances served as an opening for the editors' soapbox. But this did not happen with coeducation.

Students did write about coeducation. But they had only good things to say about it. At St. Olaf, they viewed it as a distinction for the College. The first issue of the *Manitou Messenger* reminded its readers that St. Olaf "was the first Norwegian institution [of higher education] to admit both sexes to its halls, and the management has had no occasion to regret this arrangement."[31] *Manitou Messenger* coeditor-in-chief J. P. Tandberg discussed coeducation at much greater length in a speech he delivered in November 1890 at the annual celebration of the anniversary of St. Olaf's founding, which appeared in that month's issue. He used the opportunity of this speech to protest the faculty's hostility to sexually integrated social activities, and in so doing extolled the virtues of coeducation itself. Like "church sociables, and the admittance of women into the business walks of life," he argued, coeducation developed "that unconsciousness [in relations between the genders] which is the truest sign of moral health." Men and women learning together also imparted on each other the best qualities of their respective genders. Women made men "kinder, nobler, and better"; men taught women "self-reliance and independence." The following June, Tandberg wrote another article outlining the advantages of coeducation, arguing that "St. Olaf has proved...that, here at least, co-education is a success." Most by then acknowledged that, he wrote; here he sought to convince those few, outside the College, who persisted in their opposition. Though most students probably did not formulate so carefully their reasons for supporting coeducation, Tandberg's speech and essay suggest that his classmates agreed with him: he was arguing against the faculty's interference in the extracurriculum and social life, and outsiders' hostility to coeducation, not student (or faculty) opposition to the presence of both women and men on campus.[32]

Most references in the student newspapers to coeducation and women's higher education in general actually had nothing to do with Carleton or St. Olaf. Rather, both colleges' papers often noted historical and contemporary developments in this area around the country and the world. At the very least, editors were (and expected their readers to be) interested in women's increased access to college and graduate school. But editors did not sound neutral on the issue. They seemed delighted, for example, that "[f]or the first time in the history of co-education at Cornell University, a lady is this year [1877] elected to fill a prominent place in the class-day exercises," and that 56 percent, or "[t]wo hundred and four of the 365 colleges in the United States are coeducational." The latter notice appeared in the November 1892 issues of both St. Olaf's and Carleton's papers, each of which included at least four brief items about the higher education of women.[33] Male and female students in Northfield were reading about the expansion of women's educational opportunities. The absence of any indication of opposition on either campus suggests that most, if not all, students of both genders supported or at least did not strongly resent each other's presence.

Scholars in Love

Romantic interest and relationships constituted one major form of heterosocial interaction. While this may come as no surprise, other historians have suggested a lack of dating among students of the nineteenth century. Helen Lefkowitz Horowitz, though briefly acknowledging the greater interaction between the genders at small colleges, dates "the discovery by college men that college women could be amusing" around the 1910s. Before then, she argues, men more often shunned than dated women.[34] Yet by the late nineteenth century, largely unsupervised courtship had become the norm in both the rural Midwest and America at large. A few ethnic groups, including Russians and Swedes, steadfastly held to their traditions of arranged marriage, but most adjusted to conditions in the United States by allowing young people the freedom to experiment romantically.[35] It seems unlikely that colleges, spaces notable for parents' absence, would have been anomalous in this regard. At Carleton and St. Olaf, in fact, they were not. Students' writings reflected both an active dating scene and broader interest among students in cultivating amorous relationships.

The rules suggested otherwise. Professors mandated the stringent control of students' moral and social behavior, including interactions between women and men. At least for the first decade, St. Olaf's faculty forbade students to drink, smoke, gamble, use profane language—or dance. Men must obtain the college president's permission to call on female students, and women needed the preceptress's permission before allowing male students to walk them home. Carletonians, too, had to abstain from alcohol and tobacco, watch their language, and avoid "whatever else is opposed to good manners or good morals." The faculty permitted occasional parties, but only with adult female chaparones. Men's calls on women were strictly regulated, and between 1875 and 1881, ten students faced disciplinary action for the "evening association of men and women."[36] The detailed codes of rules on both campuses seem to have indicated a very limited and closely supervised romantic life. Yet they simultaneously suggested that, contrary to scholars' prior findings, extensive student interest in each other romantically. Rules rarely forbid activities that no one wants to attempt, and we know that at least ten young people in Northfield broke the rules.

But surely more than ten. Students' accounts of college life affirmed their heterosexual romantic interest. They also revealed the ineffectiveness of the regulatory efforts by the faculties. A few Carletonians may have suffered from their indiscretions, but others on both campuses appear to have gotten away quite easily with spending time with their boyfriends or girlfriends—and without asking the president's permission. To be sure, the newspapers made only a few explicit references to dates. No wonder, given the risk of professors' wrath. Some, nonetheless, referred to individual real or fictional outings of male and female students.[37] More reflected on the dating scene generally, suggesting that many more students went out without having their stories printed in the campus press. For example, the *Carletonian*'s June 1877 issue described "the old mill" as both "a favorite summer resort for some of our college friends" and "a delightfully romantic spot for lovers."[38] J. P. Tandberg, in defending coeducation in the *Manitou Messenger*, responded to those who worried it "sometimes leads to matrimonial engagements" not by denying the charge, but instead by asking why, in fact, that constituted a problem. And two editors for that paper alluded to campus romance in an offering of humorous advice. Claiming that "[a] nervous young lady" inquired of the paper how to solve "a pricking pain in the face," the editors responded, "Tell him to take a shave."[39] Though the comment was clearly made in jest, for a reader to get the joke kissing must occur to him/her as an activity in which students engaged. Kissing very likely accompanied dating; the unshaven man here appears to have been the itching young lady's beau.

By far the most extensive discussion of dating appeared in an editorial in which Carleton senior Stella Spalding advised male students on proper behavior toward women. She appealed to Mrs. Grundy, the well-known personification of Victorian propriety, for rules her readers should follow when courting. Describing coeducation itself as "a handsome concession" on Mrs. Grundy's part, Spalding explained that a college man's conduct toward a college woman "should not be so fraternal...that you...should cease to be chivalrous." He thus must ask her out several days in advance, must not ask a second woman if rejected, and must not take her to a free show if he cannot afford to pay for one that charges admission. Most importantly, she began the article by announcing her intention to discuss questions that "the intelligent college student would like to know and fears to ask." Many of her classmates, she claimed, wondered about proper behavior leading up to dates. Many erred in that regard. Spalding sought to set them straight on the rules of an activity widespread among the student body.[40]

References to student dating formed only a small portion of the newspapers' discussion of heterosexual romantic interest. Both colleges' papers included many references to students', especially male students', concern or obsession with romantic love and the opposite gender. *The Manitou Messenger* posed the issue in another charming grammatical double entendre:

> Prof. in Grammar—"What is she the object of?"
> Student—"She is the object of him."[41]

Addressing romance more explicitly, a Carletonian cited men's accompanying women home after evening rhetoricals, a violation of college rules, as one of the faculty's reasons for moving student speeches to the daytime. But "boys will be boys," the writer pointed out, and the change did not solve the problem.[42] Plus, even in the absence of women, men spent much of their time thinking about the opposite gender. The *Carletonia* recorded that the male friends of one unfortunate lad laughed at him when he accidentally presented "the photo. [sic] of his lady-love" that he carried with him at a roller-skating rink in lieu of his ticket.[43] St. Olaf's paper made light of a student who blushed when he "made a lackadaisical confession" of his romantic feelings to a friend.[44] And two issues mentioned men who wrote love letters; in one case the scrivener's "wicked roommate" burned the letter, possibly revealing rivalry or jealousy over women among male students.[45] Either way, women as romantic objects often occupied their thoughts.

Yet women were not merely the romantic objects of men. One of the few surviving diaries from this period reveals the extent to which romance dominated the lives of some college women as well. Christina Vangan's daily account of winter term of her sophomore year at St. Olaf demonstrates both that nothing interested her so deeply and constantly as her boyfriend, and that whatever the faculty's official rules limiting female students' interaction with young men, in practice she had great freedom of movement and could see "R." (who did not attend St. Olaf) just about any time she wanted. Once, for example, she went to church late, in the hope of finding him in Northfield, and no one seems to have bothered to reprimand her. Nearly every day, Vangan mentioned having written a letter to *"my always in mind"* (emphasis in original), received one from him, mistaken someone for him, or rewritten a letter that she worried "might displease him."[46] Another day found her less generous: she was at first pleased to receive a letter from him, "but when I saw how short and little interesting it was, I put it in the stove." She forgot all grievances, however, when he came to town—especially when he trudged through the snow on "[t]he stormiest day of the winter" to see her. Soon thereafter, "many a kiss was bestowed upon me." Only a week later, though, not receiving a letter put her in such "a melancholy humor," leading her to despair that "when he does not want to write he does not want to hear from me either," that "with so many a tears [sic] moistening my pillow I slept in."[47] Her feelings as fragile as any lover's, Vangan carried on her curricular and extracurricular activities as a student at St. Olaf College almost in the background of a more important life of romance. Her student status certainly did not preclude interest in or time spent with her *"always in mind."*

And this was no secret. Campus journalists, though they focused on men's interest in women, on occasion discussed female students' heterosexual interest, too. Sometimes, women appeared merely as flattered recipients of men's attentions. This view is implicit in the examples of men's romantic interest that I cited above; in each, a woman is indeed "the object of him." The most powerful (and drolly heartrending) citation of woman as object from the woman's perspective appeared in a story taken by the *Carletonian* editors from a Massachusetts college's student newspaper:

> Not long since a junior was out riding with one of Amherst's beauties by his side, when looking up pensively into his face, she said with tears in her eyes: "O [illegible] no one loves me, Mr. B." "Some one does," he replied. "Yes?" said the lady, pressing his arm every [sic] so slightly. "Yes, Miss Lizzie," continued the wretch, "God loves you."[48]

Though originally written for a student audience far from Northfield, the Carleton editors believed it would resonate with their classmates. The author portrayed a young woman looking for love and protection under the strong arm of her companion. That writer may have appealed to men to treat women better, to women to find better men, or to both merely to laugh at this "wretch," but in any event the author and the *Carletonian*'s editors accepted the image of women as inferior partners to their boyfriends.

Such was not always the case: college women sometimes exercised power in the field of college romance. This power needed not take a silent form, as when Vangan burned her lover's letter because it was too short. A Carleton woman, for example, caused a stir among the men when she publicly "remarked that the Carleton boys were the homeliest set she had ever seen."[49] And female students could exert their power not only in the negative form of rejection, but also in the positive form of choice. They could *assert* their sexuality, not merely bestow it on romantically dominant men. In 1878, two Carleton professors organized a new student athletic group, the Carleton Archers. The announcement in the *Carletonian* did not specify whether they envisioned the group as all-male or sexually integrated. In any event, a young woman decided to join. The columnist quoted her as announcing "that at the least 'she [*sic*] should want a bow (beau) herself,' not to say anything of the arrows."[50] Not only did this woman enter the typically male world of college sports. She, according to the anonymous writer, took an active and dominating role in the world of college romance: she strode onto the archery field, weapon in hand, to find herself a masculine companion. Whether the story was an accurate account or a fiction created by the writer to criticize coeducational athletics, the writer's trepidation that a woman might take such action indicated that both women and men in the colleges expressed an assertive heterosexual romantic interest.

Organizing Men and Women

Dates were not the only extracurricular fora in which male and female students came into contact. Both informal and formal activities involved larger groups of men and women enjoying each other's presence. A number of historians have observed that the extracurriculum formed the core of nineteenth-century college students' experience. Student-organized activities played an even greater role in campus life than official, faculty-mandated coursework.[51] Although this balance shifted in Eastern colleges around the 1870s as faculties incorporated the educational activities of student literary societies into the curriculum, in Midwestern and Far Western colleges strong extracurricula dominated by literary societies survived until the turn of the century.[52] At St. Olaf and Carleton in the 1870s to 1890s, the extracurriculum remained central. Not only literary societies, but also athletics and a variety of other activities, formal and informal, dominated the lives of Northfield's college students. In many cases, those activities were, or students wished they were, sexually integrated.

To be sure, many students cared about their studies. Writers occasionally felt the need to remind their classmates to take time away from class work to engage in other individual and group activities. One, for example, regretted that few Carleton students read daily newspapers or news magazines. Many felt they were too busy with coursework to keep up with the news.[53] Similarly, two St. Olaf editors noticed that many students worried literary societies would take precious time away from their more important coursework. But that was a minority opinion. More than half the student body, they claimed, belonged to a society. Many of these may even have agreed that "society work is or should be as important as any study in the regular course."[54]

Further, not all members of the college communities shared a strong dedication to their work. Jokes about a professor's shock that a student planned to study and about a student who skipped class on the grounds of a toothache, only to be disappointed when soon afterwards he actually got a toothache, reflected at least an image on campus of the indolent student.[55] But by far the most extensive and convincing evidence of the primacy of informal and formal extracurricular activities in students' lives lies in the students' abundant references to the extracurriculum. Besides jokes like those above, writers for the campus newspapers almost never referred to classes. But every issue included brief notes and often extensive articles about a variety of other activities. The yearbooks and student diaries, too, affirmed the centrality of extracurricular life, and the archives are littered with numerous announcements of student performances and activities.

Especially at Carleton, some elements of the extracurriculum were segregated by gender. These ranged from a "walking club" formed by Carleton women to the short-lived Carleton chapter of the Phi Kappa Psi male fraternity.[56] At St. Olaf, although both women and men enjoyed croquet, they played separately.[57] Other segregated activities resulted from students' separate housing arrangements. Carleton women, who lived in a dormitory, could find a variety of magazines, dailies, and other colleges' newspapers in that building's reading room; college men, who lived off campus, read at a separate facility.[58] Campus celebrations of Halloween took less consistent forms. Some years, male and female students came together for a masquerade at the roller-skating rink or to hear their classmates deliver speeches and musical performances.[59] But more often, women and men celebrated the holiday separately and very differently. Women bobbed for apples, had their own masquerade, or serenaded the female members of the faculty. Men, on the other hand, "came to breakfast next morning [sic] with black eyes."[60] Halloween meant very different things to the two groups of students. They thus separated to enjoy the night (or not) each in its own manner.

Of all extracurricular activities, athletics and literary societies occupied the most space in both colleges' newspapers and Carleton's yearbook. Athletics usually involved the separation of men and women. More to the point, the most prominent sports involved only men. But there were exceptions, at least on one side of the river. Earlier I mentioned the Carleton Archers, which a woman apparently did attempt to join. The article did not divulge whether she achieved her object.[61] Carleton did, at times, support coeducational skiing, bicycling, tennis, skating, and possibly baseball organizations. Women also found opportunities to enjoy tennis and boating in segregated environments.[62] These mixed and women's sports clubs reflected some students' and professors' belief that physical education had a proper place in the education of both women and men. The *Carletonian* printed an article by a professor who heralded "the *right of every girl to a natural physical development*" (emphasis in original).[63] Student writers occasionally supported physical education without specifying a particular gender. They implied that athletic training should serve both male and female students.[64]

But that did not mean that men's and women's athletics achieved equal importance or attention in the student press. Competitive sports, which formed the core of the collegiate athletic scene in Northfield, constituted a masculine domain. The Carleton Athletic Association, which "has general supervision over all athletic sports and contests, excepting those governed by the Faculty," consisted only of men.[65] Though students tried such sports as archery, croquet, and leapfrog, baseball and especially football came to dominate men's interest during autumn over the 1880s.[66] Writers for the newspapers disagreed on the virtue or vice of these games. One reminded readers of "the various forms of mutilation" they caused, while others denied or flouted such charges.[67] Despite the controversy, though, by the end of the decade both papers mentioned football more than any other sport.[68] Realizing that their audience wanted to hear about the football team's games, in the 1890s Carleton's editorial team obliged with extensive reports.[69]

Unlike sports, military drilling at one college involved both men and women. Yet the genders drilled separately and in distinct manners. Drilling came to both colleges in Northfield, but from different directions. In 1888, after the male students of Carleton submitted a petition to the faculty, a professor with military experience agreed to lead them in drilling. Under the professor-turned-captain, the male students formed two companies; the College requested arms from the War Department.[70] It all had a very militaristic flavor. Drilling first came to St. Olaf in the late 1870s, with the formation of St. Olaf's Guard; this was probably the students' idea, for their captain, presumably a faculty member, tried to convince them of the group's uselessness. Perhaps he succeeded, for it fizzled out, until the faculty reintroduced drilling for men in 1889. Male students lacked the enthusiasm of their 1870s predecessors and their Carleton neighbors, but all, of course, submitted to the compulsory activity.[71] And the following year, St. Olaf's women "decided not to be out-done by the boys; they...organized a military company" of their own, also under faculty direction. According to the *Manitou Messenger*, the men supported their female classmates' initiative. But it seems never to have occurred to anyone that the women and men might drill together. Plus, the feminine version of drilling was less militaristic and "more of a calisthenic nature."[72] When women did participate in athletic activities, then, they did so separately and distinctively from the men.

Men and women often, however, enjoyed non-athletic extracurricular activities together. Sometimes these had a very informal character; a group of male and female students simply got together to have fun. One Saturday evening in 1877, for example, many of St. Olaf's students of both genders took a trip for pleasure over to Carleton.[73] In the winter months, the newspapers tell us, men and women went tobogganing together or had a snowball fight "'tween he's and she's."[74] Certain games they played required both male and female players.[75] They also played cards and drank together. On a somewhat more formal level, students at St. Olaf organized "dances and other parties" where the genders could enjoy each other's company. In this last case, the puritanical faculty stepped in to "interrupt" the students' plans, forcing them to resort to "secret meetings in solitary places."⁷⁶ Professors could not watch even public areas at all times, however, and the next school year students were writing in their diaries of parties that ended with the men escorting the women home.⁷⁷ The faculty did not relish social interaction between the genders, but students did. This discrepancy produced not only clandestine disobedience, but also "an underground current, demanding more frequent [mixed] receptions or social gatherings," which one writer saw as "an imperative necessity."⁷⁸ In the meantime, in "solitary places" or in the snow, students compensated for the dearth of faculty-sanctioned mixed activities. Indeed, they surely socialized together more often than the newspapers indicated. The editors could not have known or cared about everything every student did on the weekends. Plus, faculty hostility to coeducational activities forbade them from printing notices of their "secret meetings."

Students also established their own formal coeducational organizations. By far the most successful were the newspapers themselves. Except possibly at St. Olaf's earliest papers—two of which were published by probably all-male literary societies—nearly every year's editorial boards included both men and women, and students of both genders contributed articles. Women usually filled a minority of editorial positions, and probably never served as editor-in-chief. At Carleton, however, their representation increased over time, and, by fall of 1892, the *Carletonia* listed six women on an editorial board of eleven, including the assistant manager (see Figure 2). In 1888–89, Stella Spalding wrote the *Carletonia*'s editorials, a task not performed by the editor-in-chief. In using part of her November column to instruct her male classmates on proper dating etiquette, Spalding proved that women could use the paper to express their voices.⁷⁹ Though women's numbers were smaller on the *Manitou Messenger*, as at St. Olaf overall, they still made their presence felt. Christen Hansen, for example, argued in a November 1891 article that "[t]he teacher holds the most responsible position in society."⁸⁰ At that time women were coming to dominate the teaching profession. Hansen likely wrote in part to encourage respect for a profession increasingly associated with her own gender, and to which she likely aspired.⁸¹ The paper offered her the opportunity to publish her viewpoint for all the student body to read. At the very least, the student newspaper was the most visible coeducational organization on each campus. Arguably, it came closer than any other element of the extracurriculum to offering women and men equal voice and authority.

Figure 2

The *Carletonia*'s editorial staff in spring of 1893 included seven men and five women (*Algol*, 1893, opposite [162], Laurence McKinley Gould Library, Carleton College). http://people.carleton.edu/~ehillema/1893Carletonia

Northfield's colleges suppported several other mixed organizations. The editorial boards of Carleton's yearbook, which first appeared in 1889, included both genders.[82] St. Olaf held periodic meetings for students to arrange "programmes affecting the entire college...or [to secure] lecturers," and these welcomed both women and men.[83] The St. Olaf College Band, though it began in 1890 as an all-male group, included both genders by the spring of 1893. Although some earlier musical groups, such as the male Kjerulf Quartet and the Ladies' Octette, limited their membership by gender, others, such as the choir and the College String Band in the 1870s, may have been mixed.[84] At Carleton, the newspapers mentioned the Haydn Chorus and a brass band, but did not say whether women could join the former, and gave no hint of the gender makeup of the latter. The yearbook did, however, identify the Caecilian Club, a chorus, as mixed. This group, like those at St. Olaf, offered men and women with musical inclinations a chance to interact, much as the newspapers did for the journalistically minded. But that represented a minority of the student bodies.[85] While these organizations may have offered a select group of students a coeducational environment, the largest and socially most important extracurriculars separated men and women, forcing the majority of students to struggle for the mixed atmosphere they desired.

Ironically, one type of usually *segregated* extracurricular organization best illustrated students' desire for integrated environments. Literary societies forced students to decide whether to divide by gender into separate organizations. Students' choice of mixed groups when available, their hostility toward faculty-mandated segregation, and their manipulation of officially segregated organizations so as to promote de facto integration revealed their strong preference for coeducational activities.

The societies' *raison d'être* was, as one's constitution put it, the cultivation of "intellectual and social culture and skill in parliamentary practice."[86] They accomplished the latter through the very procedures by which they ran their meetings. The former goal led them to facilitate, in those meetings, formal debates, speeches, and readings by members on "civil and religious, literary and scientific, agricultural and commercial" topics.[87] By no means, however, did societies confine their activity to procedure and oratory. Student musical performances enlivened their meetings.[88] Early on, some societies published newspapers. First the Philomathian, then the Philomathian and Alpha Beta Phi Societies, published the *Carletonian*; the *St. Olaf's Essayist* appeared under the auspices of the St. Olaf's Literary Society, and either that or another society published the *St. Olaf's Echo*.[89] Literary societies also furnished libraries for their members' use.[90] One society at St. Olaf provided a forum to practice Norwegian.[91] At Carleton, two societies jointly hosted celebrations of George Washington's birthday and Halloween.[92] Some provided musical facilities.[93] They probably helped organize commencement debates.[94]

At Carleton, St. Olaf, and numerous other colleges of the nineteenth century, these societies stood at the center of the student-designed extracurriculum. They supplemented an official curriculum that for most of the century offered students little opportunity to develop their writing and speaking skills. Historians agree that societies played a greater part in students' lives than any other curricular or extracurricular activity at all colleges at least until the Civil War and at Midwestern and Far Western schools until the end of the century.[95] Northfield's student writers concurred. Earlier I cited two *Manitou Messenger* editors who considered the societies as important to students' education as their courses.⁹⁶ Another argued that with rote learning "alone, little can be accomplished, little can be done towards making us educated men and women in the true sense of the term." Among "many other means," this journalist contended, debate contributed to the achievement of students' primary goal of "learn[ing] to think clearly, logically and correctly." Debate also taught the "art of public speaking," a necessary skill for adult citizens engaged in democratic politics.⁹⁷ A *Carletonian* writer, too, saw literary societies' value in their political training.⁹⁸

Most students agreed on the societies' importance. In November 1891, for example, one society out of three in St. Olaf's collegiate department counted among its members over half the student body.⁹⁹ Literary societies played a greater role in more students' lives than even athletics. Many factors contributed to their popularity, but the single most important and simplest reason for their numerical superiority to sports lay in their gender inclusiveness: only men could play football, but both women and men could (and did) join literary societies. They did not always, however, join the same ones.

Society members at both colleges preferred sexually integrated literary activities. They faced very different degrees of opposition to this goal, however, at St. Olaf and Carleton. St. Olaf students, by the 1890s, could choose between mixed and segregated societies. Large numbers demonstrated their desire for integrated groups simply by joining those. By 1879, St. Olaf's preparatory students organized three societies, all of which appear to have confined their membership to boys.¹⁰⁰ Eight years later, St. Olaf was down to one society, which still consisted "exclusively of young…men."¹⁰¹

During the 1888–89 academic year, St. Olaf students' society options expanded. Men in the collegiate department founded the Alpha Beta Chi, the first society closed to preparatory boys. Preparatory girls established the all-female Utile Dulci Society; no women enrolled in the collegiate department that year (see Table 2), but collegiate women seem to have been welcome in the Utile Dulci in future years. Finally, students founded Norsk Studenter Samfund, which "conducted [its exercises] in the Norwegian language," which admitted both men and women, and whose first president was female.¹⁰² By 1889, then, St. Olaf had four societies: one for college men, one for preparatory girls and college women, one for preparatory boys, and coeducational Norsk Studenter Samfund.¹⁰³ The last, which offered a sexually integrated environment, soon won special popularity. In a sense, its gender openness almost guaranteed it numerical superiority: more students *could* join it than the other collegiate societies, so more *did*. But its membership, by 1891, included over half the student population.[104] Surely, many men and women joined to affirm their ethnic identity and to practice their Norwegian. But the extreme popularity of the mixed group probably also reflected students' desire to interact with members of both genders. Acknowledging that desire, by 1893 the heretofore male Alpha Beta Chi opened its membership rolls to women; even the female Utile Dulci involved a man in its performance of *The Courtship of Miles Standish*.[105] The Norwegian group having proved mixed societies' popularity, the others accommodated students' wishes.

Even before then, St. Olaf men and women used those societies that officially separated them to create mixed environments. Until 1889, male society members often invited women to judge their debates. The women, an alumna later recalled, founded the Utile Dulci Society partly in "indignation" at having to judge men's "debates which they neither understood nor were interested in."[106] Despite this seeming rejection of mixed society activity by the female students, however, soon thereafter both men and women sought and found new ways to facilitate mixed gatherings. By 1890, a year after the female judges left, the male Alpha Beta Chi realized that the quality of debate had declined. It attempted to remedy the situation by moving its meetings to the college chapel, where "the society hopes to get an audience to speak to and thus get a stimulus for better work."[107] In particular, the men probably made the meetings public to bring the women back in, albeit with no formal role in the proceedings. (Unfortunately, the change resulted in more "passive" but less "active" participation; apparently men who would otherwise have debated preferred to join the women in the audience. The society thus reverted two years later to "private meetings with only an occasional public entertainment."[108]) Conversely, that same year the Utile Dulci began offering "public entertainments."[109] Apparently, as long as they chose and debated their own topics, St. Olaf women were happy to have men there. Certainly all students desired to show off their talents to an audience of both genders. But the chief effect of the public fora was to bring women into a gathering of the men's organization, and vice versa. Both the women and the men seemed to enjoy debates more when their classmates of the opposite gender were watching. They easily created that condition in one coeducational society and two single-gender organizations with open meetings.

Carleton students fought a much more contentious struggle for coeducational society activity. Early on, Carleton's societies did not separate the genders. Both the Philomathian and Alpha Beta Phi Societies, founded in 1873 and 1877, respectively, included men and women from the start. Both genders played an active role in each. Women's interest formed part of the impetus for the Alpha Beta Phi's creation; the founding meeting elected three men and two women to draft a constitution, under which the membership chose a male president and female vice president. By winter term 1880, that society counted thirty-eight male and twenty-five female active members.[110] A woman served as the Philomathian's first president, and women presided for parts of five of the society's first ten years (the president's term lasted one trimester).[111] The Philomathian included performances by both men and women in its meetings, and integrated its debates. One meeting in 1882, for example, began with a song by a mixed quartette, continued with speeches on Goethe and Schiller by two men and one woman, and concluded with another musical performance by a mixed duet. Two years earlier, a particularly vigorous debate asked members to consider, "Which exerts the greater influence on the happiness of mankind, the male or female mind?" A man argued for the male; a woman, for the female.[112]

Not all Carletonians liked mixed societies. In December 1880, the "[g]entlemen only" Adelphic Literary Society appeared; two months later, it was joined by the "[l]adies only" Chrestomathian Literary Society.[113] The Adelphic's founders, some of them former members of the mixed societies, believed "that the greatest good of a literary society could not be obtained from them." The Philomathian and Alpha Beta Phi, in their view, suffered both from their size— they had so many members that each one only rarely had the opportunity to speak—and from their coeducational nature.[114] The Chrestomathians probably agreed. But these men and women were a minority. Twenty-four young men joined the Adelphic for part or all of the 1881–82 academic year, compared to at least sixty-seven in the two mixed societies. Similarly, seventeen young women joined the Chrestomathian, versus at least fifty-one in the mixed societies; the following year, those numbers grew to twenty-two and at least fifty-six.[115] Most students of both genders preferred coeducational organizations.

In December 1882, however, the faculty banned integrated literary societies, effective the next fall.[116] Students were not happy. Even before the faculty's decision, they protested the impending law. Senior E. K. Cheade, claiming to speak for "a large majority of the students" and nearly all society members, published in the *Carletonia* one month before the change a defense of coeducational societies. First, he pointed out that the expediency argument in favor of coeducation, that educators most economically used academic facilities by serving both men and women, applied equally well to the societies' libraries and pianos. Next, he refuted the two objections that professors had raised to mixed societies. First, they worried that "the gentlemen are aggressive, take the lead in all work, and do not give the ladies their proper share." Cheade denied that. Women, he argued, "do find their proper proportion of society work," and in fact demonstrated equal capacity to men in "literary and musical" endeavors. They did exhibit lesser ability in "extempore debating," but overall women and men participated equally in society work. Their "complementary" interests and abilities argued for the continuation of mixed societies.[117] Both students and faculty, then, desired equal involvement of men and women in society activity. They merely disagreed over how best to achieve that goal.

Faculty members' chief objection to coeducational societies, however, rested on their observation "that the ladies and gentlemen of Carleton seem to enjoy each other's society." During intermissions of debates, "acting in accordance with their natural and undoubted depravity," they socialized with each other. Cheade saw this as no problem at all. He brusquely denied the charge, "which originated in the cerebral ganglia of certain would-be wits," that social activity constituted the Alpha Beta Phi's sole purpose, literary endeavors serving "merely as a blind" to subvert college rules prohibiting mixed social gatherings in the evenings. In sum, Cheade argued that the faculty misunderstood the purposes and practices of the literary societies. He asked them to consider student opinion before mandating their segregation.[118] Whether or not the faculty considered their opposition, however, they nonetheless banned mixed societies.

After the division of the societies into male and female groups, students continued to resist separation. For one thing, they continued to complain. Students lamented the change as late as 1890. Alumni who remembered the good old days of coeducational societies reminded current students of the injury done to them by the faculty.[119] But students did not confine their resistance to reluctant acquiescence. Six months after the faculty's decision, sixty-eight students signed an unsuccessful petition to the Board of Trustees calling for the reinstatement of integrated societies.[120]

Furthermore, though male and female literary societies may in theory have been distinct, that did not mean that in practice they must be separate. Beginning the first year under the new policy, and continuing into the 1890s, the now all-male Philomathian and all-female Alpha Beta Phi sidestepped the rule by holding occasional joint meetings. In February 1884, they organized a Washington's Birthday celebration involving members of both societies; they repeated the event a year later, this time dressing up as such period figures as Benjamin and Deborah Franklin, Lady Castleton, and, of course, the first president.[121] On Halloween of 1892, the two organizations again met together for a socially oriented session. The two presidents "formed the reception committee," though only the male leader formally addressed those in attendance.[122] That academic year, students also organized an intercollegiate debating group, which included both men and women.[123] And in 1890, possibly assisted by declining faculty vigilance, the societies held "a session which should resemble, so nearly as possible, those held in the days of 'mixed societies.'" They invited alumni to an evening of "Society Reminiscences," which included grumbling over segregation. The president of the men's society ran the meeting, "assisted by" his female counterpart.[124] Between these special occasions, students created coeducational environments when women sang at the Philomathian's meetings; while those women may have entered immediately before and exited after their performances, they likely stayed for much or all of the officially all-male meetings, albeit silently.[125]

Contrary to the faculty's intention, women may actually have lost authority and voice in these joint meetings as a result of official segregation, assuming a mostly silent role in Philomathian meetings and a subordinate one in joint sessions. But more importantly, the choice of both women and men to hold those sessions demonstrated their continuing preference for mixed over separated societies, or at the very least for a combination of the two. It also underscores the power students had over campus life. Just as students had formed literary societies to compensate for deficiencies in the official curriculum, when professors tried to regulate those extracurricular organizations the students found ways to maintain control of their lives outside the classroom.

Students and Politics

Student political interest and participation in the late nineteenth century have received very little scholarly attention. Historians since the 1970s have emphasized connections between life on college campuses and wider cultural trends, but almost none has applied this mission to the most traditional of all topics in American national history, electoral politics. At best, researchers cite political interest as a motivation for the formation of literary societies.[126] At worst, they dismiss politics as irrelevant to life on self-contained and self-centered campuses.[127] Yet Americans of the late nineteenth century debated students' right to vote in their adopted towns, and such a debate seems unlikely if few students wanted to vote.[128] Indeed, records from Carleton and St. Olaf support a reevaluation of the usually tacit assumption of student noninterest. Students at Northfield's colleges cared about local, state, and national politics. Electoral contests enlivened campus each November, especially in presidential election years. Most remarkably, at Carleton not only men but also women played an active role in campus politics. Three decades before Minnesota's legislature granted women suffrage by ratifying the nineteenth amendment, college offered women remarkably broad opportunities for political involvement.[129] A campus that fostered a sexually integrated student life encouraged women to participate even in political activities traditionally gendered as exclusively masculine.

Students at both colleges expressed interest in elections, especially presidential elections. Students divided along the lines of the national party system. Members of the St. Olaf community, for instance, marched in a Republican parade in 1888. The campus divided into political camps to a sufficient degree that after Benjamin Harrison's electoral success a *Manitou Messenger* editor could summarize campus sentiment party by party:

> Republicans jubilant.
> Democrats gloomy.
> Prohibitionists hopeful.
> Union Labor men not heard from.
> [Equal Rights Party candidate] Belva Lockwood's influence dead as a door-nail.

Republican students probably mollified resentment when "they magnanimously treated their Prohibition [*sic*] and Democratic friends to a fine supper."[130] Four years later, partisan politics again piqued St. Olaf students' interest, beginning long before the election. In January 1892, they established the St. Olaf College Senate, a mock legislature that considered such issues as immigration laws and Indian policy, and whose participants split along partisan lines.[131] In the fall, "the stir created by the election" so dominated campus life that it forced the literary societies to postpone their activities until after the campaign.[132] In the meantime, student politicians adopted the societies' procedures; instead of a society meeting with speeches about Goethe and the normal musical interludes, they held a Republican rally with speeches on the tariff and patriotic songs performed by the chorus and Republican Quartet.[133]

Judging from the sheer number of references to elections in the newspaper, Carletonians' interest in politics exceeded even that of their St. Olaf neighbors. Both faculty and students campaigned there. "[E]nthusiastic partisans," wrote a *Carletonia* editor, interrupted "[o]ur usually quiet college circle" in 1888 with "[c]ampaign literature, campaign badges, campaign speeches and campaign tete-a-tetes."[134] Debate surrounding the next election began more than a year before the vote when, in October 1891, a literary society considered whom the Republicans should nominate.[135] In 1884, Carleton's faculty and students participated in a mock presidential election. Four years later the students again cast their ballots on campus, this time for president, governor, and congressman; they voted for president yet again in 1892.[136] The Prohibition Party was particularly active. In 1883, students formed the Carleton Temperance Union; in 1886, the more politically oriented Young Men's Prohibition Club of Carleton College succeeded it.[137] In 1888, when campus "Democrats don't dare to say much when with the crowd," Prohibitionists were so "bold" that one editor proposed that "[s]omebody ought to teach them their places." Most student debate revolved around the Republicans and Prohibitionists, with the latter's presidential candidate, Clinton B. Fisk, edging out Harrison in the campus election.[138]

College men often found their political aspirations frustrated by laws that prevented them from voting in Northfield. Age impeded some but not all. Though only those aged twenty-one or older could vote, many men attended college later then than now; one article cited twenty-five as a typical age for a man's graduation.[139] *The Manitou Messenger* related the sad story of one "ardent student politician" whom the judges told "must among other things have a wife" to vote, but officials do not appear to have often raised this objection.[140] And although a Norwegian pastor told some St. Olaf students that "Yankees" wanted to withhold from immigrants "a say in the government," students never alleged nativism as a motive of their disfranchisement.[141] The residency requirement formed the most contentious barrier to suffrage. As elsewhere in the nation, Minnesota legislators and Northfield election officials hesitated to allow students to vote in the towns where they attended college.[142] Minnesota law, as one *Carletonian* writer explained, declared that "a person leaving home for the purpose of education does not thereby lose his residence," which most judges interpreted to mean that students might vote only in their hometowns, not in the towns where they studied. Some students, hence, returned home to cast their ballots.[143] Students at Carleton even petitioned the faculty to declare election day 1892 a "[h]alf-holiday," likely so those who lived in nearby towns could travel to the polls. Their professors obligingly cancelled morning classes.[144] Unfortunately, many lived too far away to return home to vote.[145] Some of these men, literally in spite of the law, attempted to vote in Northfield.

Male students ran into friction when they arrived at Northfield's polls. Sometimes judges let them vote. More often, though, they turned away these temporary residents of the town. This very inconsistency proved one cause for student complaint. In 1888, whether students succeeded in casting their ballots depended on the ward in which they attempted to vote. Judges of the third ward allowed St. Olaf students to vote for half the day, then changed their minds. One student writer charged judges with denying students suffrage owing to partisan motives.[146] (On the other hand, two editors suggested the Republican Party would do well to enfranchise America's students, ninety percent of whom, they claimed, supported that party.)[147] Students also pointed to the inconsistency in permitting "the mass of transient laborers who have little or no taxable property, and [who] can move from place to place at will," to vote, while denying that right to "[t]he student,…[who] is obliged often to reside in a town for many years, and [who] is subject, more or less, to the laws of the town." Students better understood politics than "the meanest, dirtiest tramp," and hence deserved the franchise more.[148] One student also justified his right to vote by appealing to colleges' economic contributions to their towns. Building on the traditional association between property ownership and suffrage, he felt the "wealth" his college brought to Northfield bought its students the franchise.[149]

Armed with their carefully formed arguments, some Northfield college students successfully attained the vote. A group of St. Olaf men, having been turned away when they tried to register to vote, began a thorough study of Minnesota law. They constructed a legal argument for their right to vote, which they mailed to the state's attorney general. Agreeing with their reasoning, he overruled the local officials. Victorious, the students proudly marched back into town and became Northfield voters.[150]

Of course, not only age, marital status, and residency kept college students from the polls. However old, whether single or married, and wherever their home, nineteenth-century women could not vote. Though several states fully enfranchised women long before the nineteenth amendment of 1920, Minnesota was not among them.[151] Until the twentieth century, college students did not play a significant role in state or national suffrage movements.[152] But a perspective from within the colleges, versus from the broader movement, reveals that some of Northfield's college women found unusual opportunities for political involvement on campus. They took advantage of their chance to participate in the democratic electoral process in both direct and indirect ways.

Not so at St. Olaf. The *Manitou Messenger* said little of women's political participation. Though discussions of student interest and action may have referred to both men and women, they may just as well have referred exclusively to men, the United States' traditional political actors. Only men spoke at the Republican rally of 1892; women, by either their own choice or male dictum, may not have attended.[153] The rare mentions of women in politics in the newspaper pointed not to an abundance but to a dearth of campus interest in women's enfranchisement. Owing at least in part to their membership in the Lutheran church, notable for its leaders' and members' lack of sympathy for woman suffrage, students at St. Olaf exhibited a markedly antisuffragist bent.[154] The list of candidates' popularity among students quoted earlier in this essay identified Equal Rights Party candidate "Belva Lockwood's influence [as] dead as a doornail."[155] Her bid for the presidency in 1888 under the banner of woman suffrage and "equal and exact justice to every class of our citizens, without distinction of color, sex, or nationality" appealed to few men on campus, or at least few admitted their support after her defeat.[156] St. Olaf women did not support her, feared to express their support, or did not matter to the writer.

Around that same time, the faculty assigned a preparatory department class an essay on woman suffrage. Most of the girls argued against it on religious grounds; one of their essays appeared in the *Manitou Messenger*.[157] The author acknowledged women and men's intellectual and moral equality, but denied that this implied that women should vote. The government should expand the franchise only if doing so would improve the franchise. But with woman suffrage, fewer "good" women than "vicious" women—such as African Americans of the South—would vote. Plus, though the genders were equal, they were not the same. "God's and nature's law" assigned men one sphere of life and women another: "[m]an is to provide and to govern; woman is to encourage and prompt."[158] If a woman were to have any political role, this girl believed it should be through her husband.

A few St. Olaf students may have disagreed with this last point. In March 1889, the Prohibition Club held a declamation contest, which most likely consisted of speeches on that group's pet issue. Four women and two men competed; Thina Bjorn won.[159] She and three other young woman felt comfortable speaking to an audience on a hot political issue, and the judges felt comfortable acknowledging her superiority at political oratory over her male opponents. Three years later, when male students founded the St. Olaf College Senate, some women attended at least one meeting.[160] But these exceptions help to prove the rule. Bjorn could speak and have her oratorical ability recognized, but most of her female schoolmates who had a political voice, like the girl quoted above, used it to deny their own right of political participation. Some women attended one Senate meeting, but seem to have kept quiet and come only that once. Women at St. Olaf rarely found opportunities for political involvement and even more rarely did they choose to take advantage of them.

Life was very different across the river. Lutheran conservatism had much less an impact on Carleton's Congregational-affiliated and religiously heterogeneous campus. Reflecting the denominational difference, Carleton women enjoyed a wide range of political opportunities. Students apparently had little to say about woman suffrage in theory. Two men debated the issue in a Philomathian meeting of 1882—ironically, only minutes after inaugurating a woman as president of their society. But the newspaper rarely indicated either editors' interest in the topic or a wider campus discussion.[161] Editor Stella Spalding cited woman suffrage as a question unique to America and to the late nineteenth century, without offering her opinion.[162] Two other editors noted that Carleton's eight new woman's rights advocates in 1886 relied on "impressive looks" rather than the usual "broom stick and tongs."[163] Whatever these editors thought of woman's rights, at least a few of their classmates joined the cause.

But the limited discussion of suffrage is deceptive. Though the newspapers did not reflect a significant campus debate over women's political rights, the actions of both men and women spoke far louder than the absense of their words. Both genders helped to create opportunities for female students to take part in the action come election season. In 1886, for example, a professor led "about twenty-five girls" to a Republican rally downtown. *In loco parentis* interfered with their fun, for the women dared not stay out past their ten o'clock curfew, but until then they "listened with much interest" to the politicians who spoke.[164] Two years later, a pair of Democratic roommates sabotaged a nighttime Republican procession by turning out the lights outside the women's dormitory. Their opponents took revenge soon after by writing on the Democrats' window, "Hurrah for Harrison and Morton."[165] The adolescent nature of these pranks does not detract from their significance. These young women saw themselves as political actors. They formed political opinions and promoted their candidates, albeit in an immature fashion.

Other political activity among Carleton's women took a more mature and overt form. On election morning 1888, a female student followed the college president's address to the student body with "a rousing Republican speech."[166] The campus Democratic Club gave no accompanying oration, but operated more quietly under the leadership of a female president. On this campus, women served as leader or mouthpiece for two of the three major political parties.[167] Even more important, women at Carleton actually voted. Though Minnesota did not permit women to vote in most elections, since 1876 the state had included them in elections on school-related issues.[168] Some Carleton students took advantage of that opportunity and asserted their political identity through the one electoral method Minnesota's government offered them. But they needed not limit their political involvement to that form sanctioned by the state. The College offered them additional opportunities. As I mentioned before, in 1884, 1888, and 1892, Carleton held mock elections—open to all, *irrespective of gender*. In 1892, the female Alpha Beta Phi Literary Society held its own election in addition to the campus-wide polls.[169] In all three presidential election years, Carleton women voted.

The mock election of 1888 demonstrates particularly well the importance students attached to women's campus enfranchisement. Students, not the faculty, proposed and organized this election. At a "mass meeting" they chose one male and one female judge, and a female clerk of the election. After the election, the *Carletonia* reported the results—by gender (see Figure 3). That students identified ballots by gender and reported returns not only in total but also for "Ladies" and "Gentlemen" shows that they considered gender, and not, for instance, class year, the most important division among students not only generally but in politics specifically. And with good reason: women and men's votes differed considerably. A majority of women chose Republican Benjamin Harrison as president; a majority of men, Prohibitionist Clinton B. Fisk. The genders also disagreed about who should represent them in Congress; they selected the same candidate for governor, but women were much more divided in that race than men.[170]

Figure 3

Young men with impressive smiles gave out the ballots, but the number of doubtful voters was small. The results of the election were as follows:

CANDIDATES.	Ladies.	Gentlemen.	Total.
PRESIDENTIAL—			
Cleveland and Thurman	7	3	10
Harrison and Morton	57	35	92
Fisk and Brooks	47	51	98
GOVERNOR—			
Wilson	7	3	10
Merriam	47	27	74
Gilman	8	7	15
Harrison	49	52	101
MEMBER OF CONGRESS—			
McDonald	7	7	14
Hall	57	32	89
Fosness	47	50	97

The *Carletonia* reported the results of the campus election of 1888 by gender ("College Election," *Carletonia*, November 1888, Laurence McKinley Gould Library, Carleton College).

What do these statistics tell us? First, these women wanted to vote. The student at St. Olaf who claimed that few "good" women would vote if given the chance might have changed her mind had she peeked across the river. College women who enjoyed and defended a sexually integrated campus life felt comfortable participating in a traditionally and legally male political activity while on that mixed campus. Second, college men welcomed their female classmates into the simulated polity as stump speaker, judge, clerk, and voters—or at least did not protest loudly enough for the student newspaper to notice. Third, college women formed their own political opinions. They did not accept men's political superiority and vote according to male opinion, but instead expressed political views in opposition to the men's. Women at Carleton did not take a subordinate role through which they reaffirmed men's political hegemony. They took their place as independent, equal political actors.

* * *

Students at Carleton and St. Olaf Colleges in the years after Reconstruction created a social and political life based on free interaction between the genders. Men and women viewed each other as romantic objects and often dated. They enjoyed informal activities together, and designed a largely integrated formal extracurriculum. When faced with faculty opposition to mixed organizations, students resisted change from above. At Carleton, students of both genders joined together even in the traditionally all-male realm of electoral politics. Women and men built in these coeducational colleges open environments for women's participation in the two masculine dominions of higher education and government.

Why did women find so much more welcoming an atmosphere at Northfield's colleges than at other coeducational schools historians have studied? Geography and school size furnish at best partial answers, for segregation reigned even at some small Midwestern colleges.[171] Nor does time likely explain the difference. Though other studies of Midwestern colleges have found social segregation after my period, I see no reason for a sudden regional shift in student life in the 1890s. Specific circumstances at St. Olaf and Carleton offer more plausible explanations for their unexpected gender dynamics.

First, both began as coeducational schools. Their recent foundings brought them into existence just as coeducation, for both financial and egalitarian reasons, was coming to dominate higher education in the Midwest.[172] This in itself did not make Carleton and St. Olaf unique, for town boosters and Protestant denominations founded many colleges as coeducational institutions in the years immediately before the Civil War. But so-called coeducation did not always take the same form. In Northfield's colleges, men and women studied in the same classrooms and chose from among the same curricular offerings. Slightly older colleges, while they admitted both women and men, often relegated the former to separate "ladies' departments." Only men enrolled in the most prestigious course of study.[173] This curricular policy did not likely encourage an egalitarian spirit among the students. Northfield's colleges, meanwhile, taught through their policies that women and men deserved the same opportunities, as least while they remained in college. Recall, Carleton even advertised this decision as a particularly attractive feature of the College. Having learned this lesson in the classroom, young people brought it with them to the rest of campus.

Second, the preparatory departments may have forestalled conflict. Coeducational secondary education was the norm throughout the country.[174] Most collegiate students at Carleton had attended the preparatory department first; a similar pattern likely prevailed at St. Olaf.[175] Boys and girls who attended high school at Carleton or St. Olaf probably saw no problem with continuing their studies and lives on the same campus with the same classmates and friends, both male and female. But many colleges of the nineteenth century included preparatory departments. Outside of New England and New Jersey, in fact, only twelve American colleges in 1862 did *not*. Postbellum Midwestern colleges often began as antebellum secondary institutions.[176] This organizational element, though it surely facilitated a freely mixed student life, did not guarantee it. It did not distinguish Northfield's two colleges from their regional contemporaries with more strictly segregated campuses.

Third, men's own disfranchisement may have led them to see a common cause with politically disempowered women, bringing them to support their female classmates' inclusion in campus campaigns and elections. Yet again, this observation begs the question why a similar effect did not prevail in all colleges. For college men's disfranchisement was confined neither to Northfield nor to the Midwest.[177] Finally, we cannot deny agency or individuality to the women themselves. At colleges where women and men created distinct social worlds, initiative came from both sides. Especially in the Midwest, women did not incorporate themselves into men's extracurriculum largely because they did not want to. At such schools as Grinnell College (Iowa) and the University of Chicago, they preferred organizing their own activities. No wonder, given the ideology of separate spheres that permeated every aspect of Victorian life, including higher education.[178] The women who attended St. Olaf and Carleton felt otherwise. They wanted the men's companionship, and the men wanted theirs. Both got their wish.

So, little distinguished the colleges in Northfield, Minnesota, from those in numerous other towns of the post-Reconstruction Midwest. Only their curricular policies can account for the usual openness of gendered student life and opportunities for women. Even this notable characteristic hardly seems decisive. Nor was the absence of a ladies' department entirely unique: a number of other colleges, albeit a minority, educated women together with men.[179] I must ask, then, whether Carleton and St. Olaf really *were* unusual.

Most scholars have identified segregated atmospheres and generally hostile environments for women at nineteenth-century American colleges. But they have studied in depth only a handful of Midwestern schools. Scholars have demonstrably shown that Grinnell, Chicago, and, after 1890, the University of Michigan did foster a culture of segregation.[180] At Ripon College in Wisconsin, however, life appears to have been much like that in Northfield. Dating there seems to have been quite common. In the 1870s, the women and men's literary societies asked permission to hold joint meetings but upset their professors when they held the meetings before the faculty met to consider the applications. At least some female students voiced their partisan leanings during the presidential campaign of 1888, and a few years later women won the right to vote within the student athletic association, amid vigorous campus debate about woman suffrage in political elections. All this happened despite the presence of a distinct ladies' department. Meanwhile, at Wheaton College in Illinois, where women comprised only one third to one half of each collegiate class, all four classes in 1893–94 elected women as their presidents. John Rury and Glenn Harper have demonstrated that students at Antioch College in Ohio resisted faculty members' efforts to segregate literary societies and other elements of extracurricular life.[181] Andrea Radke's recent, unpublished research suggests that a similar pattern to that at Carleton, St. Olaf, and these other private colleges prevailed at some Midwestern and Far Western public universities.[182]

My findings suggest that scholarship on student life suffers from an insufficient sample size. A second form of coeducational student life existed in the late nineteenth century. Some colleges fit the pattern of separation described in most of the historiography, but others did not. Research on additional institutions can help us to reach a critical mass and thus formulate a more complex model of higher education in the nineteenth century, one that accounts for both the open atmospheres and expansive female opportunities at some schools, and the more restrictive environments elsewhere. At young colleges on the Western frontier, professors and students could chose the curricular and extracurricular forms they preferred. At Carleton, St. Olaf, and probably elsewhere, they chose forms that broke with the tradition of all-male higher education and stretched, if not challenged, conventions of Victorian domesticity.

Perhaps the joke with which I began this essay had a second level of meaning. The speaker rejected feminine authority, but he was poor at Latin and maybe by implication at relations with the opposite gender. The writers may have intended to ridicule this chauvinist freshman; the point may have been the futility or foolishness of resistance to women's authority. Men and women at Carleton and St. Olaf happily shared each other's company, physical space, and political power. *Lex* was both masculine and feminine.

Notes

1. M. O. Sortedahl and Anna Morterud, eds., "College Crumbs," *Manitou Messenger*, March 1887, Rølvaag Memorial Library, St. Olaf College, 11. Owing to the repetitive use of column titles, throughout this essay I give long-form citations for all newspaper articles.
2. Joan Wallach Scott, "Gender: A Useful Category of Historical Analysis," in *Gender and the Politics of History*, rev. ed., Gender and Culture (New York: Columbia University Press, 1999), 28–29, 42.
3. Rosalind Rosenberg, "The Limits of Access: The History of Coeducation in America," in *Women and Higher Education in American History: Essays from the Mount Holyoke Sesquicentennial Symposia*, ed. John Mack Faragher and Florence Howe (New York: W. W. Norton & Co., 1988), 109, 111; Barbara Miller Solomon, *In the Company of Educated Women: A History of Women and Higher Education in America* (New Haven: Yale University Press, 1985), 50–51; Elizabeth Seymour Eschbach, *The Higher Education of Women in England and America, 1865–1920*, Women's History and Culture, no. 6, and Garland Reference Library of Social Science, no. 661 (New York: Garland Publishing, 1993), 99–100; Doris Malkmus, "Small Towns, Small Sects, and Coeducation in Midwestern Colleges, 1853–1861," *History of Higher Education Annual* 22 (2002): 33–48; Ruth Bordin, *Women at Michigan: The "Dangerous Experiment," 1870s to the Present* (Ann Arbor: University of Michigan Press, 1999), 1–2; Roger L. Geiger, "The Era of Multipurpose

Colleges in American Higher Education, 1850–1890," in *The American College in the Nineteenth Century*, ed. Geiger (Nashville: Vanderbilt University Press, 2000), 142.

4. On Midwestern student life after 1890, see Lynn D. Gordon, *Gender and Higher Education in the Progressive Era* (New Haven: Yale University Press, 1990), 120, 189–90; Joan G. Zimmerman, "College Culture in the Midwest, 1890–1930" (Ph.D. diss., University of Virginia, 1978). Zimmerman observes that women at Grinnell College in Iowa preferred the segregated social life, but men protested it. Joan G. Zimmerman, "Daughters of Main Street: Culture and the Female Community at Grinnel [sic], 1884–1917," in *Woman's Being, Woman's Place: Female Identity and Vocation in American History*, ed. Mary Kelly (Boston: G. K. Hall & Co., 1979), 154–55, 163–65. Ruth Bordin has shown that male students at the University of Michigan generally welcomed women, and the extracurriculum there remained highly integrated through the 1880s. In the 1890s, however, segregation took over. Bordin, *Women at Michigan*, 101–6, 19. On the rest of the country, see Rosenberg, "Limits of Access," 113; Eschbach, *Higher Education of Women*, 106, 108; Charlotte Williams Conable, *Women at Cornell: The Myth of Equal Education* (Ithaca: Cornell University Press, 1977), 76, 124, 126; Carroll Smith-Rosenberg, "The New Woman as Androgyne: Social Disorder and Gender Crisis, 1870–1936," in *Disorderly Conduct: Visions of Gender in Victorian America* (New York: Alfred A. Knopf, 1985), 250–51. Patricia Smith Butcher refers to a nationwide backlash against coeducation within and without colleges. Patricia Smith Butcher, *Education for Equality: Womens Rights Periodicals and Women's Higher Education, 1849–1920*, Contributions in Womens Studies, no. 111 (New York and Westport, Conn.: Greenwood Press, 1989), 45. Helen Lefkowitz Horowitz acknowledges the greater social integration at small colleges. Helen Lefkowitz Horowitz, *Campus Life: Undergraduate Cultures from the End of the Eighteenth Century to the Present* (New York: Alfred A. Knopf, 1987), 200. Patricia Foster Haines notes that at Cornell University in the 1870s, women and men shared the same extracurricular organizations, though women's relative lack of participation confused their male classmates. Beginning in the 1880s, however, social segregation became the rule. Patricia Foster Haines, "Coeducation and the Development of Leadership Skills in Women: Historical Perspectives from Cornell University, 1868–1900," in *Women and Education Leadership*, ed. Sari Knopp Biklen and Marilyn B. Brannigan (Lexington, Mass.: Lexington Books, 1980), 121–22. Important exceptions to this scholarly trend, Ellen K. Rothman and Andrea G. Radke portray coeducational colleges as markedly open spaces for mixed social life, though Radke simultaneously emphasizes the limits to that openness. Radke's recent dissertation applies to Midwestern public universities a similar method of analysis to mine; her findings suggest that the argument I make in this study applies beyond the private colleges I discuss here. Christine A. Ogren argues that state normal schools in the late nineteenth and early twentieth centuries fostered mixed social environments, and John Rury and Glenn Harper argue that, from the 1850s to the 1870s, students at Ohio's Antioch College resisted faculty efforts to segregate extracurricular life. Ellen K. Rothman, *Hands and Hearts: A History of Courtship in America* (New York: Basic Books, 1984), 210–13; Andrea G. Radke, "Can She Not See and Hear, and Smell and Taste?: Women Students at Coeducational Land-Grant Universities in the American West, 1868–1917" (Ph.D. diss., University of Nebraska, 2002), 12; Christine A. Ogren, "A Large Measure of Self-Control and Personal Power: Women Students at State Normal Schools During the Late-Nineteenth and Early-Twentieth Centuries," *Women's Studies Quarterly* 28, no. 3/4 (Fall/Winter 2000): 213; John Rury and Glenn Harper, "The Trouble with Coeducation: Mann and Women at Antioch,

1853–1860," *History of Education Quarterly* 26, no. 4 (Winter 1986): 493–96, 500.
5. Helen Lefkowitz Horowitz, *Alma Mater: Design and Experience in the Women's Colleges from Their Nineteenth-Century Beginnings to the 1930s* (New York: Alfred A. Knopf, 1985), xviii; Gordon, *Gender and Higher Education*, 189–91; Linda M. Eisenmann, "Women at Brown, 1891–1930: 'Academically Identical, But Socially Quite Different'" (Ed.D. diss., Harvard Graduate School of Education, 1987), 185, 189–93.
6. Leal A. Headley and Merrill E. Jarchow, *Carleton: The First Century* (Northfield, Minn.: Carleton College, 1966), 1; Eric Hillemann, "The Founding of Carleton College: Born of Prayers, Baptized with Tears" (unpublished paper prepared for a Northfield Historical Society talk, Northfield, Minn., 22 February 2001); Delavan L. Leonard, *The History of Carleton College: Its Origin and Growth, Environment and Builders* (Chicago: Fleming H. Revell Co., 1904), 98–107; William C. Benson, *High on Manitou: A History of St. Olaf College, 1874–1949* (Northfield, Minn.: St. Olaf College Press, 1949), 22; Joseph M. Shaw, *History of St. Olaf College, 1874–1974* (Northfield, Minn.: St. Olaf College Press, 1974), 41–42.
7. "Carleton College, at Northfield—Minnesota," *Carletonian*, June 1877, Laurence McKinley Gould Library, Carleton College, 16. Similar advertisements appeared in subsequent issues.
8. St. Olaf's faculty did consider creating a separate literary track for women, but decided against the measure. Benson, *High on Manitou*, 75; photograph of Lutheran Divinity School, in Scrapbook Presented by Rev. Ole Glesne, acc. 2124, Shaw-Olson Center for College History, St. Olaf College, opposite [44].
9. Frederick Rudolph, *Mark Hopkins and the Log: Williams College, 1836–1872*, Yale Historical Publications, Miscellany, no. 63 (New Haven: Yale University Press, 1956), vii–viii, 64–85; Henry D. Sheldon, *Student Life and Customs, American Education: Its Men, Idea, and Institutions* (New York: Arno Press & New York Times, 1969, c. 1901), 125–286; E. Merton Coulter, *College Life in the Old South*, 2nd ed. (Athens: University of Georgia Press, 1951), 129–33; Thomas S. Harding, *College Literary Societies: Their Contribution to Higher Education in the United States, 1815–1876* (New York: Pageant Press International Corp., 1971), 1, 305–15, 317–19; James McLachlan, "The *Choice of Hercules*: American Student Societies in the Early 19th Century," in *The University in Society*, ed. Lawrence Stone, 2 vols. (New Jersey: Princeton University Press, 1974), 2: 485; Joseph R. DeMartini, "Student Culture As a Change Agent in American Higher Education: An Illustration from the Nineteenth Century," *Journal of Social History* 9, no. 4 (June 1976): 536–38; Roger L. Geiger, "Introduction: New Themes in the History of Nineteenth-Century Colleges," in *American College in the Nineteenth Century*, ed. Geiger, 14; Roger L. Geiger with Julie Ann Bubolz, "College As It Was in the Mid-Nineteenth Century," in *American College in the Nineteenth Century*, ed. Geiger, 81–82.
10. Headley and Jarchow, *Carleton*, 1–7, 56, 469; Hillemann, "Founding of Carleton College"; Leonard, *History of Carleton College*, 98–107, 192, 225; Sue Garwood-DeLong, "Carleton College: Archives: History: 1866–1891," *Carleton College: Private Liberal Arts College*, 19 February 2002, http://www.acad.carleton.edu/campus/archives/history/chrono/chrono1866-1891.html (23 February 2003). Carleton's nondenominational character was reflected in the library of a student literary society, which held among its collections the periodical *Catholic World*. Classified Catalogue of the Philomathian Library, Literary Societies Collection, Carleton College Archives, 19.
11. In the late 1870s, Carleton began awarding master's degrees to "graduates from the Classical or Literary Course of three years standing, who have been engaged in

literary or professional pursuits, and have sustained a good moral character." Unattributed quotation appears in Headley and Jarchow, *Carleton*, 214. Only in 1885 did the College tie this degree to a program of study.

12. These and the other data in Table 1 come from *Annual Catalogue of Northfield College*, 1868–70, Carleton College Archives; *Annual Catalogue of Carleton College*, 1870–71, Carleton College Archives; *Annual Catalogue of the Officers and Students of Carleton College*, 1872–90, Carleton College Archives; *Catalogue of Carleton College*, 1890–93, Carleton College Archives; Bureau of Education, Department of the Interior, *Report of the Commissioner of Education Made to the Secretary of the Interior for the Year 1870, With Accompanying Papers*, prepared by John Eaton Jr. (Washington: GPO, 1870), 510–11, Table 3; Bureau of Education, Department of the Interior, *Report of the Commissioner of Education*, 1871–93, prepared by John Eaton Jr., N. H. R. Dawson, and William T. Harris (Washington: GPO, 1872–95), table on colleges (number and pages vary); Headley and Jarchow, *Carleton*, 214.

13. On the more diverse national origins of Carleton students, see "Items," *Carletonian*, June 1878, p. 18.

14. Julie Peterson, "'Pluck and Perseverence': The History of Women at St. Olaf College, 1874–1914" (M.A. thesis, Sarah Lawrence College, May 1975), 7–9, 13, 16; Benson, *High on Manitou*, 22, 26, 42, 69, 144; Shaw, *History of St. Olaf College*, 42, 44, 46, 50, 79–81, 83; C[arl]. A[ugust]. Mellby, *Saint Olaf College Through Fifty Years, 1874–1924* ([Northfield, MN?]: n.p. [1925?]), 21–26, 28; Richard W. Solberg, *Luthern Higher Education in North America* (Minneapolis: Augsburg Publishing House, 1985), 229–31; Joseph M. Shaw, *Bernt Julius Muus: Founder of St. Olaf College* (Northfield, Minn.: Norwegian-American Historical Association, 1999), 234, 243–44; photograph of Lutheran Divinity School; O. G. Felland, "History of St. Olaf College," in *Quarter Centennial Souvenir, 1874–1899, St. Olaf College*, ed. and compiled by J. A. Aasgaard (Northfield, Minn.: Northfield News Printery [1900?]), in Students Enrolled, 1887–1906 folder, Shaw-Olson Center for College History, St. Olaf College, [57]; quotations from H.A.K., "Capt's Off-hand Speech before 'St. Olaf's' Guard," *St. Olaff']s Essayist*, 22 February 1879, transcript, Shaw-Olson Center for College History, St. Olaf College, 1; O. C. Narvestad, "Ought Scandinavians to Support Their Private Institutions in This Country?" *Manitou Messenger*, November 1890, 119. Hereafter, I will refer to the college as St. Olaf even when discussing the period before the name changed. Women first outnumbered men in 1917–18, presumably owing to male students' enlistment in the military. This and data in Table 2 come from St. Olaf College enrollment tables, Lars W. Boe Collection, box 2, folder 3, acc. 1, Shaw-Olson Center for College History, St. Olaf College; see also Bureau of Education, Department of the Interior, *Report of the Commissioner of Education*, 1878–88, table on secondary schools, 1888–93, table on colleges (number and pages vary).

15. Whereas literary societies published the *Carletonian*, the junior and senior classes published the *Carletonia*. Publication information, *Carletonian*, June 1880, 10; publication information, *Carletonia*, June 1881, 8

16. A. O. Sandbo and J. P. Tandberg, "Editorials," *Manitou Messenger*, November 1887, 4; Shaw, *History of St. Olaf College*, 78. Literary societies published the *St. Olaf's Essayist* and *St. Olaf's Echo*; "the students of St. Olaf's School" issued the *Student's Reporter* and *Manitou Messenger*. "Constitution of the Literary Society," *St. Olaff']s Essayist*, 2 January 1879, transcript, 1; "Committee of Managers," *St. Olaf's Echo*, 5 February 1881, transcript, Shaw-Olson Center for College History, St. Olaf College, [1]; masthead, *Student's Reporter*, transcript, Shaw-Olson Center for College History, St. Olaf College, [1]; *Manitou Messenger*, January 1887, 1 (cover).

17. Michel Foucault, *The History of Sexuality, Volume I: An Introduction*, trans. Robert Hurley (New York: Vintage Books, 1980), 42–43. Eve Kosofsky Sedgwick identifies the binary between masculine homosexuality and heterosexuality as the central constitutive element of late nineteenth- and twentieth-century Western culture. Nonetheless, gender figures more centrally than sexuality in my sources. Eve Kosofsky Sedgwick, *Epistemology of the Closet* (Los Angeles: University of California Press, 1990), 1.
18. O. C. Narvestad, "Ought Scandinavians to Support Their Private Institutions in This Country?" *Manitou Messenger*, November 1890, 119. On the multiplicity of white races in this period of American history, see Matthew Frye Jacobson, *Whiteness of a Different Color: European Immigrants and the Alchemy of Race* (Cambridge: Harvard University Press, 1998), 39–90.
19. The next known black student in Northfield, the future Harlem Renaissance poet and playwright Angelina Weld Grimké, arrived at Carleton in 1895 or 1896. Eric Hillemann, "1800s Saw Carleton's First Black Students," *Carleton Voice* (Winter 1996): 11; Mark Perry, *Lift Up Thy Voice: The Grimké Family's Journey from Slaveholders to Civil Rights Leaders* (New York: Viking, 2001), 298.
20. "College Items," *Carletonian*, June 1880, 17; A. O. Sandbo, "Why Are We Here," *Manitou Messenger*, November 1887, 7.
21. Benson, *High on Manitou*, 144; Headley and Jarchow, *Carleton*, 325.
22. Untitled, *Manitou Messenger*, November 1890, 123.
23. See, for example, "College Notes," *Carletonian*, June 1877, 11; Plainview, letter to editors, *Carletonia*, November 1882, 10.
24. "The Higher Education of Women," *Carletonian*, June 1878, 6; Shaw, *Bernt Julius Muus*, 243; Solberg, *Lutheran Higher Education*, 229. Though to my knowledge no historian has studied student ages in the late nineteenth century, Colin B. Burke notes that in the 1850s, 17 percent of students at Midwestern colleges began their studies when older than twenty-one; 28 percent, when younger than seventeen. He does not say whether he includes students in colleges' preparatory departments in the latter figure. Colin B. Burke, *American Collegiate Populations: A Test of the Traditional View* (New York: New York University Press, 1982), 127, Table 3.11.
25. "The Freshmen. *Bury the Hatchet*," *Carletonian*, June 1878, 12–13.
26. A. O. Sandbo and J. P. Tandberg, "Editorials," *Manitou Messenger*, November 1888, 115.
27. O. O. Fugleskjel and Agnes Mellby, eds., "College Crumbs," *Manitou Messenger*, November 1890, 126.
28. Ivan Ringstad and Ella Anderson, eds., "College Crumbs," *Manitou Messenger*, November 1891, 130–31, quotation from 131.
29. I borrow this adjective from Judith Butler, *Gender Trouble: Feminism and the Subversion of Identity*, 10th anniversary ed. (New York: Routledge, 1999).
30. E. K. Cheade, untitled editorial, *Carletonia*, November 1882, 8.
31. Untitled editorial, *Manitou Messenger*, January 1887, 4.
32. J. P. Tandberg, "Our Social Duty," *Manitou Messenger*, November 1890, 121–23, quotations from 122; J. P. Tandberg, "Co-education," *Manitou Messenger*, June 1891, 81–83, quotation from 81. Student newspapers, yearbooks, and other documents often named individuals by their first initial and last name only. In many such cases, I have learned their genders from Carleton and St. Olaf's online directories of alumni. Tandberg's first name, for example, was John. Carleton Alumni Directory, https://webapps.acs.carleton.edu/alumni/directory/ (for searching students by name and/or year; accessed August 2004–January 2005); Shaw-Olson Center for College History, First Thirty Years of Enrollment (1875–1905), http://www.stolaf.edu/collections/archives/sources/enrollment/ (for listing students alphabetically; accessed August 2004–January 2005).

33. "Personal," *Carletonian*, June 1877, 10; O. O. Fugleskjell, ed., "Exchanges and Clippings," *Manitou Messenger*, November 1892, 123; Luella Turrell, ed., "Exchanges," *Carletonia*, 15 November 1892, 12. The *Carletonia* claimed 204 out of only 325 colleges, or 63 percent, admitted both men and women. Both overestimated the figure, which historians today put at 43 percent in 1890. An additional 20 percent admitted only women. Solomon, *In the Company of Education Women*, 44, Table 1.
34. Horowitz, *Campus Life*, 200, 208, quotation from 202.
35. Youths, especially young women, continued to seek their parents' advice on courtship and consent for marriage. Cathy Luchetti, *"I Do!": Courtship, Love and Marriage on the American Frontier: A Glimpse at America's Romantic Past Through Photographs, Diaries and Journals, 1715–1915* (New York: Crown Trade Paperbacks, 1996), 133–35, 170–74; Karen Lystra, *Searching the Heart: Women, Men, and Romantic Love in Nineteenth-Century America* (New York: Oxford University Press, 1989), 157–64; Rothman, *Hands and Hearts*, 214–21.
36. Peterson, "Pluck and Perseverance," 10; Headley and Jarchow, *Carleton*, 336–38, quotations, including that of an undated rule, from 336.
37. Blanche E. Barney and Herbert E. Carleton, eds., "College Cullings," *Carletonia*, November 1890, 17; Bessie A. Burnham, ed., "College Cullings," *Carletonia*, 15 November 1892, 10.
38. "College Notes," *Carletonian*, June 1877, 11.
39. J. P. Tandberg, "Co-education," *Manitou Messenger*, June 1891, 82; M. O. Sortedahl and Anna Morterud, eds., "College Crumbs," *Manitou Messenger*, January 1887, 10.
40. Stella Spalding, untitled editorial, *Carletonia*, November 1888, 6–7, quotations from 6.
41. Ivan Ringstad and Ella Anderson, eds., "College Crumbs," *Manitou Messenger*, November 1891, 130.
42. Untitled, *Carletonian*, June 1880, 12.
43. C. H. Taylor and Myra Parker, eds., "College Cullings," *Carletonia*, November 1884, 15.
44. M. O. Sortedahl, ed., "College Crumbs," *Manitou Messenger*, November 1888, 123.
45. H.F.M. Dahl, ed., "College Crumbs," *Manitou Messenger*, November 1889, 107. See also M. O. Sortedahl and Anna Morterud, eds., "College Crumbs," *Manitou Messenger*, January 1887, 10.
46. Christina Vangan, diary, 28 February, 23 January, 19 February, 6 March, and 24 January 1892, transcript by Ann Metling, alumni cabinet, Christina Vangan box, acc. 2400.02, Shaw-Olson Center for College History, St. Olaf College, 15, 4, quotation from 12, 18, quotation from 5.
47. Vangan, diary, 13 February, 9 March, 12 March, and 19 March 1892, 10, 19, 20, 23.
48. "College Items," *Carletonian*, June 1880, 18.
49. Ibid.
50. "Items," *Carletonian*, June 1878, 18.
51. See note 9.
52. Harding, *College Literary Societies*, 1, 314–15, 317–18.
53. Untitled editorial, *Carletonia*, 15 November 1892, 2.
54. L. O. Johnson and A. Tollefson, "Editorials," *Manitou Messenger*, November 1891, 129.
55. O. O. Fugleskjel and Agnes Mellby, eds., "College Crumbs," *Manitou Messenger*, November 1890, 126; O. A. Tveirmoe, ed., "Exchanges," *Manitou Messenger*, November 1888, 125.

56. On the walking club, see Blanche E. Barney and Herbert E. Carleton, eds., "College Cullings," *Carletonia*, November 1890, 14. On the fraternity, which the faculty repeatedly requested students to resign from or dissolve, see members of Phi Kappa Psi to faculty, 2 October 1884; M. D. Snedicor and Carl J[?]. Brown to faculty of Carleton College, 10 May 1888; Carl J[?]. Brown to faculty of Carleton College, 16 May 1888; all in mag 79, box 1, Literary Societies: General: Men's folder, Literary Societies Collection, Carleton College Archives.
57. Photograph of women playing croquet in front of Ladies' Hall, 1888, Felland Photo Cabinet, box 22, archives no. 183, acc. 1374, Shaw-Olson Center for College History, St. Olaf College; same photograph, in Scrapbook Presented by Rev. Ole Glesne, opposite [26]. In 1889, female students complained that the men were using their croquet ground. The faculty seem to have sympathized with the women, without wishing to disturb the men: the women soon won not only a new croquet ground, but new croquet and tennis equipment. M. O. Sortedahl, ed., "College Crumbs," *Manitou Messenger*, March 1889, 42; Peterson, "Pluck and Perseverance," 23.
58. Blanche E. Barney and Herbert E. Carleton, eds., "College Cullings," *Carletonia*, November 1890, 16; Annie L. Sargent, ed., "Exchanges," *Carletonia*, November 1886, 8; Headley and Jarchow, *Carleton*, 26.
59. C. H. Taylor and Myra Parker, "College Cullings," *Carletonia*, November 1884, 16; Mary W. Wilson, ed., "Social," *Carletonia*, 15 November 1892, 8–9.
60. Blanche E. Barney and Herbert E. Carleton, eds., "College Cullings," *Carletonia*, November 1890, 16; Edith J. Claghorn and Harriet G. Brown, eds., "College Cullings," *Carletonia*, November 1888, 11; quotation from Ada Whiting and J. D. Hickok, eds., "College Cullings," *Carletonia*, November 1886, 11.
61. "Items," *Carletonian*, June 1878, 18.
62. *Algol*, 1889, Laurence McKinley Gould Library, Carleton College, 82–83; *Algol*, 1890, 101, 103; *Algol*, 1892, 96–98; *Algol*, 1893, [147–49]. Many of St. Olaf's men and preparatory boys joined the Ski Club, but women and girls were either uninterested or unwelcome. Photograph of Ski Club at St. Olaf College, 8 December 1886, Felland Photo Cabinet, box 48, archives no. 42, acc. 1374, Shaw-Olson Center for College History, St. Olaf College; same photograph, in Scrapbook Presented by Rev. Ole Glesne, opposite [10].
63. L. B. Sperry, "Some Facts and Query," *Carletonian*, June 1877, 13.
64. See, for example, "College Items," *Carletonian*, June 1880, 18; A. O. Sandbo and J. P. Tandberg, "Editorials," *Manitou Messenger*, November 1889, 99.
65. "Society Directory," *Carletonia*, 15 November 1892, 13.
66. "College Notes," *Carletonian*, June 1877, 11; "College Items," *Carletonian*, June 1880, 18.
67. Quotation from "College Notes," *Carletonian*, June 1877, 11; William J. McCarthy, "Athletics," *Carletonia*, 15 November 1892, 6; H.F.M. Dahl, ed., "Exchanges and Clippings," *Manitou Messenger*, November 1890, 133.
68. See, for example, the several mentions of the sport in M. O. Sortedahl, ed., "College Crumbs," *Manitou Messenger*, November 1888, 121–22.
69. William J. McCarthy, "Athletics," *Carletonia*, 15 November 1892, 5–6.
70. Edith J. Claghorn and Harriet G. Brown, "College Cullings," *Carletonia*, November 1888, 11; "Military," *Carletonia*, November 1888, 14.
71. H.A.K., "Capt's Off-hand Speech before 'St. Olaf's' Guard," *St. Olaf[']s Essayist*, 22 February 1879, transcript, 1; A. O. Sandbo and J. P. Tandberg, "Editorials," *Manitou Messenger*, November 1889, 99; J. P. Tandberg and H. F. M. Dahl, "Editorials," *Manitou Messenger*, November 1890, 125.
72. A. O. Sandbo and J. P. Tandberg, "Editorials," *Manitou Messenger*, November 1889, 99; quotation from J. P. Tandberg and H.F.M. Dahl, "Editorials," *Manitou*

"What Gender Is Lex?" 85

Messenger, November 1890, 125; O. O. Fugleskjel and Agnes Mellby, eds., "College Crumbs," *Manitou Messenger*, November 1890, 126.
73. M. O. Sortedahl and Anna Morterud, eds., "College Crumbs," *Manitou Messenger*, January 1887, 10.
74. H. Eliasson, ed., "Clippings," *Manitou Messenger*, January 1887, 13; quotation from "College Cullings," *Student's Reporter*, 2 February 1884, transcript, [1].
75. Ivan Ringstad and Ella Anderson, eds., "College Crumbs," *Manitou Messenger*, November 1891, 130–31.
76. J. P. Tandberg, "Our Social Duty," *Manitou Messenger*, November 1890, 122.
77. Vangan, diary, 13 February 1892, 10; Carl K. Solberg, diary, 19 March 1892, summarized transcript by Richard W. Solberg, alumni cabinet, item 15B, P590, #2, acc. 2297, Shaw-Olson Center for College History, St. Olaf College, 10.
78. Untitled, *Manitou Messenger*, December 1892, 129.
79. Women had also formed a majority of the *Carletonia*'s editorial board in fall of 1887. "Constitution of the Literary Society," *St. Olaf[']s Essayist*, 2 January 1879, transcript, 1; editorial information, *St. Olaf[']s Essayist*, 2 January 1879, 2, 22 February 1879, 1, 2, and 3 May 1879, 1; "Committee of Managers," *St. Olaf's Echo*, 5 February 1881, [1], 12 February 1881, 1, 19 February, 1881, 1; editorial information, *Student's Reporter*, 2 February 1884, [1]; editorial information, *Carletonian*, June 1877, 8, June 1880, 10; editorial information, *Carletonia*, June 1881, 8, October 1881, 8, September 1882; "Editorial Board," *Carletonia*, October 1883, 11, October 1884, 10, October 1885, 6, October 1886, 8, October 1887, 6, October 1888, 6, October 1889, 6, November 1890, 8; "Board of Editors," *Carletonia*, 8 October 1891, 1, 24 September 1892, 1.
80. Christen Hansen, "The Relation Between Teacher and Pupil," *Manitou Messenger*, November 1891, 127. Hansen was not an editor, but the *Manitou Messenger* generally included one or two women on its editorial board of seven or eight. "Board of Editors," *Manitou Messenger*, January 1887, 3, October 1887, 3, October 1888, 97, November 1889, 97, October 1890, 108, October 1891, 112, October 1892, 91.
81. On the prevalence of female teachers, see David Tyack and Elizabeth Hansot, *Learning Together: A History of Coeducation in American Public Schools* (New York: Russell Sage Foundation, 1992), 158–59, 164.
82. *Algol*, 1889, 7; *Algol*, 1890, 6; *Algol*, 1891, 4; *Algol*, 1892, [8], plate opposite [15]; *Algol*, 1893, [6].
83. Quotation from untitled, *Manitou Messenger*, November 1892, 113; Vangan, diary, 10 February 1892, 10.
84. Edward Mohn, "The St[.] Olaf Band," in *Quarter Centennial Souvenir*, ed. Aasgaard, [97]; program for the First Annual Concert of the St. Olaf College Band, 17 June 1893, in Scrapbook Presented by Rev. Ole Glesne, [7]; Vangan, diary, 4 February 1892, 8.
85. Quotation from "The Haydn Chorus," *Carletonian*, June 1878, 16; "Society Directory," *Carletonian*, June 1878, 18; "Society Directory," *Carletonian*, June 1880, 19; quotation from Blanche Barney and Herbert E. Carleton, eds., "College Cullings," *Carletonia*, November 1890, 15; *Algol*, 1892, [105].
86. Philomathian Society of Carleton College, *Constitution and By Laws of the Philomathian Society of Carleton College* (n.p., 1876), mag 79, box 3, Literary Societies: Philomathian: Constitutions, Manual, etc. folder, Literary Societies Collection, Carleton College Archives, [1].
87. "Debating," *Manitou Messenger*, January 1887, 7.
88. See, for example, President[']s Book of the Philomathian Society of Carleton College, 1882–85, Literary Societies Collection, Carleton College Archives, passim.
89. Publication information, *Carletonian*, June 1877, 8; publication information, *Carletonian*, June 1880, 10; "Constitution of the Literary Society," *St. Olaf[']s*

Essayist, 2 January 1879, transcript, 1; "Committee of Managers," *St. Olaf's Echo*, 5 February 1881, transcript, [1]. The junior and senior classes issued the *Carletonia*, which replaced the *Carletonian* in 1881, and St. Olaf's papers from the mid-1880s on claimed to speak for the entire student body. Publication information, *Carletonia*, June 1881, 8; masthead, *Student's Reporter*, 2 February 1884, transcript, [1]; *Manitou Messenger*, January 1887, 1 (cover).

90. Classified Catalogue of the Philomathian Library; "Sketch of Philomathian Society. Founded September, 1873," *Carletonian*, June 1877, 13; "The Philomathean [*sic*]," *Carletonian*, June 1878, 15; May E. Donovan, "Here and Elsewhere," *Carletonia*, November 1890, 10. I have found no references to any of St. Olaf's societies' libraries, but given Thomas S. Harding's extensive research on the topic, I would be very surprised if they did not have any. See Harding, *College Literary Societies*, 285–95.

91. L. O. Johnson and A. Tollefson, "Editorials," *Manitou Messenger*, November 1890, 129.

92. President[']s Book, meetings of 22 February 1884 and 23 February 1885, 79, 109; Mary W. Wilson, ed., "Social," *Carletonia*, 15 November 1892, 8–9.

93. E. K. Cheade, "A Proposed Change," *Carletonia*, November 1882, 9.

94. M.J.P. Thing, "Commencement Week," *Carletonian*, June 1878, 17; Headley and Jarchow, *Carleton*, 373.

95. See note 9, especially Harding's emphasis on Midwestern and Far Western societies' longevity.

96. L. O. Johnson and A. Tollefson, "Editorials," *Manitou Messenger*, November 1891, 129.

97. "Debating," *Manitou Messenger*, January 1887, 6–7.

98. "Sketch of Philomathian Society. Founded September, 1873," *Carletonian*, June 1877, 14.

99. L. O. Johnson and A. Tollefson, "Editorials," *Manitou Messenger*, November 1891, 128–29. Carleton's Philomathian Society, which was "recognized as an incorporated body" by the Minnesota government, claimed in 1877 to have enlisted about 1,250 members in its first four years of existence. However, since not that many students had attended Carleton in that time, they obviously exaggerated. "Sketch of Philomathian Society. Founded September, 1873," *Carletonian*, June 1877, 14; Headley and Jarchow, *Carleton*, 324.

100. "Constitution of the Literary Society," 1–2; Inf, untitled, *St. Olaf[']s Essayist*, 22 February 1879, 2.

101. "Debating," *Manitou Messenger*, January 1887, 6–7.

102. A turn-of-the-century account claimed that Norsk Studenter Samfund did not admit women until 1895. The *Northfield News*, however, listed a woman as its first president, and sophomore Christina Vangan recorded attending a meeting in 1892. J. E. Beum, "Manitou Debating and Literary Society," in *Quarter Centennial Souvenir*, ed. Aasgaard, [87]; Carl M. Grimsrud, "The Alpha Beta Chi," in *Quarter Centennial Souvenir*, ed. Aasgaard, [84–85]; Agnes Mellby, "The Utile Dulci," in *Quarter Centennial Souvenir*, ed. Aasgaard, [91–92]; Geo. O. Berg, "Norsk Studentersamfund [*sic*], " in *Quarter Centennial Souvenir*, ed. Aasgaard, [90]; quotation from *Northfield News*, 1 December 1888, quoted in Elise Kittelsby Ytterboe, Reminiscence from St. Olaf [c. 1938] in box C/Chronology, College History: Mohn Era, 1874–1899 folder, acc. 2700, Shaw-Olson Center for College History, St. Olaf College, 32; Vangan, diary, 15 February 1892, 11.

103. J. P. Tandberg and H.F.M. Dahl, "Editorials," *Manitou Messenger*, November 1890, 124; Grimsrud, "Alpha Beta Chi," [84–85]; Beum, "Manitou Debating and Literary Society," [87].

104. L. O. Johnson and A. Tollefson, "Editorials," *Manitou Messenger*, November 1891, 128–29.
105. Program for the First Annual Entertainment of the Alpha Beta Chi Society, 29 May 1893, [2–4], in Scrapbook Presented by Rev. Ole Glesne, [10] and [37]; program of an entertainment given by the Utile Dulci Society, 27 February 1893, in Scrapbook Presented by Rev. Ole Glesne, [35].
106. Agnes Mellby, "The Utile Dulci," in *Quarter Centennial Souvenir*, ed. Aasgaard, 91–92.
107. J. P. Tandberg and H.F.M. Dahl, "Editorials," *Manitou Messenger*, November 1890, 125.
108. Untitled, *Manitou Messenger*, November 1892, 113.
109. Quotation from J. P. Tandberg and H.F.M. Dahl, "Editorials," *Manitou Messenger*, November 1890, 124; O. O. Fugleskjel and Agnes Mellby, eds., "College Crumbs," *Manitou Messenger*, November 1890, 126.
110. "Sketch of Philomathian Society. Founded September, 1873," *Carletonian*, June 1877, 13; "Alpha Beta Phi," *Carletonian*, June 1878, 15; James W. McHose, "Report of the Rec. Sec'y of the Alpha Beta Phi. society [sic] for the Winter Term of 1880," pasted into Minutes of the A. B. Ö. Society, 1877 "—("— 82, Literary Societies Collection, Carleton College Archives, 246.
111. "Sketch of Philomathian Society. Founded September, 1873," *Carletonian*, June 1877, 13; "Society Directory," *Carletonian*, June 1878, 18; Register of the Philomathian Society of Carleton College, 1873–1915, Literary Societies Collection, Carleton College Archives, 4–30; President[']s Book, passim.
112. President[']s Book, meeting of 8 April 1882, 13. The debate about gendered mind caught the interest of more male society members than usual, leading three to volunteer additional arguments on each side. One, with perhaps calculated diplomacy, put in an argument for neither. The records do not reveal which side won. Minutes of the A. B. Ö. Society of Carleton College, meeting of 18 February 1880, 111. In a public performance in 1893, men in St. Olaf's coeducational Alpha Beta Chi Society debated the same question; again, the winner remains unknown. Program for the First Annual Entertainment of the Alpha Beta Chi Society, [3].
113. Literary Societies, and Literary Societies, 1882–[8]3, sheets of membership statistics, n.d., both in mag 79, box 1, Literary Societies: General: Men's folder, Literary Societies Collection, Carleton College Archives; quotations from "Society Directory," *Carletonia*, June 1881, 15.
114. Quotation from Adelphic Society of Carleton College, *Within Adelphic Walls* (Northfield, Minn.: privately printed by News Print, 1899), mag 79, box 2, Literary Societies Collection, Carleton College Archives, 1; Adelphic Literary Society, *Constitution and History: Adelphic Literary Society,* rev. ed. (Northfield, Minn.: Carleton College, 1906), mag 79, box 2, Literary Societies Collection, Carleton College Archives, 22.
115. Literary Societies; Literary Societies, 1882–[8]3.
116. Minutes of the faculty of Carleton College, meeting of 18 December 1892, ser. 33, box 1, Carleton College Archives, 158; Headley and Jarchow, *Carleton*, 373; President[']s Book, officer and committee rosters and meetings of 1883, 38–70; Minutes of the A. B. Ö. Society of Carleton College, membership registers of spring and fall 1883, Literary Societies Collection, Carleton College Archives, 80–81, 96.
117. No surviving documents reveals the faculty's true reasons for banning mixed societies; the minutes of the faculty mention the decision, but say nothing more. Whether or not Cheade accurately portrayed their reasons, however, what matters here is students' understanding of and opposition to the decision. E. K. Cheade, "A Proposed Change," *Carletonia*, November 1882, 9. Carleton's faculty at the time con-

sisted of eight men and eight women; of these, six men and four women attended the meeting at which they made the decision to ban coeducational societies. Minutes of the faculty, meeting of 18 December 1892, 157–58; Carleton College, *Annual Catalogue of the Officers and Students of Carleton College, Northfield, Minn., for the Academic Year 1882–83* (Minneapolis: Tribune Job Rooms, Print, 1883), bound with catalogues of 1868–84, Carleton College Archives, 4–5.

118. E. K. Cheade, "A Proposed Change," *Carletonia*, November 1882, 9.
119. May E. Donovan, "Here and Elsewhere," *Carletonia*, November 1890, 10; Flora Pike Gates, "Letter to the Alpha Beta Phi and Philomathian Societies," *Carletonia*, November 1890, 6.
120. Minutes of the board of trustees of Carleton College, meeting of June 1883, ser. 31, box 1, Carleton College Archives, 131; Headley and Jarchow, *Carleton*, 373.
121. President[']s Book, meetings of 22 February 1884 and 23 February 1885, 79, 109.
122. Mary W. Wilson, "Social," *Carletonia*, 15 November 1892, 8–9, quotation from 8.
123. *Algol*, 1893, [163–65].
124. May E. Donovan, "Here and Elsewhere," *Carletonia*, November 1890, 10.
125. See, for example, President[']s Book, meeting of 25 May 1885, 115.
126. Sheldon, *Student Life and Customs*, 125–26; Jon L. Wakelyn, "Antebellum College Life and the Relations Between Fathers and Sons," in *The Web of Southern Social Relations: Women, Family, & Education*, ed. Walter J. Fraser Jr., R. Frank Saunders Jr., and Wakelyn (Athens: University of Georgia Press, 1985), 120–21.
127. Horowitz, *Campus Life*, 49.
128. Alexander Keyssar, *The Right to Vote: The Contested History of Democracy in the United States* (New York: Basic Books, 2000), 149–50.
129. On ratification, see Barbara Stuhler, *Gentle Warriors: Clara Ueland and the Minnesota Struggle for Woman Suffrage* (St. Paul: Minnesota Historical Society Press, 1995), 175.
130. M. O. Sortedahl, "College Crumbs," *Manitou Messenger*, November 1888, 122.
131. Solberg, diary, 16 January, 18 January, 27 January, and 30 January 1892, 2–4.
132. Thos. Guisness and Ella Anderson, eds., "Pick-ups," *Manitou Messenger*, November 1892, 122.
133. Program for a Republican Rally, Under the Auspices of the Republican Club of St. Olaf College, 29 October 1892, in Scrapbook Presented by Rev. Ole Glesne, [37].
134. Stella Spalding, untitled editorial, *Carletonia*, November 1888, 7.
135. Records of the Adelphic Society, meeting of 10 October 1891, Literary Societies Collection, Carleton College Archives, 9.
136. C. H. Taylor and Myra Parker, eds., "College Cullings," *Carletonia*, November 1884, 15; "College Election," *Carletonia*, November 1888, 14; *Algol*, 1893, [159].
137. Minutes of the faculty, meeting of 28 May 1883, 204; "Prohibition Souvenir," *Carletonia*, November 1886, 7; Ada Whiting and J. D. Hickok, eds., "College Cullings," *Carletonia*, November 1886. The popularity of the Prohibition Party at Carleton is not surprising, for Northfield from the town's founding before the Civil War had been a hotbed of prohibitionist sentiment. Clifford Clark, "A Changing Landscape," in *Northfield: The History and Architecture of a Community*, ed. Clark and Carol Zellie (Minnesota: Northfield Heritage Preservation Committee, 1999), 22.
138. Quotations from Albert C. Moses, "Editor's Table," *Carletonia*, November 1888, 8–9; "College Election," *Carletonia*, November 1888, 14.
139. Wendell W. Cultice, *Youth's Battle for the Ballot: A History of Voting Age in America*, Contributions in Political Science, no. 291 (Westport, Conn.: Greenwood Press, 1992), especially 13–14; Keyssar, *Right to Vote*, 277; "The Higher Education of Women," *Carletonian*, June 1877, 6. See note 24.

140. M. O. Sortedahl, ed., "College Crumbs," *Manitou Messenger*, November 1888, 122. A *Carletonia* editor did once cite St. Olaf "students who are married men residing in Northfield" as particularly deserving of suffrage. Albert C. Moses, untitled editorial, *Carletonia*, December 1888, 7.
141. Vangan, diary, 15 March 1892, 21.
142. On the nation at large, see Keyssar, *Right to Vote*, 149–50.
143. Lex., "Suffrage for Students," *Carletonian*, June 1880, 14; Ivan Ringstad, ed., "Personals," *Manitou Messenger*, November 1892, 121.
144. Minutes of the faculty, meeting of 7 November 1892, 119; Bessie A. Burnham, ed., "College Cullings," *Carletonia*, 15 November 1892, 10.
145. Lex., "Suffrage for Students," *Carletonian*, June 1880, 14.
146. Albert C. Moses, untitled editorial, *Carletonian*, December 1888, 7.
147. C. H. Taylor and Myra Parker, eds., "College Cullings," *Carletonia*, November 1884, 15.
148. Lex., "Suffrage for Students," *Carletonian*, June 1880. See also O. A. Lewis, untitled editorial, *Carletonia*, November 1886, 7.
149. O. A. Lewis, untitled editorial, *Carletonia*, November 1886, 7.
150. M. O. Sortedahl, ed., "College Crumbs," *Manitou Messenger*, November 1888, 123. See also O. A. Lewis, untitled editorial, *Carletonia*, November 1886, 7.
151. Keyssar, *Right to Vote*, 402, table A.20.
152. Gordon, *Gender and Higher Education*, 194.
153. Program of Republican Rally.
154. L. DeAne Lagerquist, *From Our Mothers' Arms: A History of Women in the American Lutheran Church* (Minneapolis: Augsburg Publishing House, 1987), 47, 71. The central branch of the church even opposed coeducation. Geiger, "Era of Multipurpose Colleges," 142.
155. M. O. Sortedahl, "College Crumbs," *Manitou Messenger*, November 1888, 122.
156. Belva A. Lockwood, "Letter of Acceptance," quoted in Jill Norgren, "Before It Was Merely Difficult: Belva Lockwood's Life in Law and Politics," *Journal of Supreme Court History* 23, no.1 (1999): 34, see also 36.
157. M. O. Sortedahl, ed., "College Crumbs," *Manitou Messenger*, December 1888, 138.
158. "Should Women Vote?" *Manitou Messenger*, December 1888, 135–36, quotation from 136.
159. A. O. Sandbo and J. P. Tandberg, "Editorials," *Manitou Messenger*, March 1889, 34; *Northfield News*, 30 March 1889, quoted in Ytterboe, Reminiscence from St. Olaf, 34.
160. Solberg, diary, 8 February 1892, 5.
161. President[']s Book, meeting of 1 April 1882, 13.
162. Stella Spalding, untitled editorial, *Carletonia*, November 1888, 7.
163. Ada Whiting and H. K. Wingate, eds., "College Cullings," *Carletonia*, October 1886, 14.
164. Ada Whiting and J. D. Hickok, eds., "College Cullings," *Carletonia*, November 1886, 12.
165. "Political Trickery," *Carletonia*, November 1888, 12.
166. Edith J. Claghorn and Harriet G. Brown, eds., "College Cullings," *Carletonia*, November 1888, 12. Carleton's online alumni directory confirms that the speaker, Bertha Lincoln, was indeed a student. Carleton Alumni Directory (accessed 6 January 2005).
167. Carleton's Prohibition Club, as I mentioned above, limited its membership to men. *Algol*, 1889, 76.
168. William Watts Folwell, *A History of Minnesota*, 4 vols. (St. Paul: Minnesota Historical Society, 1921–30), 4: 334; Stuhler, *Gentle Warriors*, 22–23.

169. Bessie A. Burnham, ed., "College Cullings," *Carletonia*, 15 November 1892, 10.
170. "College Election," *Carletonia*, November 1888, 14.
171. Zimmerman, "Daughters of Main Street," 154–68.
172. Rosenberg, "Limits of Access," 109, 111; Solomon, *In the Company of Educated Women*, 50–51; Bordin, *Women at Michigan*, 1–2.
173. Malkmus, "Small Towns, Small Sects, and Coeducation": 33–34, 64–65 chart 4.
174. Tyack and Hansot, *Learning Together*, 114.
175. Headley and Jarchow, *Carleton*, 325.
176. Rudolph, *American College and University*, 281–82; Malkmus, "Small Towns, Small Sects, and Coeducation": 33–34.
177. Keyssar, *Right to Vote*, 149–50.
178. Zimmerman, "Daughters of Main Street," 166; Gordon, *Gender and Higher Education*, 120; Roberta Frankfort, *Collegiate Women: Domesticity and Career in Turn-of-the-Century America*, New York University Series in Education and Socialization in American History (New York: New York University Press, 1977), xiv–xv.
179. Malkmus, "Small Towns, Small Sects, and Coeducation": 64–65, Chart 4; Rury and Harper, "The Trouble with Coeducation": 484.
180. Zimmerman, "Daughters of Main Street," 154–68; Gordon, *Gender and Higher Education*, chap. 3; Bordin, *Women at Michigan*, chaps. 2–3.
181. Bertha H. Bacon and A. E. Leonard, eds., "Local," *College Days*, Ripon College Archives, Ripon, Wisc., 31–32; J. M. Geery to Lincolnian Society of Ripon College, 18 December 1871, placed in volume of constitution, by-laws, and minutes of Lincolnian Society, folder 1:11/3:8, Students—Interest Groups—Lincolian [*sic*] Society, 1867–1873 (?), Ripon College Archives, Ripon, Wisc.; "Editorials," *College Days*, 30 November 1895, 37–38; *General Catalogue of Ripon College, 1851–1900* (Ripon, Wisc.: n.p., 1900), Harry Elkins Widener Memorial Library, Harvard University, 16–17; (Wheaton) *College Echoes*, June 1894, Harry Elkins Widener Memorial Library, Harvard University, 27–37, passim; Rury and Harper, "The Trouble with Coeducation": 493–96, 500. I thank archivist Valerie Viers for her help in locating relevant sources at Ripon College.
182. Radke studies Iowa Agricultural College (later, Iowa State University), the University of Nebraska, Oregon Agricultural College (later, Oregon State University), and Utah Agricultural College (later, Utah State University). Radke, "Can She Not See and Hear, and Smell and Taste?" 12, 7. Christine A. Ogren finds mixed social environments at state normal schools throughout the country in the late nineteenth and early twentieth centuries. Ogren, "A Large Measure of Self-Control and Personal Power," 213.

The "Problem of the Gifted Student": National Research Council Efforts to Identify and Cultivate Undergraduate Talent in a New Era of Mass Education, 1919–1929

Jane Robbins

> Motivated by concerns over the future quality and quantity of scientists and engineers, after World War I the National Research Council embarked on programs to identify and cultivate undergraduate talent and candidates for graduate school in the sciences. This study documents two projects of the National Research Council, one on aptitude testing for admission and vocational counseling, the other on honors programs, that have had a broad impact on colleges and universities beyond their original objectives. It reflects on the question of how institutionalized policy and practice evolves, and offers a framework for thinking about reform in higher education as externally driven and communications-based.

When Frank Aydelotte assumed the presidency of Swarthmore College on October 21, 1921, he announced his belief that abler students could be given "harder and more independent work" than the average or below-average student, freeing them from routine examinations and allowing greater depth and breadth of study. The next academic year, the first "honors" work was introduced at Swarthmore in English and the Social Sciences, and was expanded, in subsequent years, to include Foreign Languages, Mathematics, Physics, Engineering, Classics, Education, and Chemistry.[1] Students graduating with honors received them on the basis of the nature, level, and amount of their work in broad fields, not on the traditional basis of grade-point average in a field or overall.

Aydelotte is frequently credited with introducing honors programs into the American college and university system, and the publication under his name in 1924 and 1925 of overviews of honors pro-

---

Perspectives on the History of Higher Education 24 (2005): 91-124.
©2005. ISBN: 1-4128-0517-1

grams in American postsecondary education, as well as a detailed description of Swarthmore's own experience with honors, likely supported this view.[2] But while Aydelotte was certainly one of the early adopters, champions, and important developers of honors programs in the United States, he was by no means its pioneer; University of Missouri, for example, had a rather ambitious, if failed, honors program as early as 1912. Honors work and attention to the gifted began shortly after the turn of the twentieth century as new knowledge about intellectual differences intersected with the growing problems of educating large numbers of students, and with recognition of what President H. A. Garfield of Williams College in 1908 called "the failure of our colleges to make adequate provision for men of scholarly mind and earnest purpose."[3] Stimulated by post-World War I interest in science, its rapid spread was the result more of an organized movement spearheaded by a determined group, the National Research Council (NRC), than it was either the conception or work of one man. Indeed, a few individual members of the NRC, most notably Carl Seashore of the University of Iowa, might rightly take precedence over Aydelotte in deserving credit for the spread of honors programs and their supporting infrastructure of admissions tests, special courses, and advising.

As a consortium of industrial foundations and scientists, the NRC would seem to have little concern with issues of curriculum and teaching, and therefore to be an unlikely agent for change in higher education. The motivations of the NRC, and its organized movement to enlist colleges in recruiting, maintaining, and rewarding the "gifted student," is the subject of this study. In part of their work, the NRC collaborated with and was supported by the American Association of University Professors' (AAUP) Committee G on "Methods of Increasing the Intellectual Interest and Raising the Intellectual Standards of Undergraduates"; Aydelotte, in fact, had been involved with this committee while a professor of English at Massachusetts Institute of Technology.[4] While the objectives of the NRC and the AAUP were slightly different, the impetus for their engagement with the gifted issue was the same: the declining intellectual interests of the majority of students in the new era of mass education.[5]

In the following sections I outline the origins of NRC interest in the gifted during and in the immediate aftermath of World War I (WWI), and its expansion from an admissions testing and vocational guidance issue for undergraduate college students to comprise honors programs and related initiatives to identify and encourage gifted undergraduates into research-oriented graduate education. I discuss the two related, overlapping projects that reflected this evolutionary effort, one driven by psychometrics and the other, working with the AAUP, by education; I pay particular attention to the methods used by the NRC to spread awareness of the "gifted problem," communicate recommendations, and enlist others in the cause. In a final section, I discuss the NRC as an agent of higher education reform and its marketing communications-oriented approach to achieving its own goals.[6]

I show that, while the AAUP provided much support and publishing avenues, and Aydelotte was a key member of the effort, the NRC was responsible for creating active adoption and development of honors programs and associated means of identifying and supporting the most able students throughout a broad range of institutions. Despite their internal objectives of producing better scientists, physicians, and engineers, their work was generalized to the field of higher education and many of their recommendations were harbingers of, or first-generation models for, contemporary approaches to admissions, retention, and honors work.

WWI and Its Aftermath: Background to NRC Interest in the Gifted

The NRC was founded in 1916 by a group of engineering societies to offer its services to a nation expecting to enter war.[7] An action-oriented organization of men with an eye to solving the problems of society through science and technology, when the war ended the NRC forged a broader view of its mission and activities. Anything that affected the progress of scientific research and industrial innovation was fair game for its instrumental approach to policy and change, including the institutions of higher education in which it had previously set up committees to coordinate military research. Three groups within the NRC, the Division of Anthropology and Psychology (A&P), the Division of Medical Sciences (Med), and the Division of Educational Relations (Ed Relations), came together after the war to explore related questions of college admissions and the identification and development of talented students that had been raised by wartime intelligence testing.

"Puzzling as well as intensely interesting and professionally significant" differences—in fact, "radical intellectual differences"—between physicians and engineers had been discovered through U.S.

Army testing during the war.[8] In testing of over 2500 medical officers, their "intelligence rating" was found to be lower than all other arms of the service except the Dental and Veterinary corps, and to be nearly identical with that of the Quartermaster Corps; their ratings were "strikingly" different from those of artillery and engineering officers, despite having more years of schooling and experience than any other group. Indeed, when the Army Alpha scores were converted into letter grades, only 27 percent of medical officers obtained A grades, compared to 66 percent for engineers.[9]

While it was unclear whether this was attributable to intelligence or to professional training, and the greater age and less rigorous method of selection into the armed services for the medical corps may have been factors, it seemed certain that the findings had implications for vocational guidance in colleges and universities.[10] This conclusion was underscored by the publication during the war of *A Study of Engineering Education* (the "Mann Report"), begun as a reform initiative in 1907 by a joint committee of engineering societies and the Society for the Promotion of Engineering Education (SPEE, an affiliate of the Engineering Foundation, NRC's founding donors) and informed by the results of the Army testing. While engineers had performed better than medical men on these tests, engineering was not without its own problems. Sixty percent of undergraduate engineering students failed to graduate, and only 20 percent, or half of those remaining, did more than "get by" in the fundamental subjects of calculus, physics, and mechanics. Employers found engineering graduates wanting in practical skills as well as in such traits as character, resourcefulness, judgment, efficiency, and understanding of people. They were suspect of grades as a basis for selecting new hires, and indeed, Edward L. Thorndike of Columbia had shown that the correlation between academic records and ratings by employers such as General Electric and Westinghouse on the key indicators of Technical Ability, Accuracy, Industry, Ability to Push Things, and Personality was "very slight."

One of the prominent recommendations of the Mann Report was that a new system of testing for use in college admissions be devised, one that would be both more objective and a more accurate measure of engineering ability, or aptitude, than the current tests offered by the College Entrance Examination Board. Thorndike, in fact, had developed and successfully tried out such tests on a small sample of Columbia and MIT engineering students. They appeared to measure things important to engineering of which current tests—and school methods—took no account, such as advanced reading, diagramming, language skills, and certain laboratory-type problems. Furthermore, they appeared to provide knowledge *before* college entrance of where a student would be at the end of his freshman year.[11]

Alarmed by the Mann Report findings and eager to capitalize on the wave of support for science and engineering in the aftermath of the war, the NRC turned to the General Education Board (which had been a member of the group that produced the Mann Report) for assistance in studying the results and the prospects for research generally.[12] In 1920, Ed Relations began a Survey of Research Conditions in Colleges and Universities; they were shortly joined by A&P, the history of whose committee name reveals the honing of NRC's interest in discovering the gifted. It began as "Organized Search for Research Talent," was renamed the "Committee on the Superior Student," and finally, by 1925, the "Committee on the Gifted Student Problem." Between 1920 and 1922, of the 320 institutions surveyed and 116 visited during this project, the committee found ample encouragement that research was being enthusiastically embraced by institutions of all kinds, and that facilities, at least at the largest universities, were excellent; the problem was a lack of good graduate students.[13] The brightest new baccalaureates routinely chose paying positions in industry or to study traditional professions, leaving those presumed to be less motivated and less bright to enter graduate school in the sciences, where attrition was high.

As a consequence of these wartime and postwar findings, admissions and vocational guidance became a priority for the NRC for both undergraduate and graduate education, with the goal of producing more baccalaureate engineers and more graduate students in the sciences.[14] Two projects, representing different methodological approaches but nevertheless overlapping and compatible goals, were conducted in tandem. Together they represented a sizable effort to attack the problem of identifying and cultivating talent in America's colleges and universities through a combination of testing, ratings, and improvement of teaching, learning, and advising on programs and careers.

The Psychologists' Project:
Predicting College Success for Vocational Guidance

The Division of Anthropology and Psychology (A&P) established the Committee on the Prediction of Success of Students Entering

Higher Institutions in December 1919. A cooperative project on college admissions with the Society for the Promotion of Engineering Education (SPEE), it was an extension of the work already underway by the SPEE to investigate the use of intelligence and engineering aptitude measurements as means of predicting the likely success or failure of students applying for admission to colleges or engineering schools.[15] SPEE worked primarily with the Pennsylvania State Educational Association and the Carnegie Institute of Technology (now Carnegie Mellon) under the direction of L. L. Thurstone, but Carnegie Institute served more as a central compiler and analyst of a rather large pooled trial of intelligence testing of engineering ability and the ability of students to do college work involving some forty psychologists, engineers, and teachers; men, women, and various populations, including Indian children and, as was planned, Mexican children living at the U.S. borders, were part of the trial. By 1919 SPEE had tested about 9,000 students during their regular entrance examinations. It was believed that the results of these tests would not only help determine who might most usefully be selected for certain kinds of training, but also be useful in sectioning classes; understanding the reasons why a particular student was or was not performing well in his or her school work; opening admissions to a larger group capable of doing college work who were presently excluded while eliminating those presently admitted who could not; and any racial or other individual differences. In these ways the project was the direct outgrowth of both the Mann report and the work of Edward L. Thorndike, particularly his book *Individuality*.[16]

At virtually the same time the Division of Medical Sciences of the NRC was interested in pursuing a similar vocationally oriented testing study, prompted by the same Army testing findings. They soon joined in the project, whose subtitle became, "Cooperative Research on Methods of Determining Probable Success or Failure of Applicants for Admission to Engineering Schools, Medical Schools, and Colleges." Carnegie Foundation for the Advancement of Teaching was approached for funding expected to be around $15,000, with some plans for also approaching Rockefeller once Carnegie was in. But while some Carnegie board members were favorable to the idea, several others were known to be "hostile to most of the ideas advanced in the Mann Report" and concerned about conflict of interest with giving money to the NRC as a whole. Funding ultimately came from the NRC and SPEE itself as well as Thurstone's own pocket.[17]

Thurstone's work was meticulous and thorough, and suggested substantial benefits from the use of "mental tests," as intelligence or aptitude tests were often called, along with other measures then in use. Having completed mass tabulation of returns on 154 colleges and 27,000 students (of which about 10,000 were engineering students at forty-three schools and included all entering liberal arts students at the University of Pennsylvania, University of Texas, Northwestern, and many small liberal arts schools such as Dickinson and Ursinus), in the fall of 1920 he sent a progress report to the NRC.[18] Test data had been analyzed in relation to, for each student, high school scholarship in five subjects and high school average; age at admission; high school; method of admission (exam, certificate, both); regular entrance exam scores in various subjects; number of withdrawn students and reasons (e.g., health, conduct, finances, grades, unknown); freshman scholarship for both semesters by subject; and special information for certain schools or states as appropriate (e.g., New York State Regents' Examination records or class ranks). He planned to retest the students in their sophomore year and track success out ten years. From this work, Thurstone felt confident that he could recommend to colleges that:

- The intelligence exam had demonstrated its predictive value both alone and relative to other measures. It should not replace customary entrance requirements, which aid in understanding students' preparation, but had "by merit earned a legitimate place in a system of college admission."
- The intelligence test had greater predictive value in liberal arts colleges and normal schools than in engineering colleges; however, even with engineering students the intelligence test was a better predictor of college success than the "average high school scholarship for four years."
- All engineering colleges should administer such psychological examinations in order to provide vocational guidance. In this spirit of vocational advising, these tests should not emphasize memory, and problems in algebra, physics, and geometry "should be simple" problems that indicate whether students like to think along the lines needed in the profession, as these simple problems had the highest predictive validity.

Throughout his work Thurstone maintained the importance of simplicity and aptitude not dependent on subject knowledge, such as "interpretation of a paragraph of Prose,...analogies among ordinary words," the ability to determine whether "a simple argument is true or false," and problems based on diagrams, which was the basis of his own thirty-minute intelligence test to be given with subject-matter tests.[19]

Thurstone's extensive work was aided and complemented by equally extensive experimental work administering tests to freshmen in other colleges. Many used the Thurstone test, others a similar test such as the Army Alpha, Binet-Simon, Thorndike, or even a college's own test developed by its own psychologists (e.g., Dartmouth's Completion of Definitions test). During a meeting of the American Psychological Association, Carl Brigham of Princeton invited a number of those experimenting with the tests to the Nassau Club in Washington, D.C.—a site of much NRC high-level decision-making—for a dinner and informal report on the status of their work. The experiences of the individual schools using these diverse instruments were quite consistent with Thurstone's findings as to validity. As hoped, the tests had also been found to be useful for advising lazy but intelligent (underperforming) students, diagnosing delinquency, to support/deny cases of dismissal or reinstatement, to determine workload, and for vocational counseling and other advising purposes. And they had another potential benefit: the saving of administrative costs from admitting students who could not do the work. Stanford, for example, spent 20 percent of its annual budget on instructing students on probation or who would eventually be dismissed for poor performance. The University of Iowa, similarly, noted that the lowest 10 percent of testers eventually dropped out or were dismissed, and Ohio University pointed out how clearly the results showed that students of low intelligence consume "administrative time and energy." Everyone was encouraged to collect their latest data together for submission, through Carl Seashore of the University of Iowa, to the NRC for analysis.[20]

Within the year, the College Entrance Examination Board had decided to adopt Thorndike's version of the test. Intended to "make a rather effective and accurate test at the point of decision between acceptance or rejection for college entrance" and, hopefully, to have a good effect on high-school instruction, it followed the design principles of testing fundamental rather than high-level abilities. With the SPEE project winding down, A&P made a decision to broaden the committee's mandate to comprise industrially oriented vocational guidance for all students.[21] Under the continuing leadership of Mann and Thurstone, the committee forged an ambitious program to promote student-oriented research and services in colleges. It held two invitational conferences on vocational guidance, supported by the Carnegie Corporation of New York, at which formal recognition of the need for student "personnel work" in colleges and universities was recognized and several initiatives were outlined. These included continued work on placement and entrance testing, including development of a high-school equivalency exam so drop-outs might be guided into college, and the development of manuals for schools on establishing vocational guidance and guidance materials for students. The major recommendation, however, was to establish a central Bureau of College Personnel Research. This group would collect and analyze data on student characteristics for the purpose of matching such characteristics to occupations.[22]

For Seashore, this end to the focus on test development and validation, now successfully handed over to others, allowed him to move on to his growing interest in the work identified during his survey work with Ed Relations: supporting the gifted student *after* he was identified.[23]

The Educationists' Project: Honors and the Gifted Student Problem

As Carl Seashore of the University of Iowa would later put it, the driving force behind the expansion of the gifted student work was that graduate schools were getting the "culls." This was partly because of retention problems at the undergraduate level, but also because the most promising new graduates were being hired for paying jobs in business, public affairs, or teaching.[24] Seashore attributed this in large part to an unfortunate tendency toward mass treatment of students in colleges and universities, particularly in schools with more than 100 entering freshmen. Since the 1918–1919 academic year, he had been trying to promote a more systematic approach to identifying and attracting into graduate work talented students at his own school, primarily through the use of a rating scale for evaluating upperclassmen for research promise. Similar to those used today in both high school and college faculty recommendations, the scale looked for an assessment of a student's characteristics compared to all other students ever taught, expressed in a percentage (top/bottom 0–100 percent, later changed to A-E). Beyond mental tests, Seashore believed it was important to understand such characteristics as perseverance and energy, initiative, logical memory, emotional stability, imagination/creativity, abstract reasoning ability, precision, intellectual honesty, moral attitude, craving for independent search for the truth, and physical habits and control. Many of these were comparable to the articulated needs of employers.[25]

The gifted program got its start in 1920 when Seashore raised concerns that the Survey of Research Conditions was not yielding enough information about students. A University of Iowa colleague of Seashore's, George Stewart, professor and head of the Department of Physics, made some preliminary visits to sixty-seven institutions to ascertain what, if any, attention was being paid to the "problem of the gifted student." Stewart's mandate included introducing the idea of identifying talented students with an instrument such as Seashore's scale during the last two years of undergraduate work (Seashore had only used the scale with men, although acknowledged that there "might be reason for including some women").[26] During these visits, Stewart, as the NRC's agent, also encouraged schools to set up their own committees on gifted students and arranged for "correspondents," faculty members who could report back to the NRC on their progress and the attitudes of other faculty. He made his report of these visits, limited largely to his own locale of the central region of the country in April 1921.[27]

The findings from the early visits informed both subsequent work on the gifted and the first phase work on testing conducted by the psychologists. Stewart had learned that faculty tended to spend more time helping students of mediocre ability, and to assume that superior students will succeed without their help. Students were not receiving early information on careers, and seniors were not receiving career advice; he viewed the senior year as a critical one in terms of graduate education and career planning, and thought there should be a test for seniors. There was inadequate availability of advanced courses. None of the colleges visited was doing enough to identify and encourage superior students, with some but not enough using testing for the purpose, and there was virtually no data on whether students of ability were dropping out and if so, why. In his report, Stewart laid out a range of activities for the NRC, such as regular information bulletins for faculty, institutions, and students on topics ranging from careers to the running of advanced coursework, and development and distribution of psychological tests and rating scales for identification and vocational guidance early and at senior year (pursued by A&P in the first phase). He strongly recommended further visits to schools to consult with faculty, appeal to students, and collect data from school records for analysis. He and Seashore saw this communications link as permanent and professional, grounded in a marketing approach using mailing lists, follow-ups to mailings, and charges for publications to communicate value.

Around the same time that Stewart was conducting his visits, the Division of Educational Relations began working on some "overlapping issues" of student engagement, retention, and advanced work for undergraduates with the AAUP's Committee G, Methods of Increasing Undergraduate Intellectual Interest and Raising the Standards of Undergraduates. Committee G's objectives were twofold: to restore intellectual meaning to education and, not incidentally, to maintain faculty interest and satisfaction. It was as an early leader of this team, now headed by Ernest H. Wilkins, professor of romance languages and literature at the University of Chicago, that Aydelotte began his investment in the possibilities of American honors work while at MIT.[28]

As a first project, Ed Relations and Committee G, which it partly funded, had begun developing a list of sixty-seven methods for improving education for undergraduate students. These methods were oriented to controlling not only the quality of students and their college experience but also the quality of professors and student administration. At the classroom level, they included interdisciplinary courses, courses that related to current issues, "companionable" alternatives to lectures, small sections, guidance and supervision in independent and non-laboratory study, elimination of nonintellectual subjects, and special initiatory courses for freshmen. To support these measures, institutions would need to recruit professors of high intellectual and moral standards, and provide pedagogical training and mentoring in teaching. The committee also identified a wide range of characteristics at the curricular, administrative, and student services levels: the use of preceptorial systems; higher standards for admission, retention, and graduation; course planning and election in advance; a system of concentration and distribution; special sections, courses, or honors work for the ablest students, with allowance for credit or election of courses in proportion to quality of work; general examinations; creation of an active student life of activities, publications, and resources of an intellectual or cultural or social character; faculty-student clubs and discussions; the integration of undergraduates and graduates in some courses and activities; and elimination of both faculty and students who consistently performed below par.[29]

Seashore approached Ed Relations with his ideas of focusing this work on identifying the gifted student. Although some in A&P felt the work in Ed Relations was "too intangible" and "distant" from A&P's measurement approach, Seashore had respect for what they were doing and, almost from the beginning, work on the gifted became a cooperative project. Though A&P would retain its committee in name with Seashore as chair (and E. L. Thorndike a member), the real work was done within Ed Relations, and Seashore himself devoted all his efforts on the subject to that division. He also became the major influence on the content and direction of the division's work. Building on Seashore and Stewart's earlier program of visiting colleges and forming faculty committees to attend to the question of identifying and supporting the gifted, Ed Relations redefined their own work as a complement to Seashore's and his ideas.

Working together, Seashore and Ed Relations developed a strategy of honors work and its components at a Conference upon the Problem of the Unusually Gifted Student at the NRC on December 23, 1921, attended by conference committee members Seashore, Wilkins, Aydelotte, S. P. Capen of the American Council on Education, J. Crosby Chapman of Yale University, J. J. Coss of Columbia University, L. T. More of the University of Cincinnati, A. A. Potter of Purdue University, G. W. Stewart of the University of Iowa, J. J. Tigert of the U.S. Bureau of Education, Vern Kellogg and Albert Barrows representing Ed Relations and NRC administration, and a few invited guests. There were six presentations on the state of honors work in the United States, particularly in comparison with honors work in England, the state of current knowledge in identifying and developing students of exceptional ability, and the role the NRC could play in assisting institutions of higher education to find and support such students. This role was wide-ranging. Developing proper assessment instruments, assisting universities to attract outstanding professors, and stimulating interest among undergraduates in research with grants and prizes were obvious possibilities. But the NRC might also encourage institutions to become specialized in some way to avoid waste and unnecessary duplication of curricula, and suggest to them the kinds of problems that needed solutions.[30]

Beyond the notion of extra work with high grades to be recognized at graduation, honors work was conceived of as being something far more attractive to and challenging for students. Admission into honors work should be based on excellence in a particular subject rather than overall grades, and the test of success should be a comprehensive examination to demonstrate ability in and overall grasp of a subject rather than memory and rote knowledge attainment. With the goal of encouraging the best work of which students were capable, the view was that honors work should include relief from the ordinary academic guidelines and restrictions (including class attendance), resulting in less lecture-type work and more independent reading and thinking of greater difficulty and depth. There should be ample collaborative work and social engagement with faculty as well as personal encouragement and recognitions. These might include conferences, small gifts (e.g., books, association memberships), junior- or senior-year fellowships (without a service requirement), and broader access to facilities and equipment.

At the heart of this perspective was the view that the kind of methods, routine, and supervision needed by the mediocre student were a hindrance to the abler one. As Seashore put it, "school actually often succeeds in discouraging initiative, cutting the wings of imagination, lowering ideals, and recognizing inferior standards, so that the superior student comes out from the system not much different from the inferior." Yet "differences in capacity tend to increase in proportion to the complexity of the task," and among a hundred college freshman, the five most able can do five times more work than the five least able, and the few at the upper end "may be capable of rendering more than ten times the *average* output for the class, while the one or two at the other extreme are quite certain to fail."

In this perspective lay the rationale for the assessment and sorting components associated with the gifted project, bolstered by the reality that, in many institutions at the time, two or three times more students applied than could be accommodated, and the belief that promise of intellectual and moral leadership should be the basis of selection. In practical terms, given the difficulty of measuring the latter, this meant consideration of the ability to succeed in college through testing, sorting of groups into ability, and rating of more subjective characteristics.

The approach to testing and sorting was grounded in recent psychometric knowledge and pragmatism. It replaced an idealized view of schooling as a great equalizer with the notion that each student would function best, be happier, and be treated most fairly at his highest level of achievement among peers; it was seen as vital to motivation that he be free to move, at any point, if he showed he belonged elsewhere. "Colleges should profit by the lesson we have learned in treating morons," Seashore said. This lesson was that placing someone in an environment in which he did not belong resulted in rebellion, unproductivity, and unhappiness.

To put their plans into action, the committee agreed that the information and ideas being developed on the gifted should be disseminated to the faculty of colleges and universities in as concentrated, vigorous, and persistent a way as possible. They were united on the importance of personal visits to institutions, such as carried out earlier by Seashore's Iowa colleague George Stewart, for communication and building networks of people in support of the project. Aydelotte and a few others, however, objected to sending a psychologist given the tendency of some faculty to "disregard the value of work being done by psychologists today." And while a few members questioned the wisdom of constructing a single recommendation for honors work, the committee was unanimous in the conviction that wide circulation throughout the country to plant the information discussed during the day was needed. Rather than just a "periodical bombardment with a series of independent publications," however, Wilkins suggested that there might be one extensive bulletin generally followed by more detailed publications on the specific topics of the conference, such as sectioning or rating scales. It was, as Seashore noted, "important to consider carefully the manner of going before the public." They also decided to prepare bulletins for seniors on careers and other issues of concern, to conduct extensive experimental research on aspects of the gifted problem, and in general serve as an advisory or clearinghouse service. All in all, the decisions reflected Stewart's findings and recommendations in his April report.

The group agreed that the superior student had long been neglected, both in colleges and in elementary and secondary education. They were determined to change that. Working with the AAUP, and perhaps other interested parties such as the Association of American Colleges and the Bureau of Education, they would attack what Edwin Wilkins called "the most important single problem within the field of higher education."[31]

Strategy in Action: Activities of the Gifted Student Groups

Following the conference, in 1922 the Gifted Student Project began to execute its plans for raising consciousness about the need to better identify and serve the undergraduate. It embarked on a five-year period of intense visiting, conference, publication, and speaking activity, much of it backed by the Commonwealth Fund and General Education Board, and some by the NRC itself. From the range of possible methods to identify and support the gifted, best represented by the previously published AAUP list of sixty-seven, a narrower focus was chosen for emphasis and expansion. Honors work was the foundation, supported and complemented by college qualifying and placement testing and early identification of talent, sectioning of classes, rating of individuals, initiatory courses taught by senior faculty designed to stimulate freshmen's intellectual interest, student interviews and advising throughout the undergraduate years, faculty-student comradeship, orientation/information for scientific careers, personnel service (student life and career counseling activities), special coursework and differentiation of teaching methods at the upper levels, and independence of progress/move away from the credit hour. This selection reflected the combined interests of A&P and Ed Relations.

The visits were the cornerstone of the project. Despite the concerns expressed at the conference about having a psychologist as the visitor, Seashore was appointed to the task. He proved to be a committed and, at least in public, diplomatic ambassador on the issues of testing and the gifted to a wide range of educational institutions, simultaneously promoting attention to, and theoretical and economic rationales for, supporting the gifted while assuring its non-interference with the privileges and opportunities of others. Between 1922 and 1927, he visited 120 colleges and universities around the country. These visits served the dual purpose of introducing the NRC, largely unknown outside the East or by smaller, less research-oriented institutions, and of focusing the attention of faculty, students, and administrators on the gifted and on the potential for careers in research. The dual purposes were so well served that Seashore took to referring to them as "National Research Council Days" or "Gifted Student Days," reflecting the fact that institutions would organize entire days around his visit in recognition of the prestige of the NRC, which guaranteed a serious hearing of what he had to say. Convocations of the entire student and faculty bodies were common, supplemented by research lectures, conferences with administrators and deans, faculty dinners, and sometimes extended meetings with presidents or boards. Invariably, the visits sparked interest in self-examination and further contact among the institutions, and Seashore, like Stewart in the first visits, never left without establishing a formal contact for further correspondence on institutional activities, often at the level of dean or president. The timing of these visits could not have been better. The postwar period was a "psychological moment" to introduce the new ideas, a period of reconstruction when schools were "groping for information" as interest in the gifted was emerging, and colleges were finding that they were "engaged in mass production by methods suitable for primitive institutions; that the first concern of all institutions was to take care of the 'cripples'; that the bright student was held in leash by the poor student and often by a mediocre faculty."[32]

Seashore's reports on his visits indeed showed, through comments on each institution, a higher education field in transition, but in more ways than through mass education alone. Commenting on a trip to twenty-four schools out West, he noted that several state universities had managed, as he put it, to have "gone through the political fire and struggle of pioneer days," and to now have wrenched free of politics and to be admirably on their way to growth and improvement; he counted the Universities of New Mexico, Utah, Idaho, Oregon, and Arizona in this group, despite lesser opinions of their reputations by some. A number of state colleges were fighting for recognition as full-fledged universities—beyond the capacity of their faculty if not their facilities. Seashore was generous with both praise and criticism, and attributed the healthy direction of a college—or its opposite—directly to the leadership of the institution, believing that the president of the institution was far more important than it had been in earlier times: "the maker, or un-maker, of the institution." Whitman, Lewiston State (a two-year institution), Occidental, and Pomona were variants of "splendid" small colleges; Reed was in "a serious crisis" of governance and division that threatened its future, and Mills was a kind of "higher fitting [*sic*: finishing] school" for girls. He had scathing criticism for the University of California system: Berkeley did things "educationally on the principle of 'what the traffic will bear,'...a most unprecedented situation" in terms of admission and curriculum, and Southern Branch (UCLA) was a "miniature of Berkeley and in some respects worse." The University of Southern California, "a mushy, overgrown institution run in a small college caliber, with a large university constituency and bold claims for recognition," was only successful because of the problems in the region with the state system. Stanford was "an inspiration." On a trip through the East and Midwest, he noted that with the "exception of Bryn Mawr, everyone was attempting mass education," but that Northwestern, Purdue, and Columbia were doing a fine job on the "personnel work" of maintaining contact with and morale in the student body. He thought much more highly of Antioch than Flexner had—and wrote Flexner to tell him so—and found Rochester very substantial for an urban school. In the South, with few exceptions Seashore found a strong religious atmosphere, poor finances, low admission standards, high freshman ejection rates, and rampant grade inflation, especially in the graduate schools.[33]

While Seashore traveled the country for face-to-face contact with institutions, believed to be absolutely essential to the success of the project, he also mounted a publishing and speaking campaign. This was carried out in large part in cooperation with, and the substantial effort of, the AAUP, which offered, through their own Committee G and the association publications, an excellent complement to Seashore's promotional activities and access to a large audience. One of the first publications for which the AAUP *Bulletin* served as outlet was an annotated bibliography, compiled with Seashore in mind by Committee G in cooperation with the NRC, of where faculty could find discussion of the identified methods for supporting intellectual interests among undergraduates. This bibliography, which covered 255 articles, books, and university reports on education appearing in the philosophical, religious, social, and institutional literature between 1901 and 1922, was published in 1923.[34] Committee G members also developed a series of papers for the *Bulletin* on key methods of interest to the gifted project, including, among others, initiatory courses for freshman, which received a great deal of interest; special sections for the ablest; interdepartmental courses; improvement of admissions standards; and general examination and testing. Seashore contributed the paper on sectioning on the basis of ability for the *Bulletin*. It was based on two earlier papers he had written for *School and Society*, one a general discussion, circulated to the deans of 190 institutions for their comment, and one a report on this feedback and the experience of such diverse institutions as Princeton, Vassar, Montana State, the University of Missouri, Georgetown, the University of Chicago, and Purdue on its use.[35] Many schools reported following Seashore's plan exactly; indeed, sectioning had "swept the entire country" since the visits began.[36]

During his years as a visitor Seashore was, in fact, a prolific spokesperson for the Gifted Student Project, taking over the role that had been filled in earlier years by his predecessor George Stewart and Ed Relations member Albert Barrows.[37] He spoke to the Association of American Universities and the National Association of State Universities, and published numerous additional articles in *School and Society* and other publications.[38] Over 1,000 reprints of his first speech to the Association of the American Universities (AAU), "The Gifted Student and Research," were distributed to the presidents, deans, and selected faculty of 480 colleges and universities; included in the mailing was a reprint of Seashore's "Sectioning Classes on the Basis of Ability."

A comparable effort was made on the goal of encouraging the gifted into careers in research. Seashore wrote an "Open Letter to College Seniors" about going to graduate school, and the use of his pet rating scale for judging the characteristics rather than the grades of promising research talent. In 1922 alone 15,000 copies were sent to 520 institutions, and in 1923 an offer was again made to send as many copies as institutions required; by 1927, over 74,000 copies had been distributed. (By the end of the program, plans were underway to develop a comparable "Open Letter to Freshmen," to get them thinking about research careers from the start and offer advice on course selection during the first years.) In addition, prominent scholars in a dozen scientific fields were retained to write papers on opportunities in their fields; authors included astronomer Harlow Shapley of Harvard, physicist Augustus Trowbridge of Princeton, anthropologist Clark Wissler of the Museum of Natural History, chemist W. D. Bancroft of Cornell, and mathematician C. J. Keyser of Columbia. The NRC sent sets to 220 institutions, resulting in a general call for more and prompting the NRC to revise and repeat the series. Eventually there were twenty such papers, totaling 113,900 copies in circulation. In 1927, fifteen of these papers were bound together with the "Open Letter to College Seniors" and distributed to approximately 340 educational institutions and public libraries at their request.[39]

But perhaps the major publication to come out of the project, and certainly the best known, was Frank Aydelotte's report on honors colleges, the results of a survey conducted by the NRC. Prompted, to some extent, by a new series of articles on advanced work that Aydelotte was running in the *American Oxonian*, in June 1922 the NRC sent out a letter to 450 colleges and universities asking them whether any system of honors had been established in their institutions, and to please report back on its nature and usefulness. The NRC heard back from such diverse institutions as Denison, Dickinson, Knox College, Middlebury, NYU, Princeton, Southern Presbyterian University, Wesleyan, Johns Hopkins University, and the University of Colorado. Aydelotte, a member at large of Ed Relations, was asked if he would put the data together. A first printing of 3,000 copies of *Honors Courses in American Colleges and Universities* was published as an *NRC Bulletin* in February 1924, describing thirty-five programs in which additional or partly substituting work was offered as honors work, often involving a comprehensive exam and thesis (placed in Appendix A), and nine with full-time, specialized upper-level courses and independent study culminating in a comprehensive exam (placed in Appendix B).[40] The NRC distributed a total of 1,737 copies for free, with offers to send more if desired; among the recipient list were 615 college and university presidents, 467 deans of arts and sciences, special contact lists of both Seashore and Aydelotte, and 553 Oxford scholars.

The report was warmly welcomed and prompted a growth of interest throughout the country. Numerous institutions requested additional copies (the University of Michigan, for example, asked for 100, with most asking for another 5–35) or additional information about running a program; these schools ran the gamut from teachers colleges to military schools, religious schools, even high schools. Student, alumni, and trade publications asked for information, and wrote articles. Most of all, the publication of *Honors Courses* motivated Rockefeller's General Education Board to fund a kind of "demonstration project" at Swarthmore, a full try-out of the honors idea, the results of which could be analyzed and published. The announcement of this funding alone spurred increased interest in colleges around the country.[41]

With the *Honors Courses* report in hand, another popular NRC method for promoting change was put into play: the conference. Choosing the Midwest as the venue for its first drive—both for its high proportion of public "mass" universities and the belief that the relatively innocent and unjaded character of the Midwestern student made him a promising clean slate for development—the NRC invited the presidents of institutions showing greatest interest in cultivating the superior student to a two-day conference on March 17–18, 1925, at the University of Iowa. Sixty institutions were invited (based on response to the distribution of *Honors Courses*), and ultimately forty-nine presidents, deans, and professors from forty-one colleges and universities attended. The program, under the direction of conference committee Aydelotte, Mann, Seashore, and Kellogg, was a day of five presentations, two on "The Need of [*sic*: for] Honors Courses in Mid-West Colleges and Universities," and three on "Factors Determining Types of Honors Courses"; the second day was devoted to discussing committee reports and efforts to formulate principles for constructive work toward the goal of serving the superior student.

The speakers made the case for honors work through a range of research and stories, compellingly illustrating the dual problem of often staggering attrition rates (for example, only 23 percent of the entering liberal arts students at Iowa made it to their senior year) and declining numbers of students over four years possessing B averages or above. The blame for this was divided between the mediocre and distracting curriculum of distributed requirements that had been the political compromise replacing Eliot's wrong-headed elective system, and the attitude of "the inalienable right to an academic degree" that had overrun the colleges with students who had no idea why they were there except that it was the thing to do. These students were unable to do college work, and their presence resulted in the best students doing only the barest amount to stay a little ahead and surely contributed to the dropping out of good as well as poor pupils. While there was some discussion about "re-educating" the public about who should get a college degree or that only those able to handle honors work should go on to the upper years of college, the overall sentiment was that individual attention to all students was the solution. For the most talented, honors work of a challenging and completely flexible nature should be provided; for others, the best education that they could handle. The most talented were not necessarily A students, but those who had an interest in something and could drive toward a goal; they could be identified by any combination of overall grades, outstanding ability in a single area, evidence of real interest in intellectual work and study, and evidence of leadership, moral, and other character traits. There were disagreements, concerns, and wonderings about whether undergraduate education would be turning into graduate education, whether elite schools would (or should) crop up serving only honors students to create a hierarchy of institutions within a state, and whether the techniques of honors work might be beneficially applied to every student.

There were two points of uncommon agreement: the urgency of getting hold of promising students at the earliest possible moment, though at any point in college that they may be found; and the pivotal importance of the faculty. Teachers, indeed, were seen as the key to the entire honors idea, and whose interest would determine whether the gifted were properly identified and supported or not, as often the real issue was getting students to work and to value intellectual achievement. Not the lecturing scholar who often teaches upper-level students but the kind with real teaching and advising skills, who cared about students and could encourage, motivate, and teach by critical rather than didactic approaches. Such teachers should be made available to new students from the start. But everyone there knew that they were defining a problem as well as a need: "American education has gotten away from the faculty. The more administrative machinery you set up, the more you break off the contact between the student and the faculty." All efforts would be in vain without dedicated teachers.[42]

The conference made a big impression on attendees. Writing only a week later, H. Glicksman, Office of the Assistant Dean, College of Letters and Science at the University of Wisconsin, wrote Aydelotte: "I returned from Iowa City full of enthusiasm about the reading for honors system, as you are now employing it at Swarthmore. Yesterday I finished a rough draft of a report to the faculty, in which I recommended the scheme for trial at Wisconsin." Word of the conference got around, and more requests for information came in. The NRC immediately began planning a second conference for the Pacific Coast area.

With such enthusiasm, following the conference a revised and updated edition of *Honors Courses in American Colleges and Universities* was published and a first run of 3,500 again distributed aggressively, together with a summary of the conference. In the one year since the publication of the first edition, the number of institutions providing honors work had at least doubled in both categories of program to a total of ninety-three: from thirty-five to seventy-five institutions where additional work beyond the regular curriculum was required for honors, and from nine to eighteen where honors constituted a different, more difficult, and largely independent course of study, with many schools moving in this hoped-for direction.[43] Like its predecessor, this edition yielded many more information requests, including from law schools and high schools, and extensive discussion in the press. Schools such as MIT, Stanford (which had been a laggard in the honors idea), and the University of Oklahoma sent their proposed programs in to the NRC or to Aydelotte requesting feedback.

The need to provide special work for exceptional students had clearly been felt in institutions at all levels, as adopters ranged from the modest to the elite at both public and private colleges and universities. But as of 1925, some pattern could be seen in connection with the type of program adopted—that is, whether a school had been categorized into Appendix A or B under Aydelotte's personally strict, though objectively far from obvious, criteria. While Appendix A included institutions as diverse as Amherst, Bradley Polytechnic, the College of Puget Sound, Connecticut College for Women, Oberlin, Johns Hopkins University, Kalamazoo College, Princeton University (a minimal program), and Yale, the majority in this category were the large state universities. Several of these, including the Universities of Illinois, Minnesota, North Carolina, Vermont, and Virginia, required the full complement of additional coursework (often without extra credit toward a degree), comprehensive exam, and thesis. It may be that state universities, one of the prime targets of NRC attention, indeed saw honors programs as a way of serving the gifted within their state-mandated mission to serve all. Appendix B, in contrast, contained almost all private institutions, many of them elites: Barnard College, Brown University, Carleton College, Harvard University and Radcliffe College, Smith College, Swarthmore College, Vassar College, to name the most prominent. None of these required a thesis (although it might be an option); the key was that it offered substantially separate work from the regular program. That already academically challenging institutions should offer honors work of this type may at first seem counterintuitive. It may be, however, that with the focus on what Aydelotte recommended be drive and interest rather than "cleverness," and with their own desire to provide an individualized education and to maintain their already established reputation as being feeder schools for research institutions, these schools felt a need equal to those with more intellectually diverse student bodies.

Passing the Baton:
The End of the Gifted Student Project within NRC

The movement to attend to the gifted in colleges, and to promote honors and various forms of assessment and advising as the means of doing so, had bred interest in many quarters and many other agencies, creating a network of activities and support. Several new national agencies had arisen to share in and coordinate with the NRC in gifted student work, with one of the original project purposes, that of clearinghouse, "being taken over in a very happy way." Seashore, while ending his own stint as visitor, believed the visits should continue on an annual basis, and that the secret to their success was that the NRC and the foremost leaders of higher education shared an interest in a vital issue that made focus on the gifted student an easy sell: the future scholar and researcher.

Nevertheless, the time had come when it made sense to integrate and solidify efforts to present a "solid front" to postsecondary institutions. At a meeting on April 23, 1927, Ed Relations voted to call a conference to initiate joint continuation of the gifted work, and to seek additional funding. The first joint conference of representatives of the principal interested agencies convened later that year, consisting of the NRC; Carnegie Institution of Washington; American Council of Learned Societies; Institute of Economics; Social Science Research Council; and the American Council on Education. A second conference followed in April 1928. Among the changes in direction were a decision to expand out from the initial goal of finding students for the natural and physical sciences to include the humanities (in practice, much honors work started in these fields), and to further broaden purposes by convening from time to time to raise and work on, primarily through the American Council on Education, pressing issues in regard to the advancement of research and scholarship.

With this transition, the gifted student project became more diffuse, with no clear locus of responsibility, and, with Seashore's withdrawal from the visiting role, no missionary leader. The consequence was that the project was left without a focal point for raising funds or to attract someone who would, as Seashore had done, devote the necessary time to visiting. Though the NRC voted to update *Honors Courses* through renewed visitation in April of 1930 and to seek another $15,000 to continue the gifted work in June, by October of that year funds had not been found. The NRC decided that, for the future, the NRC should not be seen as the backer of further work, and that an outside publisher should be found for the next revision of *Honors Courses*, with the joint committee taking over more responsibility; an outside publisher would "indicate for one thing that people generally have a real interest in the matter."[44] A year later, funds still had not been found, and *Honors Courses* was now seven years out of date.

Ed Relations had, with the decision to relinquish control and move the project out to a broader cooperative group, refocused on its traditional domain, graduate rather than undergraduate education. Its new concern was restricting teaching and the demands of graduate students for specialized courses in order to free faculty for more research; the worry was that "overcrowding in the curriculum" in graduate school "may be interfering with the best interest of research in such schools."[45] Other concerns included "gaps" in scientific fields in the colleges, and the relation of the Ph.D. degree to college teaching.

Through this combination of factors, attention to the gifted did not exactly come to a halt, but it was slowed. Ultimately, visitors were recruited from among Swarthmore faculty and, supported by Carnegie Corporation and the General Education Board, a new survey of honors work (including in high schools) was conducted during 1940, and was eventually published near the end of the World War II. It had taken about ten years for the gifted work to regain strong organizational footing after the NRC withdrew its leadership, but, further prompted by postwar efforts at recovery and global economic competition, work on the problem of the gifted student begun by the NRC in the days following the previous world war enjoyed renewed interest in the 1950s and 1960s.[46]

Conclusions and Discussion

Looked at in institutional terms, "great things," as Seashore reflected, were achieved in support of identifying and supporting the talented, and Aydelotte considered the spread of the honors idea to be "the most important educational development of the period between the two wars."[47] Honors work had been incorporated into

The "Problem of the Gifted Student"   115

nearly one hundred schools, many of them the small colleges or public institutions targeted by the project; admissions and placement testing, sectioning of classes on the basis of ability and initiatory courses had been widely adopted; and the importance of continuous advising, vocational counseling, and research on students had been established and substantially institutionalized.

At the very least, the NRC's significant external programmatic reach shaped and influenced the future of these mainstays of college administrative procedure and curriculum. Today, honors programs are thriving in American colleges and universities, particularly in state universities and others with a tradition of accepting students of varying degrees of ability and academic record. Honors programs are no longer limited to serving the gifted as a means of making faculty work more satisfying or identifying and developing the talented next generation of scientists or social leaders, although these remain important. They have, in addition, become a way to enhance institutional prestige and move up in the rankings by attracting students, often with great financial support, to attend schools they might not otherwise have considered—and to attract faculty and both private and public funding as well.[48]

But perhaps a more remarkable achievement of the NRC is that so previously little-known an agency raised the consciousness, and was adopted as expert, on issues fundamental to the running of undergraduate colleges and arguably outside the purview of an industrially funded and oriented body such as the NRC—issues that, up to that point, had received little to no attention by most college leaders. The process by which the NRC achieved its remarkable influence is worth considering as a lesson in how educational reform, and fundamental change in administrative practice in education, might occur. Several elements are observed in what is perhaps best described as a largely technocratic approach to policy change, and a pattern of effective NRC behavior:[49]

- The NRC began with a clearly articulated, interest-driven agenda. It had identified an "internal" problem (insufficient numbers of engineers and talented future researchers) to be solved. It located a "cause" in the external environment (neglect of the superior undergraduate student), for which it chose a "solution set" (a combination of testing, curricular intervention, and vocational guidance).
- The NRC scanned the environment—for indications of any movement in the desired direction, for ideas, and for allies to be brought on

board in the effort; these allies ranged from early actors such as Aydelotte, to AAUP's Committee G, whose views of the purpose of education differed but who shared some views about its means. Through surveys and visits, the NRC both collected information and raised consciousness and activity where none had previously existed.

- The NRC used a primary execution strategy of persistent expert communication, blanketing the field of higher education through conferences, speeches, articles, pamphlets, and books. It became the "guide" to which colleges turned for information on the issues, resulting in *communicative isomorphism*, or change toward common behavior as a result of a largely communicative process. By this means, a very few dedicated individuals convinced of the value of their message—primarily Seashore, Aydelotte, and Mann—were, by working under a legitimizing organizational umbrella, able to effect broad change.[50]
- The project capitalized on a "window of opportunity" of postwar uncertainty and overwhelming mass education—what Seashore had called "a psychological moment." Institutional prestige and a sense of urgency lent credibility and persuasiveness; despite its own arguable lack of special knowledge about the best way to run educational enterprises, the NRC was accepted as an expert in what for institutions was new and confusing territory.[51]

There is a paradox in the perspective of mass education having created difficulty in finding and recruiting talented students into scientific careers. Arguably, mass education was created, in part, via the Morrill Acts to develop more people for scientific and technical careers. That the enormous increase in the influx of students should then be viewed negatively as having translated into a paucity of students for scientific careers is ironic indeed, and begs the question of whether the issue was not that students had not the aptitude but that they were simply not interested. The second phase of the gifted student project, in trying to locate and cultivate interest among any reasonably well-performing student, seemed to recognize the lack of interest, and viewed it as something fixable. But the problem of not being able to attract and hold students into the sciences remains today, at both the undergraduate and graduate levels; in engineering in particular, attrition remains above 50 percent, with still higher percentages expressing loss of interest in the field as reasons for leaving, despite persistent financial and programmatic efforts.[52]

The NRC's approach thus appears to have been effective at institutionalizing its desired policies, but not necessarily at achieving the goals of those policies to increase the numbers of graduates in science and engineering, and thereby more practicing engineers and qualified applicants for graduate and academic careers. One can wonder whether another movement, that to limit faculty teaching time at the graduate level in preference for research, may have, in moving down into the undergraduate college, worked in opposition to the goals of the gifted work, which had a well-acknowledged dependence on skilled and dedicated teaching. Whatever the reasons for its failures to remedy the problems in the sciences, the gifted work altered the thinking about fundamental issues in higher education in ways in which its original ends have largely been forgotten while the means of testing, honors, and advising have become taken-for-granted components of all undergraduate education.[53]

Notes

1. Robert C. Brooks, with an introduction by Abraham Flexner, *Reading for Honors at Swarthmore: A Record of the First Five Years, 1922–1927* (New York: Oxford University Press, 1927), 7–8.
2. Paul G. Friedman and Reva C. Jenkins-Friedman, *Fostering Academic Excellence Through Honors Programs*, New Directions for Teaching and Learning, Jossey-Bass Higher Education Series (San Francisco: Jossey-Bass, Inc., 1986), 6. The publications are Frank Aydelotte, *Honors Courses in American Colleges and Universities, Parts 1 and 2*, Bulletin of the National Research Council (Washington, D.C.: National Research Council of the National Academy of Sciences, January 1924 and April 1925) and Brooks, *Reading for Honors at Swarthmore*, op. cit. Three other works by Aydelotte on the subject are Frank Aydelotte, *The Oxford Stamp, and Other Essays: Articles from the Educational Creed of an American Oxonian* (New York: Oxford University Press, American Branch, 1917); Frank Aydelotte, *The American Rhodes Scholar at Oxford* (Philadelphia, 1925)—he was himself a Rhodes Scholar—and Frank Aydelotte, *Breaking the Academic Lock-Step: The Development of Honors Work in American Colleges and Universities* (New York: Harper & Brothers, 1944). See also J. J Coss., ed., *Five College Plans: Columbia, Harvard, Swarthmore, Wabash, Chicago* (1931). Lectures given at Columbia University summer session, 1931. H. E. Hawkes et al., "New York: Columbia University Press and Symposium on the Outlook for Higher Education in the United States," in A. Flexner, F. Aydelotte, and F. J.E. Woodbridge, *Proceedings of the American Philosophical Society*, vol. LXIX, no. 5 (1930).

    In addition to works referred to in the text, on honors and independent study see also William N. Haarlow, *Great Books, Honors Programs, and Hidden Origins: The Virginia Plan and the University of Virginia in the Liberal Arts Movement*, Studies in the History of Education (New York: RoutledgeFalmer, 2003); David W. III Beggs and Edward G. Buffie, *Independent Study*, Bold New Venture (Bloomington: Indiana University Press, 1965); College of Wooster Committee on Educational Inquiry, *The Independent Study Program in the United States*, A Report on an Undergraduate Instructional Method, Robert H. Bonthius, F. James Davis, and J. Garber Drushal, in collaboration with Frances V. Guille and Warren P. Spencer (New York: Columbia University Press, 1957); Paul David Goldstein, "Honors Programs in Higher Education" (Ed.D. thesis, Teachers College, Columbia University, 1968), 115; Timothy P. Cross, *An Oasis of Order: The Core Cur-*

riculum at Columbia College (New York: Columbia College). Full text at www.college.Columbia.edu/core/oasis, 1995.
3. Garfield to Aydelotte, 14 November 1923. Swarthmore College Archives. Frank Aydelotte, Presidential Papers, Series A, Box 51, Folder NRC Correspondence 1923 (7–12).
4. It was while at MIT that Aydelotte came to share the interests in engineering education that were the driver of the NRC gifted work. See, for example, Frank Aydelotte, ed., *English and Engineering: A Volume of Essays for English Classes in Engineering Schools* (New York: McGraw-Hill, 1917).
5. On the growth and problems of mass education, see particularly Martin Trow, *Problems in the Transition from Elite to Mass Higher Education*, Report of the Carnegie Commission on Higher Education (Novato: McGraw-Hill Book Company, 1973); Martin Trow, "From Mass Higher Education to Universal Access," *Minerva* 37 (Spring 2000): 1–26, and Trow's many articles on related subjects of admissions testing, stratification, and underprepared students. Also see Laurence R. Veysey, *The Emergence of the American University* (Illinois: University of Chicago Press, 1965), especially his chapter II, "Utility"; Eric Ashby, *Any Person, any Study: An Essay on Higher Education in the United States* (New York: McGraw-Hill, 1971); David O. Levine, *The American College and the Culture of Aspiration, 1915–1940* (Ithaca, N.Y.: Cornell University Press, 1986); Helen Lefkowitz Horowitz, *Campus Life: Undergraduate Culture from the End of the Eighteenth Century to the Present* (Illinois: University of Chicago Press, 1987).
6. Except as noted, this study is based on the archival records of the National Research Council, National Academy of Sciences Archive, Washington, D.C., and records are from Division files, indicated in the citation by Division name (Div.), folder name, and year. Documents are shelved accordingly. There are no records for Committee G in the AAUP archives housed at George Washington University.
7. On the founding of the NRC, see Rexmond C. Cochrane, *The National Academy of Sciences: The First Hundred Years, 1863–1963* (Washington, D.C.: National Academy of Sciences, 1978); Lewis E. Auerbach, "Scientists in the New Deal: A Pre-War Episode in the Relations Between Science and Government in the United States," *Minerva* (Summer 1965): 457–82. George Elery Hale et al., *The National Importance of Scientific and Industrial Research*, Bulletin of the National Research Council 1, no. 1 (Washington, D.C.: National Research Council/National Academy of Sciences, 1919) embodies the founders' rationale for the new organization.
8. Henry Christian, Division of Medical Sciences, to W. V. Benghan, Division of Anthropology and Psychology, 20 January 1920. A&P: Committee on the Prediction of Success of Students Entering Higher Education (hereafter A&P: COPSSEHE) 1919–22.
9. Margaret V. Cobb and Robert M. Yerkes, *Intellectual and Educational Status of the Medical Profession as Represented in the United States Army*, Bulletin of the National Research Council 1, no. 8 (Washington, D.C.: National Research Council, February 1921), 458–59, 462. See also U.S. War Department, *Army Mental Tests: Methods, Typical Results and Practical Applications* (Washington, D.C., 1918). Yerkes was professor of medicine at Yale University, and later chair of the NRC Medical Sciences Division. The study also looked at results by school and type of curriculum/school. Schools classified as "homeopathic" had a higher median score than both the "regular" schools, which included the most prestigious medical schools, and the "eclectic." The range among traditional schools was substantial, with a few, such as Harvard, Johns Hopkins, Columbia, and Rush at the high-scoring end.
10. Note that these findings coincided with the rise of and reform movements in modern professional education in engineering and medicine. See, as general background,

Richard J. Storr, *The Beginnings of Graduate Education in America* (Arno Press, 1969) and the work on professionalization, including Burton Bledstein, *The Culture of Professionalism: The Middle Class and the Development of Higher Education in American* (New York: Norton, 1976); Magali S. Larson, *The Rise of Professionalism: A Sociological Analysis* (Berkeley: University of California Press, 1977); Randall Collins, *The Credential Society: An Historical Sociology of Education and Stratification* (New York: Academic Press, 1979); Andrew D. Abbot, *The System of Professions: An Essay on the Division of Expert Labor* (Illinois: University of Chicago Press, 1988); and Eliot Freidson, *Professional Powers: A Study of the Institutionalization of Formal Knowledge* (Illinois: University of Chicago Press, 1986). For engineering education history, see James G. McGivern, *First Hundred Years of Engineering Education in the United States, 1807–1907* (Spokane, Wash.: Gonzaga University Press, 1960). For medical education history, see Vern L. Bullough, *The Development of Medicine as a Profession: The Contribution of the Medieval University to Modern Medicine* (New York: Hafner Publishing, 1966); Kenneth M. Ludmerer, *Learning to Heal: The Development of American Medical Education* (New York: Basic Books, 1983); Thomas Neville Bonner, *Becoming a Physician: Medical Education in Britain, France, Germany, and the United States, 1750–1945* (New York: Oxford University Press, 1995); Kenneth M. Ludmerer, *Time to Heal: American Medical Education from the Turn of the Century to the Era of Managed Care* (New York: Oxford University Press, 1999). Reform reports in both fields also provide important historical records. In addition to the Mann and the SPEE reports on engineering cited further on, see, for example, Dugald Caleb Jackson, *Present Status and Trends of Engineering Education in the United States: A Report Supported by the Carnegie Foundation for the Advancement of Teaching* (New York: Committee on Engineering Schools, 1939); American Society for Engineering Education, *The "Grinter Report" on Evaluation of Engineering Education* (Washington, D.C.: ASEE, 1955); Edwin J. Holstein and Earl J. McGrath, *Liberal Education and Engineering* (New York: Institute of Higher Education, Teachers College, Columbia University, 1960); President's Science Advisory Committee, *Meeting Manpower Needs in Science and Technology, A Report* (Washington, D.C.: The White House, USGPO, 1962); American Society for Engineering Education, *Goals of Engineering Education, Final Report of the Goals Committee* (Washington, D.C.: ASEE, 1968); William H. Corcoran, chair, "Engineering Education: Aims and Goals for the Eighties," Engineering Foundation Conference, 26–31 July 1981 (United Engineering Trustees, Inc., 1982); NRC Committee on the Education and Utilization of the Engineer, *Engineering Graduate Education and Research* (Washington, D.C.: National Research Council, 1985); NRC Committee on the Education and Utilization of the Engineer, *Engineering Undergraduate Education* (Washington, D.C.: National Research Council, 1986); Joseph S. Johnston Jr., Susan Shaman, and Robert Zemsky, *Unfinished Design: The Humanities and Social Sciences in Undergraduate Engineering Education* (Washington, D.C.: Association of American Colleges, 1988); NRC Board on Engineering Education, *Engineering Education: Designing an Adaptive System* (Washington, D.C.: National Academy Press, 1995). Some principal reform documents in medicine include Abraham Flexner, *Medical Education in the United States and Canada*, Bulletin no. 4, A Report to the Carnegie Foundation for the Advancement of Teaching (New York: Carnegie Foundation, 1910); Abraham Flexner, *Medical Education in Europe*, Bulletin no. 6, A Report to the Carnegie Foundation for the Advancement of Teaching (New York: Carnegie Foundation, 1912); John Deitrick and Robert Berson, *Medical Schools in the United States at Mid-Century*, Carnegie Report (New York: McGraw-Hill, 1953); Association of American Medical Colleges, *Planning for*

Medical Progress Through Education (Washington, D.C.: AAMC, April 1965); Carnegie Commission on Higher Education, *Higher Education and the Nation's Health: Policies for Medical and Dental Education*, Special Report (New York: McGraw-Hill, 1970); Institute of Medicine, *Medical Education and Societal Needs: A Planning Report for the Health Professions* (Washington, D.C.: National Academy Press, 1983); AAMC Panel on the General Professional Education of the Physician, *Physicians for the Twenty-First Century: A Report of the Panel on the General Professional Education of the Physician and College Preparation for Medicine* (Washington, D.C.: AAMC, 1984); Robert Q. Marston, M.D. and Roseann M. Jones, eds., *Medical Education in Transition: Commission on Medical Education: The Sciences of Medical Practice* (Princeton, N.J.: Robert Wood Johnson Foundation, July 1992).

11. Charles Riborg Mann, *A Study of Engineering Education*, Prepared for the joint committee on engineering education of the National Engineering Societies, Bulletins of the Foundation, no. 11 (New York: Carnegie Foundation for the Advancement of Teaching, 1918), ix–x, 34–36, 48–53.

12. For background on this organization of which Abraham Flexner was secretary at this time, see Raymond Blaine Fosdick, *Adventure in Giving: The Story of the General Education Board, a Foundation Established by John D. Rockefeller* (New York: Harper and Row, 1962). The work on foundations generally is of interest, as reforms are often funded, even initiated, by them. See Robert Arnove, *Philanthropy and Cultural Imperialism* (Bloomington: Indiana University Press, 1980); Ellen Condliffe Lagemann, *Private Power for the Public Good: A History of the Carnegie Foundation for the Advancement of Teaching* (Middletown, Conn.: Wesleyan University Press, 1983); Howard S. Berliner, *A System of Scientific Medicine: Philanthropic Foundations in the Flexner Era* (New York: Tavistock, 1985); Robert E. Kohler, "Science, Foundations, and American Universities in the 1920s," *Osiris* 2, no. 3 (1987): 135–64; Steven C. Wheatley, *The Politics of Philanthropy: Abraham Flexner and Medical Education* (Madison: University of Wisconsin Press, 1988); Ellen Condliffe Lagemann, *The Politics of Knowledge: American Research Universities Since World War II* (New York: Oxford University Press, 1989); Robert E. Kohler, *Partners in Science: Foundations and Natural Scientists, 1900–1945* (Illinois: University of Chicago Press, 1990); Joan Roelofs, *Foundations and Public Policy: The Mask of Pluralism* (Buffalo: SUNY Press, 2003); and Brian J. Low, "The Hand That Rocked the Cradle: A Critical Analysis of Rockefeller Philanthropic Funding, 1920–1960," *Historical Studies in Education* 16, no. 1 (Spring 2004): 33–62.

13. In the late nineteenth and early twentieth century, the physical and human capacity for research had undergone a "significant transformation" through a "building boom" and a "spectacular" expansion of facilities at state universities. Roger Geiger, "The Conditions of University Research," *History of Higher Education Annual* 4 (1984): 5, 21; see also Roger L. Geiger, *To Advance Knowledge: The Growth of American Research Universities, 1900–1940* (New York: Oxford University Press, 1986). The NRC conducted another survey of research during 1926 and 1927 to ascertain medical researchers' needs as a basis for a program to increase research funding. Again, most researchers of the time were quite satisfied with their circumstances, and had no expectation of receiving large sums to support their research. Pressed to state their needs, these were either nonexistent or almost invariably modest indications of what would make their work easier, often small outlays for equipment or, at the higher end of several hundred to a few thousand dollars, assistance in tasks from lab cleaning to research (in Central Policy Files 1924–31: Div: Ed: Survey of Universities re Funding Needs for Medical Research 1927, 1926).

14. The emphasis was on vocational guidance (career steering) rather than vocational education per se, although the two are clearly related and the honors emphasis did create a distinct educational track. On vocationalism in education, see Marvin Lazerson and W. Norton Grubb, eds., *American Education and Vocationalism: A Documentary History, 1870–1970* (New York: Teachers College Press, 1974); H. Kantor, *Learning to Earn: School, Work, and Vocational Reform in California, 1880–1930* (Madison: University of Wisconsin Press, 1988); and W. Norton Grubb and Marvin Lazerson, *The Education Gospel: The Economic Power of Schooling* (Boston: Harvard University Press, 2004). A classic critique of vocationalism is Robert Maynard Hutchins, *The Higher Learning in America* (New Haven, Conn.: Yale University Press, 1936).
15. The testing experiments discussed herein were forerunners of the SAT, which was introduced on June 23, 1926. See Nicholas Lemann, *The Big Test: The Secret History of the American Meritocracy* (New York: Farrar, Straus, and Giroux, 1999). The work of the SPEE during the decade covered in this study was ultimately published in a comprehensive report, Society for the Promotion of Engineering Education, *Report of the Investigation of Engineering Education*, 2 vol., includes a supplemental report on technical institutes, 1928–29 (Pennsylvania: University of Pittsburgh, 1930).
16. W. V. Bingham to Alfred D. Flinn, 6 January and 14 January 1920; Memorandum to NRC on Cooperative Research on Methods of Determining Probable Success or Failure of Applicants for Admission to Colleges and Enabling Schools, 14 December 1919, no signature; Memorandum, W. V. Bingham to Dr. Angell, 17 January 1920 in A&P: COPSSEHE 1919–22; Wissler to Raymond Dodge, no date, probably February 1921. Bingham was chair of A&P as well as director of the Division of Applied Psychology at Carnegie Institute of Technology; Flinn was secretary of the Engineering Foundation; Angell was chair of the NRC; Clark Wissler was subsequent chair of A&P. See Edward W. Thorndike, *Individuality* (Boston: Hodes Michele, 1911).
17. Bingham to Dr. Angell, op. cit.; "Memorandum of Correspondence with the Carnegie Foundation for the Advancement of Teaching," 5 October 1920, no signature. Funding became further complicated when Thurstone began, quite unexpectedly, realizing a profit on sales of the tests intended to merely cover costs—i.e., demand was higher than projected. He invested it in further research, but it made both the NRC and others uncertain how to handle the question of appropriating funds. A precedent of making royalties from tests had been established with the National Intelligence Tests, and there was concern about how the "spoils" might be divided among the many institutions that had supported the work (Wissler to Bingham, 14 February 1921).
18. "The Present Status of the Admissions Research by L. L. Thurstone," Report attached to letter, W. V. Bingham to NRC Division of Anthropology and Psychology, 25 October 1920.
19. "Intelligence Tests for College Students," pamphlet, L. L. Thurstone, Department of Psychology, Carnegie Institute of Technology, Pittsburgh, Pa., 15 April 1920.
20. "Notes on Experience in the Use of Mental Tests in College," C. E. Seashore, in A&P: Conference on the Use of Mental Tests in College, 30 December 1921. The detailed institutional knowledge of a school's student characteristics and outcomes as a basis for decision-making during the period is making a resurgence; it has been consistently common in engineering. At the time, such analyses were made public. See, for example, Arthur Kenneth Goodman, *The Relationship of Intelligence and Classification Test Scores to Mortality and Scholastic Ratings: A Continuation of a Study of 438 Freshmen of the Class of 1932 at CSTC*, 3rd Report, Study 95 (Fall,

Winter, and Spring quarters 1928–29), a Report to Dr. Thomas J. Machlup, Dean of Men and Director of Freshman Studies (Colorado State Teachers College, 1929). "Mortality" was the contemporary term for drop-out rate.

21. H. C. Bingham to Seashore, 24 April 1922, Letter and Report of Committee on Prediction of Success of Students Entering Higher Education; Memorandum Concerning Sample A of the New Type of Examination, in Algebra and Quadratics, Prepared for the College Entrance Examination Board (CEEB). The CEEB established a Commission on Psychological Tests, and in 1925 the Board moved to "conduct psychological tests by means of machinery under the control of the Board" through a relationship with "the National Research Council or some other agency" that would prepare the tests (College Entrance Examination Board, *Twenty-fifth Annual Report of the Secretary* [New York: 1925], 33–34).

22. L. L. Thurstone and Charles R. Mann, "Vocational Guidance for College Students," Reports of two conferences at the National Research Council, in *Reprint and Circular Series of the National Research Council*, reprinted from *Journal of Personnel Research*, vol. III, no. 12 (Washington, D.C.: National Academy of Sciences, 1925), 421–448.

23. Seashore continued his interest in assessing the gifted, however, and developed a series of tests for identifying musical skills such as pitch that became widely known as the "Seashore measures of musical talent." See C. E. Seashore, *Studies in the Psychology of Music* (Iowa City: University of Iowa, 1932).

24. Seashore to G. M. Stratton, 27 January 1926. "All the practical interests are digging into the undergraduate schools, motivating students with reference to the professions, industries and commerce, and all have the advantage of material remuneration to offer. The result is, we are in many respects getting into our graduate schools the 'culls.'"

25. Seashore to Kellogg, 21 January 1920. Ed Relations: Gifted Student: Beginning of Program 1920.

26. Seashore to Kellogg, 21 January 1920. Kellogg was secretary of the NRC and head of Educational Relations. As the gifted project proceeded, women were included in its intent.

27. George W. Stewart, *Encouragement of Superior Attainment and Superior Ability in Colleges*, Report presented to the Division of Educational Relations of the National Research Council (18 April 1921).

28. The goal of increasing what was seen as insufficient interest in and exposure to intellectual subjects drove the introduction of several early general education curriculums at this time, such as Columbia's general honors and great books program introduced in 1920 (Cross, *An Oasis of Order*).

29. Ernest H. Wilkins, "Interests and Standards of Undergraduates. Preliminary Report and A Tentative Definition of the Purpose of Undergraduate Education," *Bulletin of the American Association of University Professors* VIII (1922): 61–69.

30. These latter efficiency goals were to become fixtures of external reform pressures, particularly during the Depression; see Richard Novak and David Leslie, "Retrospective: A Not So Distant Mirror: Great Depression Writings on Governance and Finance of Public Higher Education," *History of Higher Education Annual* 20 (2000): 59–78.

31. Abstract of minutes and Transcript, "Conference upon the Problem of the Unusually Gifted Student, December 23, 1921," Ed Relations.

32. Seashore to Kellogg, 1 March 1927, Ed Relations: Gifted Student: General 1925–27; this was a summary of the status of the project at the end of the visits.

33. Seashore to Kellogg, 23 December 1924, letter with attached report on visit to the west; Memo from C. E. Seashore, "Some Observations Made during Visits to

	Universities in November for the Division of Education Relations of the National Research Council," November 1922, January 1923, February 1926, and April 1926 trips, Ed Relations: Gifted Student: Trips: Seashore C. E. Reports, 1921–26. There are many interesting observations in these and other trip reports.
34.	*A Bibliography of Methods of Increasing the Intellectual Interest and Raising the Intellectual Standards of Undergraduates*, Circular Reprint, Bulletin of the American Association of University Professors IX, no. 8 (Washington, D.C.: December 1923). Though to some extent hand-picked for a purpose, this bibliography does offer a good snapshot of the prominent education literature of the early twentieth century.
35.	C. E. Seashore, "Sectioning on the Basis of Ability," *Bulletin of the American Association of University Professors* IX, no. 6 (October 1923): 9–24; C. E. Seashore, "Sectioning Classes on the Basis of Ability," *School and Society* (1 April 1922): 353 ff; C. E. Seashore, "Comments on the Plan for Sectioning Classes on the Basis of Ability," *School and Society* 16, no. 410 (4 November 1922): 514ff.
36.	Report, Trip to Midwest, 5–27 November 1923. Seashore Trips: 1921–26.
37.	George Walter Stewart, "A Problem in the Education of College Students of Superior Ability," *School and Society* XIV, no. 439 (19 November1921); Albert Barrows, "Studying for Honors in American Colleges and Universities," *School and Society* XIII, no. 328 (9 April 1921): 432–34.
38.	C. E. Seashore, "The Gifted Student and Research" (paper presented at the Association of American Universities, 24th Annual Conference, Washington, D.C.: National Research Council, 1922), 12; C. E. Seashore, "Progressive Adjustment Versus Entrance Elimination in a State University" (speech given at the National Association of State Universities, Washington, D.C., 13–14 November 1922); C. E. Seashore, "College Placement Examinations," *School and Society* XVI, no. 515 (8 November1924); C. E. Seashore, "Recognition of the Individual," *Bulletin of Engineering Education* XV, no. 1 (September 1924); C. E. Seashore, "The Placement Examination as a Means for the Early Discovery and Motivation of the Future Scholar" (paper presented at the Association of American Universities Annual Conference, New Haven, Conn., 29–31 October 1925); C. E. Seashore, "The Individual in Mass Education," *School and Society* XXIII, no. 593 (6 May 1926): 569–76.
39.	The numbers are drawn primarily from the following: Memorandum to the Members of the Division of Educational Relations, National Research Council, 30 January 1923; Distribution of Bulletin #40 (no date); and Minutes from the Informal Conference on the Gifted Student Problem, 24 October 1927.
40.	Frank Aydelotte, *Honors Courses in American Colleges and Universities*, Bulletin of the National Research Council (Washington, D.C.: National Research Council of the National Academy of Sciences, January 1924).
41.	"Since the announcement of the donation by the Rockefeller Foundation to Swarthmore to try out scientifically a series of honors courses, there is a growing interest in other schools to know what such honors courses are." J. H. Moore, A. B., Dept. of Latin and Greek, Lincoln Memorial University, to Secretary of Swarthmore College, 16 March 1925. Personal Papers of Frank Aydelotte, D007 (Series 3), Box 69, Correspondence, NRC 1921–25, Friends Historical Library, Swarthmore College, Swarthmore, Pa. Abraham Flexner suggested the idea of the try-out to Aydelotte at a social function.
42.	Minutes and transcript, Honors Courses Conference at Iowa City, Iowa, 17–18 March 1925, 56 pp.
43.	Aydelotte, *Honors Courses in American Colleges and Universities, Part 2*, 7–8.
44.	Barrows to Aydelotte, 11 October 1930, Aydelotte Papers, Box 50, NRC 1930.

45. Report of Permanent Secretary to the Executive Board, National Research Council, 12 June 1928.
46. The updated report was *Breaking the Academic Lock-Step*, op.cit. After Sputnik there was a resurgence in interest in gifted students; the Inter-University Committee on the Superior Student, funded by Carnegie Corporation of New York and founded by Joseph Cohen of University of Colorado, who had run an honors program there since 1928, published a newsletter called "The Superior Student" from 1958 to 1965. The National Collegiate Honors Council succeeded this group beginning in 1966 when the Carnegie grant expired (Friedman and Jenkins-Friedman, *Fostering Academic Excellence*, 6). See also, from this period, Arthur E. Traxes, ed., "Selection and Guidance of Gifted Students for National Survival," A report of the 20th educational conference, New York City, 27–28 October 1955, held under the auspices of the Educational Records Bureau and the American Council on Education (1955); Charles Chester Cole, *Encouraging Scientific Talent: A Study of America's Able Students Who Are Lost to College and of Ways of Attracting Them to College and Science Careers* (New York: College Entrance Examination Board, 1956); College of Wooster Committee on Educational Inquiry, *The Independent Study Program in the United States*; University of the State of New York, *Regent's Program for Meeting Needs in Science, Technology, and Education of the Talented* (Albany, 1958); Beggs and Buffie, *Independent Study*; Joseph W. Cohen, ed., *The Superior Student in American Higher Education*, Carnegie Series in American Education (New York: McGraw-Hill, 1966).
47. *Breaking the Academic Lock-Step*, IX, op. cit.
48. Friedman and Jenkins-Friedman, *Fostering Academic Excellence*, 8. In this sense, some honors programs have violated the original ideas that, first, students should not be admitted into honors until their junior year and, second, that average test scores and grades should not form the basis of admission.
49. The NRC engaged in a similar approach on the subject of university patenting. See Jane Robbins, "Solving the Patent Problem: Cognition, Communication, and the National Academy of Sciences in the Evolution of University Patent Policy, 1917–1966" (Ph.D. diss., University of Pennsylvania, 2004). One question is whether this approach is generalizable to external change efforts by other groups.
50. Communicative isomorphism is my own term, reflecting the view that "organization emerges in communication (and nowhere else)": James R. Taylor and Elizabeth J. Van Every, *The Emergent Organization: Communication as Its Site and Surface* (Mahwah, N.J.: Lawrence Erlbaum Associates, Publishers, 2000), 4. On other types of isomorphism in institutions, see Paul J. DiMaggio and Walter W. Powell, "The Iron Cage Revisited: Institutional Isomorphism and Collective Rationality in Organizational Fields," in *The New Institutionalism in Organizational Analysis* (Illinois: University of Chicago Press, 1991).
51. On these aspects of policymaking, see particularly D. McAdams, J. D. McCarthy, and M. N. Zald, eds., *Comparative Perspectives on Social Movements: Political Opportunities, Mobilizing Structures and Cultural Framings* (New York: Cambridge University Press, 1996) and Frank Fischer, *Technocracy and the Politics of Expertise* (Newbury Park: Sage Publications, 1990).
52. Larry J. Shuman, Cheryl Delaney, et al., "Engineering Attrition: Student Characteristics and Educational Initiatives" (Meeting, American Society for Engineering Education, 1999).
53. See John Meyer and Brian Rowan, "Institutional Organizations: Formal Structure As Myth and Ceremony," *American Journal of Sociology* 83, no. 2 (1977): 340–363, on taken-for-granted routines and legitimacy of practice.

Reds, Race, and Research: Homer P. Rainey and the Grand Texas Tradition of Political Interference, 1939–1944

Susan R. Richardson

The dismissal of Homer Rainey from his post as president of the University of Texas stands as one of the most celebrated and misunderstood academic freedom cases of the twentieth century. To varying degrees, scholars have treated the Rainey episode as (1) an isolated event inspired almost exclusively by discontent with the New Deal; (2) a devastating blow that injured UT's reputation as a viable research university for years to come; and (3) a simple story of good versus evil. This study argues: (1) that Rainey's dismissal was part of a long and grand history of political conflict between the Texas government and UT; (2) Rainey's dismissal was a short-term setback that would prove to be a turning point for UT; and (3) Rainey was, in the words of Walter Webb, neither "superman" nor "the real Moses." This study begins with an overview of Texas culture and political structure, provides a brief history of UT and its relationship with Texas policymakers, describes the events that precipitated Rainey's removal from office, and concludes with an analysis of the relations between UT and the State of Texas in the aftermath of the Rainey tragedy.

On November 1, 1944, the University of Texas (UT) Board of Regents fired President Homer Price Rainey, after a five and a half year power struggle. The Rainey episode attracted national attention and remains one of the most celebrated academic freedom cases of the twentieth century. Two major issues were at stake: (1) the governing board's role in the day-to-day operations of the institution; and (2) the principles of academic freedom as defined by the American Association of University of Professors (AAUP).

With numerous book and dissertation chapters, Rainey's 1971 memoir, Alice Cox's 1970 dissertation, a host of firsthand accounts, and some two thousand pages of legislative testimony already in existence, one might conclude that there is little left to say about this ugly event. This abundance of published material, however, fails to demonstrate three important points. First, the Homer Rainey episode was not an isolated example of political interference at UT, but rather one segment in a long saga of political conflict that began in the 1880s. Second, the Rainey scandal resulted in more than the dismissal of a university president, subsequent censure from the AAUP, and a probation sentence from the Southern Association of Colleges and Schools (SACS). Although devastating in the short-term, Rainey's departure proved to be a turning point: the last gasp of the bitter brand of political interference that had plagued UT since its establishment. Third, most accounts have depicted Homer Rainey as a complete innocent in his conflict with the Regents. Authors have leaned heavily on Rainey's 1971 memoir, accepting it as an objective source. Rainey's version of the ordeal is neither objective nor complete, particularly since he recalled the details twenty-seven years later. This study will point out errors in Rainey's tale and the manner in which these discrepancies have distorted, however mildly, the events at UT between 1939 and 1944.[1]

This study begins with an overview of Texas culture and political structure, provides a brief history of UT and its relationship with Texas policymakers, describes the events that precipitated Rainey's removal from office, and concludes with an analysis of the relations between UT and the State of Texas in the aftermath of the Rainey tragedy.

Understanding Texas Culture and Politics

Scholars have placed Texas in both the South and the West in attempts to decipher the complex social, political, and economic systems of this enormous state.[2] Politically and culturally, Texas was Southern during the slow dismantling of segregation, and certainly during the years under study in this study, was Southern. The majority of Texans resided in the eastern portion of the state between 1830 and 1900. These transplanted Southerners moved gradually westward and planted the ingredients for racism, states rights ideology, anticommunism, and religious fundamentalism throughout the state.

Economically, the state began to separate itself from the former Confederacy at the turn of the twentieth century. The size of Texas and the availability of uncultivated land meant a lower farmer-to-acre ratio and higher wages for tenant farmers and sharecroppers. With fewer workers to till the soil, Texas farms relied less on skilled workers and more on machines. Texas farms therefore modernized more like states outside of the South. Unlike most of the South, Texas had a more fluid economic system. Much of this openness could be attributed to the oil boom that began with the Spindletop discovery in 1900 and catapulted Texas to be the top producer of oil in the nation by the 1930s. Texans enjoyed elephantine profits and almost nonexistent government control over petroleum in the 1910s and 1920s. V.O. Key noted that by 1950, 158 of the State's 254 counties were involved in commercial petroleum production. Taxes and drilling procedures arrived with the New Deal, but Texans continued to profit in spite of what they described as socialist-inspired federal intervention.[3]

Similar to its culture, the Texas political structure possessed distinguishing features. Civil rights activist Virginia Durr declared to fellow iconoclast Maury Maverick, Jr. that she could not "make head nor tail out of Texas politics." Her home state of Alabama was easy because power revoled around white supremacy. Texas was far more mysterious and complex.[4]

Using Daniel Elazar's three-category typology of state political culture, Nimmo and Oden, and later George Green, labeled Texas as traditionalist and individualist. Texas was traditionalist in that it was governed by a smug group of oligarchs committed to protecting the status quo. The state was individualistic in that those in power believed that the government's role was to protect the interests of the most assertive groups and individuals. Because of the traditionalistic-individualistic qualities of Texas political culture, David Nevin observed that Texas politicos placed material self-interest above the common good. Therefore, the state boasted rapid growth in construction and oil fields while it was woefully deficient in its funding and development of public schools, social services, roads, and public utilities.[5]

No Texas political faction could be described as a machine, at least not of the Chicago or New York variety complete with a spoils system and elaborate bloc voting networks. Texas was too large for its powerbrokers to organize. In addition, Texas lacked the rigid factional and regional loyalties found in states such as South Carolina and Mississippi with upcountry and low country divisions.[6]

The most cohesive Texas power network, described by Green as "the Establishment," was an informal group of men who met in various cities and established the Texas Democratic Platform over poker games, whiskey, and cigars. The power elite would then handily gain the support of small businessmen in real estate, oil, construction, and automotive firms who shared their fears of labor unions, federal regulations, and academic subversives. The Establishment was influential, but not exclusive. Before the state Democratic primary, there were as many as twelve gubernatorial candidates in some elections. Power could shift quickly since governors served two-year terms until the 1960s. A political outsider could easily enter the Establishment if he shared the interests of the power elite. This is precisely how W. Lee O'Daniel (1939–1941) secured the governor's race in 1938. While O'Daniel presented himself as one of the common-folk, he was encouraged to enter politics by some of the wealthiest corporate bigwigs in Texas.[7]

The Grand Tradition of Political Interference in Texas Higher Education

UT clashed with the state government and citizens over the issues of political interference and institutional autonomy from the beginning. Ashbel Smith, an influential board member and Yale graduate, stated to the *Austin American Statesman* in April 1881 that UT would only succeed if protected from political interference. As sound as this principle may have been, the state media was outraged when the Regents adopted a motion to make their meetings private. A writer for Austin's *Daily Democratic Statesman* wrote in November 1881 that closed meetings were undemocratic, sinister, and denied citizens their rights to govern their own institutions.[8]

Prior to the Rainey debacle, the worst episode of political conflict occurred between 1915 and 1917, when Governor James Ferguson (1915–1917) ordered the dismissal of several faculty members and attempted to close UT.[9] Ferguson had long distrusted the administrators and faculty at UT and labeled them as elitists who believed they were above the law. Specifically, Ferguson described the UT faculty as "butterfly chasers," "day dreamers," and "educated fools." Ferguson also found fault with academic programs such as journalism, which he called wasteful fluff, and faculty who traveled to out-of-state meetings. Exchanges between Ferguson, the Regents, and University officials grew increasingly harsh when the governor vetoed the University's appropriation in 1916. The conflict ended when the Texas Senate voted to impeach Ferguson in the summer of 1917 and convicted him of ten charges, including bribery, mismanagement of public funds, and his actions against the University.[10]

Governor Ferguson's philosophy of state/university relations is concisely described in his angry letter to Regent Rabbi M. Faber:

> Your bold statement that the Governor of the State has no right or authority to interfere or inquire into the management of the University proves conclusively the arrogance which has attained to a marked degree in the institution, and shows how far the idea has gained credence that the people are to have nothing to do with this institution except shoulder and pay high appropriations to be turned over to a set of men to continue their unholy spree of establishing an educational hierarchy.[11]

In spite of the fact that the Legislature, as well as most Texans, disapproved of Ferguson's handling of the University, this incident influenced relations between the state and UT officials for decades to come. Lawmakers, and even the Regents, believed that UT faculty thought themselves exempt from the law and therefore insulated from criticism regarding the way they spent state funds, administered the institution, or expressed their political beliefs.[12]

Political tension erupted once again in February 1923 between the executive branch and UT when President Robert Vinson (1916–1923) announced that he was leaving to accept the presidency at Western Reserve University in Ohio. The Regents discussed the appointment of long-time dean, Harry Benedict, as the interim president, but then seemed to lean towards Governor Pat Neff (1921–1925) to replace Vinson. Regents H. J. Lutcher Stark and Fred Cook appeared to support Neff and additional supporters stated that a man of Neff's morals and fiscal conservatism could help build the people's trust in the University. The faculty, in contrast, was outraged by the suggested appointment because Neff was not an academic. Similarly, the Ex-Students Association issued a statement at its June 1923 meeting. In this letter, alumni argued that a former governor would lure political enemies within firing distance of the college. Neff's foes would use the institution as a target to attack the former governor.[13]

The Regents met once again in May 1924 to select a president. A number of alumni, including noted folklorist John Lomax and Houston businessman and former UT Regent Will Hogg, attended the meeting. After hearing an emotional message from Hogg, who pleaded and allegedly cussed at the Regents to reject Neff, the Regents promised the former students that they would not select Neff. The Regents promptly turned around and elected Neff president of the University seven to two during their afternoon meeting. Dissenters Sam Cochran and Frank Jones resigned as Regents after the vote.

Neff, in turn, declined the offer. After Guy Ford, graduate dean at the University of Minnesota, and Herbert Bolton, history professor at the University of California, declined the presidency, Texas Railroad Commissioner Walter M. Splawn (1924–1927) accepted the job. The faculty were not pleased by Splawn's appointment, and at least a few believed that Neff pressured the Regents to appoint his political crony. The conflict provides more evidence that tensions were high between alumni, certain vocal faculty members such as Harry Benedict, Frank Dobie, Eugene Barker, and the more politically motivated Regents along the lines of Lutcher Stark, who remained on the Board until 1945.[14]

One the most scandalous episodes involving the dismissal of a leftist faculty member during the pre-Rainey era occurred between 1932 and 1936. Geneticist Hermann Muller was forced to resign (or be fired) after he penned *Out in the Night: A Biologist's View of the Future*, a eugenicist's homage to communism.

In early 1932, Muller suffered from a nervous breakdown, allegedly caused by his marital difficulties. Two UT students reportedly found a stupefied Muller wandering in the hills west of Austin. Muller's doctor diagnosed him with "melancholia" and concluded that Muller had attempted suicide. Soon after this strange episode, Muller was awarded a Guggenheim Fellowship to conduct research in Germany during the 1932–1933 academic year. Just before Muller left for Germany, the UT Regents learned that he had links to the Communist Party.[15]

President Harry Benedict called for Muller's dismissal, but Robert Batts, chair of the Regents, worried that Muller might commit suicide if he were fired. The Regents agreed to let the matter go for the year that Muller was in Germany. At the end of his stay, Muller requested an additional year's leave from UT in order to complete his research. Benedict assumed that Muller was remaining in Germany, but Muller intended to spend 1933–1934 at the Soviet Institute of Genetics. It is not known when Benedict and the Regents learned of Muller's whereabouts, but they granted him an additional leave for 1934–1935 and 1935–1936, certainly knowing by this point that he was in the Soviet Union.

The Regents and Benedict became troubled by Muller's location in late 1935 when *Out in the Night* appeared. It was bad enough that Muller wrote a book praising the promise that genetic engineering held for controlling human evolution. It was worse that he spoke admiringly of the Soviet system of governance, a system he would later denounce upon learning of Stalin's atrocities. The worst part of *Out in the Night* was the title page that included the University of Texas underneath Muller's name. The world now knew that the University of Texas employed a communist. At least, Walter Elmer Pope knew. In early January, Pope, the State representative from Corpus Christi, alerted Texas newspapers to the presence of professors who were teaching "rank communism" at UT. Benedict dismissed Pope's charges and welcomed a legislative investigation. On January 30, 1936, the *Daily Texan* printed a matter-of-fact, noninflammatory article on its front page that described *Out in the Night*. Muller's affiliation was becoming increasingly public. With support from the Regents, President Benedict informed Muller of his options: Muller could return to Austin and face a hearing regarding his membership in the Communist Party or he could resign. Benedict and Muller both knew that a hearing would have been nothing more than a kangaroo court, so Muller saved everyone some time by resigning first.[16]

Recounting the Muller episode several decades later, Regent J. R. Parten said that Benedict and the Board believed Muller's departure was necessary in order to avoid an ugly political ordeal. If the University defended Muller, it could risk losing its legislative appropriation. According to Parten, President Benedict believed Texans were too narrow-minded to accept a communist on the UT faculty. UT, as well as Muller, would be better off. Ten years later, Muller won the Nobel Prize for medicine for work he conducted at UT.[17] His institutional affiliation was listed as Indiana University.

At various times and for disparate reasons, the University of Texas found itself embroiled in politics. While the players would change, political clashes remained the norm. Governor Ferguson went after UT and the Regents because he questioned, among other things, their accounting procedures and the content of the curriculum. Governor Neff, the Regents, and other politicos fought the faculty and vocal alumni who protested the Regents' choice to hire Neff, a politician with no academic leadership experience, as president. The Muller episode demonstrated the power that one legislator could have over faculty publications and job security. In this case, the Regents and President Benedict worked in concert. UT frequently found itself in a sticky web of political interference; sometimes it was the governor versus the Regents, other times it was the Legislature versus dissident faculty. In the Rainey case, the governor, his Regents, and a small-but-powerful set of Texas businessmen joined forces to take on the UT president and his most politically liberal faculty members. What made the Rainey conflict different? It was the most egregious and the most public attack upon presidential/faculty governance and academic freedom in the history of UT. It grew out of a growing discontent with the New Deal.

Texas Politics and the New Deal

Governor O'Daniel and his successor, Coke Stevenson, packed the UT Board of Regents with men who went on to leave the Texas Democratic Party and form the Texas Regulars in 1944. The Texas Regulars and their most vocal supporters kicked off their initial campaign against the New Deal, communism, and the academics that allegedly stood for both in 1939. Many of the Regulars belonged to "the Establishment" and would monopolize Texas politics through the end of the fifties.[18]

While the New Deal had many foes in Texas, Governor James Allred (1935–1939) warmly accepted these federal programs. In addition, Allred introduced initiatives for the elderly and children, but the Legislature refused to fund them. Allred also attempted, albeit unsuccessfully, to introduce a state income tax, raise crude oil taxes, and reduce public utility rates. Allred did not seek reelection in 1938, but had he entered the race, he would have faced a formidable opposition from the corporate lobby.[19]

Texans generally opposed federal intervention and the New Deal, fearing that they would destroy the Texas brand of minimally regulated capitalism and rugged individualism. Besides the aforementioned regulation of oil, the financially and politically powerful of Texas despised New Deal programs designed to help homeowners from losing their mortgages and small business owners from losing their livelihood by providing them with alternatives to dealing with banks. The Works Progress Administration (WPA) gave individuals jobs so that they did not have to rely on local charity. New labor standards particularly alarmed factory management and landowners because they tampered with management-labor and landlord-tenant relationships. It was easier for Texans to oppose the New Deal because the state was less severely affected by the Depression. During the 1937–1938 downturn factory payrolls dropped 5 percent in Texas as compared 27 percent nationally. Texas farm income stood at 79 percent of the 1929 index as compared to the national figure of 69 percent.[20]

In his seminal 1949 study of Southern politics, V. O. Key argued that Texans not only opposed the New Deal, but also waged "the most bitter intra-Democratic fight along New Deal and anti-New Deal lines in the South."[21] The liberal cadre of Texans, such as Allred and U.S. Congressmen Maury Maverick, experienced severe setbacks in 1937 and 1938 following debate over an anti-lynching law and a protracted fight over a wages and hours bill. Maverick lost his congressional seat in 1938 after distinguishing himself as the only Southerner to vote for the anti-lynching bill. Both of these measures were extremely unpopular in Texas and led many who had tolerated the New Deal to abandon it altogether.[22]

As previously stated, the majority of men who waged war on Texas colleges joined the Texas Regulars in 1944 and took advantage of the growing opposition to Roosevelt in the state.[23] It galled many that Roosevelt had served three terms and was seeking a fourth. Under Roosevelt, Texas had to endure excessive wartime restrictions and federal regulation—especially the price controls on oil. Gasoline rationing was highly unpopular in Texas where then-Governor Coke Stevenson stated that gasoline was as important as "the saddle, the rifle, the ax, and the Bible that won Texas for the society we now have."[24] To make things worse, Roosevelt's vice president was no longer John Nance "Cactus Jack" Garner, the borderline New Dealer from Texas, but leftist Henry Wallace.

W. Lee O'Daniel served as the Regulars' chief spokesperson as governor and later as U.S. senator. A number of businessmen were active: E. B. Germany, Hugh Roy Cullen; UT Regents John Bickett, Orville Bullington, Dan Harrison, H. H. Weinert, Scott Scheiner, and D. F. Strickland; Texas A&M Directors Neth Leachman and Robert Briggs; Texas Tech trustee Karl Hoblitzelle; HUAC chairman Martin Dies; and Coke Stevenson.[25] Armed with a war chest and control of the major newspapers and radio stations in Houston and Dallas, the Regulars promoted their eight-point platform:

(1) Restoration of the Democratic Party to the integrity, which has been taken away by Hillman, Browder, and others.
(2) Protection of honest labor unions from foreign-born racketeers who have gained control by blackmail.
(3) Return of state rights which have been destroyed by the Communist-controlled New Deal.

(4) Restoration of the freedom of education.
(5) Restoration of the supremacy of the white race, which has been destroyed by the Communist-controlled New Deal.
(6) Restoration of the Bill of Rights instead of rule by regimentation.
(7) Restoration of government by laws instead of government by bureaus.
(8) Restoration of the individual appeal for justice, instead of a politically appointed bureau.[26]

The Regulars lost the election in part because most voters wanted to support the Democratic Party in all posts below the presidential level. Nevertheless, the Establishment endured. They could not manipulate presidential politics, but their ideas remained popular in Texas as evidenced by continued aggression towards labor unions, anti-communist witch-hunts of the late 1940s and the early 1950s, and alliance with the Dixiecrats in 1948.[27]

Loyalty Oaths and Legislative Investigations

The Texas Legislature introduced a number of measures designed to regulate education and political activity in the late 1930s and early 1940s. SB 359 became law in 1937 and compelled witnesses to testify before legislative bodies and committees under heavy penalty and a denial of privileges for any individual who refused. During the regular session of 1941, the House introduced a bill to make it legal for citizens to kill members of the Communist Party. This initiative died in committee, but the state did pass a law barring communist candidates from appearing on the ballot.[28] The Texas Senate passed a loyalty oath for educators in 1941. SB 38 mimicked the language used in the federal Smith Act passed in June 1940 and specified that any educator discovered advocating subversive principles would be promptly dismissed following a hearing. Senate Bill 38 was a reaffirmation of a clause printed in the 1939–1941 appropriations bill.[29]

The Texas House and Senate both formed un-American activities committees in 1941, the Senate during the regular session and the House during the first called session in September.[30] These "Little Dies" committees were patterned after the House Un-American Activities Committee (HUAC) headed by East Texas Congressman Martin Dies.[31] Neither of these "Little Dies" committees endured beyond a few months and fizzled in part because Martin Dies abandoned his investigations in Texas just as these committees were organized. The Legislature, however, did not give up on its search for subversive activities.

The Legislature expressed its outrage over an editorial entitled "Russia is Wiping Out Seven Sins for a Bright Future" in the February 5, 1943 edition of the *Daily Texan*, the UT student newspaper. On behalf of fellow disgruntled legislators, Representative L. H. Flewellen organized an investigation soon after the offensive article appeared. Addressing his colleagues in the House, Flewellen declared that he was most upset that religion was included among the seven sins. The student author declared that the Soviets were winning the war in part because they had eliminated the crutch of superstition. Following a brief discussion, the House enthusiastically adopted a resolution instructing the Regents and Homer Rainey to determine whether faculty censors approved the article. The House further resolved to require the *Texan*'s editor to dedicate a portion of the editorial page to articles that reinforced the ideals of God and democracy, and minimized the alleged accomplishments of the USSR.[32]

In his May 1, 1943 response to the House, Rainey stated that the student author had selected ambiguous language and did not mean to disparage Christianity. He conceded that editorial policies were in need of repair, but at the same time, the *Daily Texan* was a student-run paper that was monitored, but never censored by the faculty. Rainey concluded: "We cannot conceive a better way of encouraging young people than that of permitting them much latitude in the expression of their thoughts." Legislators were likely troubled by Rainey's opinion, but the House abandoned its investigation after receiving his letter.[33]

The Issue of Race

While Texas boasted a small African American population relative to the rest of the former Confederacy (14 percent), Jim Crow still thrived in the Lone Star State. The Ku Klux Klan, for example, gained a number of state legislative seats and one U.S. Senate seat in the 1920s. Texas disfranchised its African American voters with the introduction of the poll tax in 1903 and maintained an all-White primary for the Texas Democratic Party until 1944, when it was struck down by the U.S. Supreme Court in *Smith v. Albright*. This decision reinforced Texan as well as Southern fears that the national Democratic Party had established links to the civil rights movement.[34]

African Americans possessed few, even modest, educational opportunities in Texas circa 1940. Conditions at historically black Prairie View College, for example, had been dismal since it was established as a branch of Texas A&M in 1878. Rainey and Texas A&M President T.O. Walton joined W. R. Banks, principal of Prairie View, and other educational leaders in late 1941 to form the Bi-racial Conference on Negro Education in Texas (BCNET). BCNET published a major report titled "Senior Colleges for Negroes in Texas" in April 1944 and concluded that Prairie View, the state's only public college for African Americans, suffered from substandard funding and that graduate and professional education was woefully inadequate. BCNET did not support integration, but the committee's report called for a dramatic plan to equalize opportunities and facilities so that Texans could begin a long journey towards addressing the race problem. The committee contended that desegregation was not a viable solution because whites would resist. Even if blacks were permitted to attend white schools, they would not feel comfortable attending these institutions.[35] In the end, BCNET recommended improving quality at Prairie View rather than pumping money into the out-of-state scholarship program.

The BCNET report outraged UT Regent Orville Bullington, who declared that no African American would ever attend the University as long as he was part of the institution, "regardless of what Franklin D., Eleanor, or the Supreme Court says, so long as you have a Board of Regents with as much intestinal fortitude as the present one has." Bullington also worked to nullify the anti-discrimination clause in the University's Navy V-12 contract.[36]

A number of white citizens favored greater educational and employment opportunities for African Americans, but virtually none advocated integration during these years. Interracial cooperation, not desegregation, was the goal in these pre-civil rights years. For example, UT faculty member C. L. Cline wrote an article in the *Interracial Review* in support of greater educational opportunities for blacks, but only in segregated classes. Specialized training, particularly at the UT medical school, would benefit African American individuals, as well as the nation, in wartime.[37] These were cautious years when even the most liberal of Texans questioned the pace at which blacks were moving towards desegregation. In a letter to his son, the liberal-minded Maury Maverick, Sr. worried that African Americans were stirring their communities up and offending whites to the point that they were risking their lives.[38]

Academic Freedom in the 1930s and 1940s

No other state university governing board micromanaged teaching and research as much as the University of Texas Regents, although politicians in other states investigated their state universities in search of communists and fascist subversives. Such investigations violated the standards set by the AAUP (American Association of University Professors) in its 1940 statement on academic freedom and tenure.

At the time that the AAUP was founded in 1915, academic freedom meant three things. First, faculty members needed the freedom to research and teach absent government and public interference. Second, faculty members had the right to express their views as private citizens without the threat of dismissal. Finally, the academic community was entitled to corporate freedom—meaning that the professorate should be treated as an autonomous entity where academics exclusively decided what should be taught, what should be researched, and what constituted good research.[39]

According to Walter Metzger, the men who formed the AAUP did not fashion themselves as a labor union, but an organization whose job was to codify academic freedom and tenure. Despite the AAUP's insistence that they were not a labor union, many governing boards viewed the AAUP as such. This was particularly true of the UT Regents, who explicitly referred to the AAUP as a CIO union.[40]

In October 1940, AAUP members expressed concern that the war in Europe might prompt governing boards and legislative committees not only to dismiss alleged communists, but also professors who might hold views that were merely deemed different.[41] The AAUP's alarm over growing threats to academic freedom came during a wave of government-initiated investigations of faculty members. The AAUP was also disturbed by the passage of the Smith Act, a statute passed in 1940 by the federal government that declared it illegal for individuals to "teach and advocate the overthrow of the government of the United States by force and violence."[42] Indeed, UT possessed a long tradition of political interference, but state and national anxieties over the New Deal and the war would intensify the conflict.

New Leaders for Texas and the University

Texans welcome two ideologically opposed leaders in 1938. Texans elected W. Lee "Pass the Biscuits Pappy" O'Daniel, a former flour salesmen and bluegrass musician, as their governor in November. O'Daniel campaigned in favor of the Ten Commandments, the Golden Rule, old-age pensions, and tax cuts. Unlike James Ferguson, he made little mention of public education in his campaign and communicated no concern about the UT faculty or the institution's curriculum.[43]

Regents appointed by Governor Allred named Homer Rainey as president one month after O'Daniel's election. Rainey, however, was not the Regents' first choice. After the beloved Harry Benedict (1927–1937) suffered a stroke and died in route to an appropriations meeting before the Legislature, the Regents launched a national search to find a new president. Regents Parten, Randall, Aynesworth, and Waggener picked Luther Gulick, a professor of public administration at Columbia University, as their top choice. Gulick never expressed enthusiasm for the position and dragged his feet for several months before he agreed to visit Texas for the first time to view the UT campus. Despite Gulick's hesitancy and subsequent refusal to accept the presidency, the Regents voted unanimously to hire him after his campus visit in early November 1938.[44]

The Regents then turned to their second choice, Homer Rainey. Lotus Coffman, president of the University of Minnesota and national educational reformer, had suggested Rainey for the position upon hearing of Benedict's death. Coffman believed that Rainey, who had served as president of Franklin College (1927–1931) and Bucknell (1931–1935), possessed the administrative skills necessary for the job. Coffman also noted that the forty-one year old native Texan could provide the youth and regional perspective required to lead UT. By May 1938, Coffman had a change of heart. He confided to Regent J. R. Parten, "If there is need for a two-fisted fighter, I should doubt whether Rainey should be considered." Despite concerns from Coffman, as well as from Regents Randall, Stark, and Weinert, the Regents voted unanimously to hire Rainey. While Coffman worried about Rainey's leadership skills, particularly when compared to Gulick's abilities, the dissenting Regents possessed reservations about his political beliefs.[45] Contrary to these Regents' assessment, Rainey was not a radical liberal. As a moderate Democrat, Rainey supported the New Deal, interracial cooperation (not desegregation), and antitrust laws.

Born in 1896 in rural Northeast Texas, Rainey grew up poor. After graduating first in his class at Lovelady High School in 1913, Rainey attended Austin College, a small liberal arts college in nearby Sherman. Rainey was ordained as a Baptist minister in 1917, graduated from Austin College in 1919, and briefly pitched for the Houston Buffs baseball team. He left Texas for Illinois where he earned a master's degree in 1923 and a Ph.D. in 1924 at the University of Chicago. Following three years on the faculty at the University of Oregon, Rainey served as president of Franklin and then Bucknell. One biographical sketch of Rainey described him as "an innovative leader" while at Bucknell.[46] Rainey centralized the fragmented faculty, increased admissions standards, divided the curriculum into lower and upper divisions, and introduced a large-scale building program.[47] Bucknell then abandoned much of Rainey's expensive program after he abruptly left Bucknell in 1935 to assume a position in Washington as director of the American Youth Commission, part of the American Council on Education. The Rainey that the Regents hired in 1938 was neither a Robert Maynard Hutchins nor a Frank Porter Graham, but he was an experienced administrator with ambitious plans for the University of Texas.

Rainey's Plans for UT

Rainey addressed the Regents for the first time on February 4, 1939. He would officially assume the presidency in the summer, but Rainey seemed eager to begin once he completed his duties as head of the American Youth Commission. During this February meeting, Rainey declared that UT and the citizens of Texas failed to understand one another. The University existed to serve the State through excellent teaching and research, but it did not do a good job conveying this mission to the people. Citizens, in turn, did not always acknowledge the ways in which UT's extension and degree programs served Texas. UT would not become a great research university until legislators and citizens deemed the institution to be a worthy investment. The Regents largely agreed.[48]

Rainey returned to Texas on May 5 to attend the dedication of the McDonald Observatory in Fort Davis. On the 468-mile trip back to Austin, he shared his strategy for improving UT's status as a research university with progressive-minded Regent J. R. Parten. Rainey was inspired by the progress that the University of California had made in the 1920s and 1930s by attracting young academic stars with the promise of extensive research facilities and healthy compensation packages, and he wanted to try a similar, albeit more ambitious, strategy at UT. Rainey wanted to convince an established scientist from a top research university to exchange their better-equipped laboratory at a top-tier research university for a chance to lead an inchoate or even nonexistent program at UT. Parten appreciated Rainey's enthusiasm, but he believed that the plan would be difficult to pull off since the Legislature had approved a maximum salary of $6,500 for distinguished professors. The only position that paid more was the newly created vice presidency, which offered $14,000. Few leading scientists would consider a position with administrative responsibilities, so Rainey suggested that the Regents reduce these aspects of the position and provide this individual with large segments of research time and the best facilities that money could buy. Rainey suggested Arthur Compton, the Nobel Prize winning physicist (1927) from the University of Chicago. Parten agreed with Rainey's choice and promised to secure support from the other Regents. Not surprisingly, Arthur Compton rejected Rainey's offer. Rainey and Parten would wait until after the biennial budget process to contact their second choice.[49]

Rainey submitted his first budget recommendations to the Regents in July 1939. After a few adjustments, the Regents approved a budget that gave UT $255,000 of additional funds to work with in 1939–40 over 1938–39. Funds ($126,650) were dedicated for fifty new faculty and staff positions, as well as salary increases ($41,000) for sixty-one professors and associate professors. The Board allocated $207,867 to the Division of Research. The Regents also approved Rainey's proposal to establish the University Research Council (URC). The URC, composed of the dean of the Graduate School and representatives from the various departments and schools, would solicit research applications and award grants to the general faculty. UT requested $900,000 for this initiative, but the Legislature reduced the amount to $25,000. Despite the reduction, the $25,000 provided UT with its first state funds designated for research. The Legislature still approved salaries as line items, but the University would be able to allocate research dollars at its own discretion.[50]

Encouraged by a stronger research budget, Rainey returned to his search for a star scientist in September 1939. Arthur Compton was unwilling to leave the University of Chicago, but he volunteered gossip that E. O. Lawrence was looking to leave the University of California. Berkeley physicist Leonard Loeb had wooed the twenty-seven year old Lawrence away from Yale in 1928 with the promise of a promotion to associate professor, state-of-the art facilities, and the opportunity to teach graduate students. Lawrence invented the cyclotron in 1929, became director of the Berkeley Radiation Laboratory in 1936, and won the Nobel Prize for physics in 1939.

Lawrence's accomplishments placed him in a powerful bargaining position. According to Compton, Lawrence now wanted a bigger cyclotron, but the University of California was unable to finance the $8 million machine. Rainey thanked Compton for the information and proceeded to Berkeley to tempt Lawrence.[51]

As Rainey and Lawrence toured the Radiation Laboratory, Lawrence mentioned that he was about to embark on a fundraising trip in search of private foundation support for the new cyclotron. The two went back to Lawrence's office where Rainey offered him the vice president's position and suggested that the UT Regents could match any amount of foundation support that Lawrence could obtain. Lawrence agreed to consider Rainey's offer and arranged to visit the UT campus on October 16, 1939. At the same time, Lawrence informed Berkeley president Robert Sproul of the Texas offer. Lawrence embellished upon the Texas deal by adding that Rainey "could guarantee the necessary funds for such an undertaking *immediately.*" Sproul pledged to fight for Lawrence.[52]

According to J. R. Parten, the Regents agreed to build Lawrence's 184-inch cyclotron and purchase additional equipment with money in the AUF and the help of foundation support. Parten shared this information with Lawrence, who promised Parten that he would come to Texas and recruit four of his colleagues as well. Lawrence then returned home to the news that the Rockefeller Foundation would provide matching funds for the cyclotron. He immediately alerted Rainey and Sproul that they were free to fight over him.[53]

This fight never took place. James Elkins, cofounder of the Vinson and Elkins law firm in Houston, balked at the suggestion that the State of Texas needed a publicly funded "atom-smashing machine." Elkins warned Regent E. J. Blackert that the Legislature would kick the Regents across the state line if they dared to squander tax dollars in this manner. Upon hearing Elkins' judgment, the Regents agreed to withdraw their support for the Lawrence deal in the interest of upcoming legislative requests. Rainey and Parten refused to give in and appealed to the recently formed M. D. Anderson Foundation in Houston. Once they received an answer of no from Anderson, Rainey reluctantly reneged on the deal with Lawrence.[54]

In the midst of his failed attempt to recruit Lawrence, Rainey prepared his inaugural address to the people of Texas. In this speech delivered in early December 1939, Rainey introduced his vision for UT. He proclaimed that UT had and should continue to embrace the

AAUP's principles of academic freedom. This statement, and his declaration that UT faculty must commit more time to organized research and that the Legislature should increase appropriations for all Texas colleges and schools, were no different from Harry Benedict's inaugural address. What distinguished Rainey's speech were the biting criticisms of the State's business elite. Rainey first took aim at the booming lumber and petroleum industries:

> We have been a wasteful people. Our ancestors came from an old continent of meager holdings to the richest land in the world and the result was a Roman holiday. Three-fourths of our timber is gone...two-thirds of our known oil reserves....[55]

He proceeded to call for state corporate taxes:

> The surest way for industry to limit its markets and goods in the future is to curtail the opportunities for education. Business leaders who advocate a reduction in educational expenditures are shortsighted and are committing a slow but sure economic suicide.[56]

Rainey ended his address with a call for institutional autonomy:

> The regents and administrators of the University should be given full power to develop the institution...they should not be hampered in their movements by too close a control.[57]

While Rainey hoped for administrative autonomy accompanied by trust and support from the Regents, he would soon face Regents who would do everything they could to hamper his leadership.

Early Troubles, 1939–1940

Rainey made his final attempt to gain a world-class scientist in June 1940. The Regents and Rainey hosted the 1934 Nobel laureate in chemistry, Harold Urey. During his two-day visit to Austin, the Columbia University chemist inspected a number of the science departments and provided recommendations for improvement. The Regents were impressed by Urey and authorized Rainey to hire him as vice president and professor of chemistry. In spite of Rainey's assurance that the administrative duties would be minimal, Urey had no interest in taking such a post and declined the offer. Rainey abandoned his strategy after this stinging rejection.[58]

In addition to his failed quest to acquire a big name scientist, Rainey handled a debacle brewing at the medical branch in Galveston. The Regents held a series of initial meetings to discuss academic deficiencies and other controversies in Galveston, October 7–9, 1939. After studying the issues presented in October 1939, Rainey submitted his report on the Medical School to the Regents at a special session, January 13, 1940. Rainey warned that conditions at the medical school were so poor that the program was on the verge of losing its Class "A" rating from the American Medical Schools Association (AMSA). The president listed thirteen deficiencies. The first eight dealt with the medical school's low ranking among sixty-four programs in a survey conducted by the AMSA. The areas cited by Rainey included organization and administration, faculty qualifications for teaching and research, faculty salaries, educational programs in pre-clinical and clinical studies, clinical facilities, and financial support.[59]

Rainey also cited an inadequate physical plant and the lack of accreditation by numerous specialty boards as major problems. He believed that all of the medical school's problems were attributable in part to its disjointed organizational structure. Four separate boards managed the Medical School: the Regents, the Smith and Sealy Foundation, the Hospital Board of Managers, and the Executive Committee of the Faculty. The Hospital Board consisted of officials from the city and University, so that UT did not possess direct control of its own hospital. For decades, the University leased the hospital to the City of Galveston, who determined the admission of patients and undermined the authority of doctors employed by the medical school. While the Smith and Sealy Foundation was charged with disbursing funds to promote teaching and research, it was not empowered to dictate policy or manage the medical school. The Foundation's role had been confused with that of the Regents over the years. The general faculty had little say in the administrative and curricular matters because a five-member Executive Committee made most of the decisions for the entire faculty, and this body remained largely unchanged from year to year. The dean of the Medical School had little, if any, control over this body. The Regents made minor changes to Rainey's claims and appointed a committee to study the issues in greater detail.[60]

Rainey and Regent Fred Branson met with individuals from Galveston Board of Commissioners, Smith and Sealy, and the Hospital Board of Managers on November 25, 1940. During this meeting, the Galveston officials agreed to place Sealy Hospital back in the hands of the University. Galveston would then pay $40,000 to UT to provide medical services for charity cases.[61] In spite of this victory, the medical school troubles would continue between 1940 and 1942 over the performance of its dean, John Spies. Following a number of investigations into his effectiveness, his tact, and his Americanism, the Regents would fire Spies on August 1, 1942.

Despite his unsuccessful effort to nab a Nobel laureate and the evolving medical school conflict, Rainey's first year and a half were generally calm. The Regents who hired Rainey, particularly J. R. Parten, Leslie Waggener, and George Morgan, still possessed a good deal of influence on the Board. Rainey and the Regents were unified in their goals of increasing faculty salaries and research funds. The Regents, however, would soon reintroduce politics into the day-to-day management of the University to a degree that would rival the Jim Ferguson era.

The Regent Packing Process

A nine-member board that was appointed by the governor and confirmed by the Texas Senate governed UT. Each Regent served a six-year, staggered term, which meant that three new Regents were appointed every two years. Governors served two-year terms, so each governor had an opportunity to appoint regents. If a governor served for two or more terms, he could appoint the entire board. This structure allowed Governor O'Daniel to gain political control of the University in 1941.[62]

Rainey's relatively peaceful tenure ended in November 1940 when O'Daniel was reelected governor. In his campaign, O'Daniel announced that he had alerted FDR to a possible Fifth Column in Texas.[63] It is widely believed, but impossible to prove, that O'Daniel marshaled Texas businessmen and lawmakers in January 1940 at what became known as the "Houston Gag Conference." Plans were allegedly formulated there to restrict academic freedom, eliminate faculty, and cut questionable curricula.[64] Rainey, Parten, and J. Frank Dobie would later cite the "Gag Conference" as definitive evidence that the Regents calculated and plotted to eliminate Rainey and certain liberal faculty. Parten claimed that Fred Branson mentioned the "Gag Conference" casually during a golf game. Branson denied that the meeting with O'Daniel ever occurred and stated that he could not recall the golf course conversation with Parten. Even though the tale is impossible to verify, Parten, Rainey, and Dobie—none of whom had firsthand evidence—took a mere rumor and added colorful description. A number of writers such as Ronnie Dugger, Alice Cox, George Green, and of course, Homer Rainey, cited the "Gag Conference" as fact.

Around the same time as the supposed Houston meeting, O'Daniel appointed Fred Branson, employee of high-powered Galveston financier Maco Stewart, and reappointed long-time Regents Kenneth Aynesworth, physician from Waco, and Marguerite Fairchild, civic volunteer from Lufkin. During Branson's first meeting in May 1940, he introduced a motion to fire Robert Montgomery, a full professor of economics and an advocate for public utilities, in order to hire several assistant professors. Long-time Regent Lutcher Stark seconded Branson's motion. Stark then moved to strike the salary of J. Frank Dobie, the Texas folklorist and frequent critic of Texas conservatism. Neither of these motions carried; however, both suggested to Chairman J. R. Parten, as an independent oilman and enthusiastic supporter of the New Deal, that Governor O'Daniel was fomenting a coup.[65]

In early 1941, O'Daniel announced the nomination of new Regents Orville Bullington, a railroad and banking tycoon, and Dan Harrison, an oil baron and cattleman. At the same time, O'Daniel removed Allred appointees J. R. Parten, and George Morgan, a Columbia University Ph.D. and president of Cardinal Oil. The Texas Senate immediately approved Fred Branson in 1940, but a number of members initially opposed Bullington and Harrison in 1941. Both men voted for Wendell Wilkie as president in November 1940 and Bullington had run as the Republican candidate for governor in 1932. The Texas Senate met in closed session for over two hours on January 30, 1941 and asked the two men if they were willing to "hire and fire a lot of new people and if they were against the Communists and other isms." San Antonio banker D. K. Martin, who stated in his nomination letter that he was alarmed by the "unscrupulous, designing, subversive professors who have been diggin' in in our schools more than we dare to admit," endorsed Harrison. The Senate approved Bullington and Harrison once it was satisfied that the Wilkieites would not take control of the University.[66]

The Regent-packing program continued even after O'Daniel was elected to the U.S. Senate in a special election in August 1941. Lieutenant Governor Coke Stevenson became governor and was elected in his own right in November 1942. Leslie Waggener, son of UT's first president and director of a Dallas bank that was in constant conflict with the major Dallas oil companies owned by Texas Regulars, stepped down from the Board in March 1942. That same year, Stevenson appointed additional regents D. F. Strickland, a movie theater lobbyist, John Bickett, general counsel for Southwestern Bell, and W. Scott Scheiner, a banker and rancher. With five O'Daniel and Stevenson appointees and H. J. Lutcher Stark, the prickly, twenty-three year member who often cast the dissenting vote, the Regents were poised to assent control of Rainey and his liberal faculty. The inevitable conflict began at the medical branch.

Medical Branch Dean John Spies

The first investigation into Dean Spies' performance occurred on July 9, 1941. During this investigation, the Regents and Rainey examined Spies' "tact, diplomacy, and administrative ability in dealing with the Faculty in his charge." Despite concerns over his abilities, the Regents reelected Spies to his post at the July 26 meeting.[67] Spies would continue to lead the medical school, but Rainey remained dissatisfied with the administration and academic standing of the unit. In a resolution issued September 29, 1941, Rainey, identified the organizational reporting structure as a major culprit. Rainey lacked the proper authority to supervise the dean and oversee the medical school faculty. Instead, the Regents formed a committee to oversee the dean and medical faculty. Although Rainey did not state this, he insinuated that the Regents had overstepped their boundaries and asked for this committee to be abolished. The Board discussed Rainey's resolution, but voted to postpone any decision until the next meeting.[68]

Members of the medical school faculty appeared before the Board on October 25, 1941 to present a recently drafted policy statement. This group called for a reorganization of the Executive Committee of the Faculty. The committee would consist of four members who could serve no more than two years in succession. They also recommended that the general faculty be given the ability to make recommendations directly to the Regents and the president if they disagreed with the actions taken by the Executive Committee and the dean. The Board elected to take this proposal under advisement. During this same meeting, Rainey asked for a final vote on his resolution presented at the September 29th meeting. After much discussion, the Board rejected Rainey's request to eliminate their medical school committee, but accepted other parts of his resolution that affirmed the president's authority over the dean and the medical school.[69]

Rainey and the Regents rejected the medical faculty's proposal on the grounds that the new powers circumvented the dean and the

Executive Committee. They did not seem to have a problem setting term limits on the Executive Committee, but the proposed rules seemed to highlight, not solve, the conflicts that existed between the dean, Executive Committee, and the general faculty at the Medical School.[70]

Problems at the medical school persisted in 1942. The recently formed Texas HUAC launched an investigation of activities at the medical school and presented its report on February 28, 1942. Aside from the medical school's failure to train competent doctors to assist in the war effort, the House Committee found no evidence of un-American activities at the medical school. The little HUAC recommended that the Regents dismiss Dean Spies and any counterproductive faculty so that the rest of the faculty could commence with plans to make UT's medical program "first class." The Committee blamed the Regents for allowing the situation to degenerate at the medical school and urged them to loosen their control and grant Rainey the authority he required to manage the unit.[71]

During this same meeting, the Regents reviewed a statement signed by fifty-one faculty members, and the associate and assistant deans, calling for Spies' removal. The Regents agreed to hear further evidence in support of Spies' removal as well as his defense on March 16, 1942.[72] The medical school faculty declared that they had already presented ample evidence calling for Spies' dismissal, so the Regents cancelled this meeting. In the midst of the controversy, Fred Zapffe of the Executive Council of the Association of American Medical Colleges (AAMC) warned Rainey that a review team had recommended probation.[73]

The saga lingered on in May 1942, when a clearly frustrated Rainey presented an extensive list of recommendations concerning the medical school. As for Spies, Rainey urged the Regents to fire or affirm him immediately so that the faculty and Spies could move on and make peace. Rainey called for seven general actions to improve the academic quality of the medical program. These actions included the expansion of courses, introduction of fields not currently offered, and initiation of research projects in the areas of biophysics and biochemistry. He suggested that the University establish a dentistry program and expand its nursing and pharmacy schools. After hearing Rainey's proposal, the Regents voted to proceed with a hearing regarding Spies and other problems related to the medical school.[74]

The Board fired Spies on August 1, 1942 and replaced him with Chauncey Leake on August 8. Leake quickly identified some quick solutions to the administrative and curricular problems at the Medical School. He suggested that the school limit its enrollment to better match facility and faculty size and that it subsequently develop an expansion program. Leake provided the medical branch with stable leadership through 1955 and was largely responsible for improving the unit's reputation in the 1940s and 1950s.[75]

While problems at the medical branch may seem peripheral to the challenges to academic freedom that largely occurred at the Main University in Austin, the facts of this situation are an important example of the power struggle between Rainey and the Regents. Rainey would cite his lack of authority over the medical branch in his list of sixteen grievances to the Regents in 1944. Issues at the medical school were only a small part of the conflict.

Foil at Forty Acres[76]

Rainey and the Regents experienced little conflict beyond the medical school issue between the winter 1941 meeting and January 1942. In early 1942, the Regents challenged a report from the University Bureau of Municipal Research titled *Municipal Utilities in Texas*. In this report, the Bureau of Municipal Research highlighted the benefits of municipally owned utilities. According to Rainey, the Regents were so outraged by this report that they threatened to abolish the Bureau.[77] There is no record of this disagreement in the Regents' minutes, but it is certainly possible that such an exchange occurred in the unrecorded executive session.

Later in the summer, the Regents fired economics instructors J. Fagg Foster, Wendell C. Gordon, and W. N. Peach.[78] These men made a statement to correct false claims that were made at an anti-labor rally in Dallas. Karl Hoblitzelle, a Dallas movie mogul, organized the meeting to protest the National Labor Relations Act (1935) and the Fair Labor Standards Act (1938)[79] in the decidedly anti-labor *Dallas Morning News*.[80] The advertisement contained a picture of large Japanese soldiers aiming rifles at U.S. soldiers who were holding toy guns. The ad stated that American soldiers were dying because the union-controlled government would not permit anyone to work over forty hours per week. Hoblitzelle sponsored a meeting that he claimed was organized by mothers of servicemen and invited all who wanted to express their opinions on the matter in an open forum.[81] The three economics professors who attended the meeting intended to read the law that provided overtime to individuals who worked in excess of forty hours, but were forbidden time to speak and notified a reporter. Hoblitzelle witnessed the exchange and notified his friend D. F. Strickland, who brought the three in for interrogation. Six regents were present at this meeting with the faculty, and Senator O'Daniel called twice from his office in Washington.[82] O'Daniel's successor, Coke Stevenson, chose to watch the proceedings from a distance. To Rainey's dismay, the men were fired in a vote of four to one.[83] These dismissals prompted an investigation by the AAUP in July 1942.[84]

A number of organizations, including the Democratic Club of Tarrant County (Fort Worth area) and the Austin League of Women Voters, sent letters of disapproval to Governor Stevenson after the Regents fired the economics instructors. The Tarrant County group argued that the three instructors did nothing but honorably represent an opposing viewpoint at a public meeting. Likewise, the League of Women Voters accused the Regents of denying the three their right of free speech. The League's president, Mrs. Alfred Taylor, accused Stevenson and O'Daniel of packing the Board of Regents with opponents of academic freedom. Stevenson defended his appointee, D. F. Strickland, who the governor appointed for his knowledge in law and medicine and his potential to resolve problems at the medical branch.[85]

Following the Regents' dismissal of the three economics instructors, a group of faculty assembled to discuss what this action meant for academic freedom at UT. This faculty group contacted the Regents and requested a meeting. Representing this faculty assembly on September 25, 1942, Roy Bedichek, Frank Dobie, the noted and outspoken Texas folklorist, J. M. Kuehne, and Frederic Duncalf expressed their disapproval of the Regents' actions and presented them with a petition containing fifty faculty signatures. The petition claimed that that the Regents had failed to provide adequate reasons for why the instructors were dismissed. Since the Regents had provided them with limited information regarding their reasoning, the faculty had just enough information to believe that the penalty was too harsh. Lack of knowledge would only create distrust of the Regents from both the faculty and the public. Primary spokesman Roy Bedichek added that while the Board had infringed upon academic freedom, the faculty were largely concerned about the negative publicity that

UT had incurred as a result of the Regents' dismissal of the instructors. The Regents discussed the petition, but the minutes contain no details.[86]

Faculty disgust over the Regents' behavior began to spread. H. Bailey Carroll of the Texas State Historical Association quipped to Roy Bedichek that an individual had to meet four requirements to gain a seat on the Board: "(1) Strike oil; (2) inherit lumber; 3) marry rich; (4) and this may overlap the other three—Buy an office for the governor."[87]

During the January 30, 1943 meeting, D. F. Strickland introduced a motion to amend Chapter I, Part II, Section 3 of the Regents' rules and regulations, which then stated that the Regents could not remove a professor or associate professor from his/her position until a five-member advisory committee composed of the General Faculty had conducted an investigation and submitted a recommendation to the Board's Complaint and Grievance Committee. Strickland reintroduced his proposal at the March 27, 1943 meeting. Strickland suggested that the Regents forward this rule to the State attorney general and ask him to rule on the legality of such a provision. In addition, Strickland wanted the attorney general to rule on the legality of the rules pertaining to tenure and promotion. Strickland was quick to clarify that he was not interested in changing the tenure guidelines, but he believed that the current rules violated state statutes. Rainey then requested that the Board permit J. W. Calhoun, Eugene Barker, and R. W. Slayton to meet with the Regents on behalf of the General Faculty to draft such a petition to the attorney general jointly with the Regents. The Regents granted Rainey's request.[88]

The joint committee unanimously concluded that Section 3 was ambiguous and set about to revise the rule in its entirety. This new tenure rule stated that those who demonstrated competence

> are given assurance that they may feel secure and independent in their positions and that they will be promoted upon the basis of merit as circumstances permit. Unless otherwise stipulated in advance in the letter of appointment, it is the intention of the Board that the term of service of a professor or associate professor will be continued during good behavior and satisfactory service, of an assistant professor will be two years, and an instructor or other member of the teaching staff will be one year. Three months' notice of intention not to reappoint an assistant professor or an instructor will ordinarily be given, but failure to give such notice will not constitute reappointment.[89]

As for termination, the Board would provide written justification for dismissing a faculty member and would provide that person with a hearing before a committee of five faculty members approved by the Board "in consultation" with the president. The Board could act on its own if an emergency existed. Strickland also pointed out that the Board included portions of Section 3 on the backside of the appointment forms sent to faculty. He believed that the Regents should discontinue this practice (although his reasons are not recorded in the minutes). The Regents approved the revised rules and Strickland's proposal to remove the guidelines from reappointment forms. Strickland then moved to deny a salary increase for economics professor E. E. Hale for the 1943–44 year. Scott Schreiner seconded Strickland's motion, but the action failed to carry.[90]

T. Whitfield Davidson, U.S. district judge from the Texas Northern District in Dallas, wrote Regent John Bickett in September with the warning that Rainey and the faculty had asked the AAUP to intervene in the matter of tenure. Davidson reminded Bickett of an article in the *Daily Texan* where the author stated that professors were protected from dismissal. Given that the University had hosted Oscar Ameringer, a German socialist and opponent of the lend-lease policy, and allowed faculty to glorify Sacco and Vanzetti, providing faculty with unconditional tenure accompanied by unbridled academic freedom, which the AAUP would certainly demand, would damage the University and corrupt student minds.[91]

Ralph Himstead, general secretary of the AAUP, sent a telegram to the Regents in the fall of 1943 and requested a meeting with the Board to discuss the 1942 dismissal of the three economics instructors. The Regents agreed to allow Himstead to attend a meeting. According to Orville Bullington, this meeting never materialized. Bullington concluded that the AAUP had decided to work through the Southern Education Conference. He believed that the various so-called radicals outside of UT had cooked up a conspiracy theory that the Regents were in cahoots with Karl Hoblitzelle. These "Roosevelt worshippers" believed that Hoblitzelle acted on behalf of the Regents when he denied the economics instructors the opportunity to speak at the Dallas rally in 1942. According to Bullington, he did not know Hoblitzelle and such accusations were ridiculous.[92]

The Regents then turned to the curriculum in January 1943 and banned *The Big Money*, the third volume in John Dos Passos' *U.S.A.* trilogy. The Regents had expressed concern over its use in English courses, so the faculty in that department elected to place the work on the sophomore supplementary reading list. Led by Regent Bickett, the Regents conducted a hearing with English department faculty and threatened to fire the person who placed the book on the supplementary reading list. When the English faculty insisted that the decision came from a committee and not an individual, the Regents banned the book due to the author's use of sexually explicit language and sympathetic stance towards labor unions.[93]

Rainey believed the Board was growing increasingly distrustful of him and the faculty. For example, the Regents insisted on reviewing all research proposals, especially those submitted by departments in the social sciences and humanities. The Regents began to scrutinize and postpone or reject projects that the University Research Institute had already. Of the thirty projects that appeared on the June 27, 1942 docket, twenty were approved (seventeen in natural sciences, two in social sciences, and one in humanities). Of the three proposals that were postponed, two had been previously approved.[94] Although the Regents did not record their reasons for rejecting research proposals, none of the seven rejected proposals had obvious New Deal or socialist/communist elements.[95] Later, Rainey would accurately list the spurned proposals, but he failed to note that two of the postponed projects and two of the rejected programs were later approved.[96]

The Regents continued to read all faculty research proposals and rejected many that promoted the "wrong" ideas. The Regents zealously opposed a proposal submitted by English professor G. L. Joughlin to investigate the impact that the Sacco-Vanzetti case had made on American literature. Bullington stated that this case had already been glorified in the public and the Regents would not fund any project that promoted the "communist murderers." The Board rejected Joughlin's proposal on September 29, 1944.[97]

On October 1, 1944, D. F. Strickland allegedly called Vice President J. Alton Burdine and told him that the Regents were going to put a stop to Rainey's speaking engagements around the country. According to Burdine, Strickland believed that Rainey was making disparaging remarks about the Regents in churches. Burdine called Rainey immediately and within several days, the supposed Strickland-Burdine conversation was leaked to the press. Strickland denied ever having this conversation with Burdine.[98]

Rainey could no longer contain his frustration. On October 12, 1944, the beleaguered president called a faculty meeting where he issued a list of sixteen grievances directed at the Regents and called for a meeting with the Board to discuss them. According to Rainey, the sixteen wrongs were caused by the absence of academic freedom and the Regents' failure to acknowledge administrative authority. Most of Rainey's charges were taken directly from the Regents' meeting minutes and are summarized below:

Rainey's Sixteen Grievances[99]

1. On June 1, 1939, Regent Weinert asked Rainey not to re-nominate J. C. Dolley to the athletic committee. Weinert provided no reason for his request and Rainey believed Weinert simply did not like Dolley. Rainey stated that it was his privilege as president to hire his own staff and Weinert had interfered.
2. On March 16, 1943, Regent Strickland responded to Rainey's request that he withdraw a resolution to change the tenure rule. In this letter, Strickland suggested that Rainey had overstepped his bounds as president of UT by challenging the actions of a Regent.
3. A former Regent (Rainey did not provide the name) introduced a motion to eliminate economics professor Robert Montgomery during a 1940 budget meeting. The motion did not carry, but Rainey was upset that the Regents would have fired Montgomery without a hearing.
4. During the same 1940 budget meeting, Regent Stark called for the dismissal of Dean Shelby, Roy Bedichek, and R. J. Kidd. Stark admitted that he blamed these men for changes in the University Interscholastic League (UIL) rules that kept his sons from playing football at Orange High School. Stark's motion failed.
5. The Regents voted to dismiss economics instructors J. Fagg Foster, Wendell Gordon, and W. N. Peach for speaking out at the anti-strike rally in Dallas during the summer of 1942.
6. On January 8, 1943, the Regents voted to remove Dos Passos' *The Big Money* from the supplemental reading list for sophomore English.
7. Regent Strickland spent several months in 1942 complaining to Rainey about the un-American attitudes espoused by several UT faculty members. Strickland then presented a loyalty oath to the Regents in January 1943. Rainey pleaded with the Regents to defeat the resolution and they complied with the president.
8. Strickland also introduced a revised tenure rule at the January 1943 Board meeting.
9. The Regents fired Arthur Brandon, director of public relations, in 1943.
10. Between 1941 and 1944, the Regents rejected funding for an array of social science research projects that they deemed politically offensive.
11. The Regents repeatedly denied a request to establish a school of social work at UT. According to Rainey, the Regents rejected the request because the school would nurture socialism.
12. In 1942, the Regents attacked the Bureau of Municipal Research after its staff published a report citing the merits of publicly owned utilities.

13. On September 25, 1942, the Regents passed a rule to forbid the use of University funds for faculty travel.
14. The Regents reduced the University's State appropriation request for the 1944–1945 biennium by $230,000. Rainey and Regent Strickland presented the reduced budget to the Legislature during which time Strickland disparaged the University. One state senator asked Rainey if he thought that Strickland was even in favor of UT's success.
15. The Regents barred Rainey and other administrators from attending executive sessions.
16. The Regents handled the Dean Spies episode poorly. They failed to include Rainey in major decisions regarding Spies and the difficulties at the medical school.

One day after Rainey issued his statement, Strickland allegedly declared that Rainey had finally pushed too far and that the Regents would make haste in dealing with him. Between October 12 and October 27, the campus community mobilized in support of Rainey. A large group of faculty pledged their support for their embattled president and formed a committee consisting of Frederic Duncalf (history), Theophilus Painter (zoology), and Robert Stayton (law) to work with the Regents. The Ex-Students Association assembled a similar committee.[100] None of this support would help Homer Rainey.

The Regents, the recently formed faculty committee, a student committee, representatives from the Ex-Students Association, the Texas Senate, and the AAUP assembled at the Rice Hotel in Houston on October 27. One hundred and fifty miles removed from the University, the Regents conducted routine business and heard testimony from Rainey supporters. Two days into the meeting, the assembly received word that Regent Kenneth Aynesworth had died in Waco. The Regents adjourned until October 31 in order to attend Aynesworth's funeral. Upon returning to the Rice Hotel, the Regents called the faculty and Ex-Students committees into an executive session. Rainey and Vice President John Alton Burdine were not invited to join the exchange. The Regents spent the majority of this executive session responding to Rainey's charges, perhaps as a way to win the faculty and alumni over to their side. Instead, the committees believed that Rainey could stay on if he tempered his grievance statement. The faculty and alumni communicated this to Rainey, who sat down that night and composed a statement, which is excerpted below:

> It is a matter of sincere regret to me that a critical situation has developed between the Regents and myself…in referring to individual members of the Board I have done so in their official capacities only…. I did not intend to reflect upon the motives of individual

members or former members, living or dead, or to question their personal integrity, and anything in my statement which might be so construed I am glad to withdraw.... I recognize the authority of this Board under the Constitution...and I shall be happy to work with this Board of Regents in accordance with these aforementioned laws, rules, and regulations.

Furthermore I heartily approve of the suggestions made by the Faculty Committee and endorsed by the Ex-Student Committee that the Board of Regents appoint a Committee from teaching faculty to serve in a liaison capacity for the purpose of considering future problems of Board and administrative relationships, and differences of policy or functions that may arise between us.[101]

On the morning of November 1, Rainey submitted his statement to the faculty and alumni, who then delivered it to the Regents. The committees expected the Regents to embrace Rainey's letter, but were shocked when the Regents stated that they would accept nothing less from Rainey than a total retraction of the sixteen-point grievance statement. The faculty and alumni left the meeting to inform Rainey of the Board's ultimatum. The weary president had run out of options. Rainey could write a groveling letter, but he could not withdraw his charges. After subsequent talks between the faculty/alumni group and the Regents, Rainey was summoned to the executive session. Lutcher Stark introduced a motion to fire Rainey without a hearing. Scott Schreiner seconded Stark's motion. Dan Harrison, D. F. Strickland, Orville Bullington, and Hilmer Weinert voted yea, John Bickett abstained, and Marguerite Fairchild cast the lone vote against the motion. As if they knew they had just taken part in a sinister deed, Bickett, Weinert, and Harrison resigned on the spot.[102]

The state and national press quickly published several articles in which they criticized the Regents, but Governor Stevenson refused to show public support to any side and simply stated that he had been taught to keep his lips away from a hot coffeepot.[103] Prior to Rainey's dismissal, Stevenson privately told one of the Regents that he supported their decision to restrict Rainey's freedom to govern because Rainey had forced the University to succumb to the "foreign...undemocratic...and totalitarian" bureaucracies from the AAUP and the American Medical Association.[104]

Perhaps the most dramatic response came from the student body. On November 2, 1944, approximately 5,000 of the nearly 9,000 students on campus gathered in the streets of Austin and marched behind a coffin labeled "academic freedom" to Chopin's "Funeral March" performed by drummers and trombonists from the Longhorn band. The students paraded through the rotunda of the Capitol building and delivered the coffin to the steps of Governor Stevenson's mansion. The next day, students gathered again and formed a mile-long parade. Led by a banner brigade clutching a sign that announced "Academic Freedom Is Dead" and a car sporting wounded veterans, hundreds of students and Austinites marched in support of Rainey.[105] Student opposition to the Regents, Stevenson, and O'Daniel was not new. Following the appointment of Harrison, Bullington, and Branson in 1941, students circulated a handbill that included a picture of two cigar-smoking elephants clad in silk top hats. The elephants stood in a pool of oil next to a derrick. Even in 1941, students worried that the new Regents would make the university into a political battleground.[106]

The scandal attracted national attention. In one of the most quoted articles on the subject, *New Republic* writer Bernard DeVoto observed that thousands of Texans believed that the Regents fired Rainey because they had to protect the state from a dangerous threat:

> The communists were responsible for the New Deal and they intend to inflict a labor dictatorship on us. They want to debauch your daughters with free love and marry them to Negroes. They want to destroy private enterprise and white supremacy. They want to destroy initiative and profit, business and freedom, the individual and the United States. And for this the evil things they teach at the University are responsible. Get rid of the communist professors—who are all homosexuals and New Dealers anyway—and everything will be right once more.[107]

DeVoto exaggerated, but this was the manner in which Americans received the story—the UT Regents were a group of fat cat, paranoid, racist, cowboys who cared nothing about the education of its youth. The Regents, who dismissed the troublemaking Rainey to make their jobs easier, did nothing but damage the University's reputation. It was this national scorn and attention that would encourage future UT Regents to break the long, grand tradition of political interference at UT.

The Hearing

The State Senate Education Committee initiated an investigation of the events in mid-November, but these hearings did not result in any action or recommendation. The hearings did however, reveal a great deal about the Regents' opposition to the New Deal, communism, and desegregation of the university.

Orville Bullington submitted a written statement to the committee in which he responded on behalf of the Regents to a number of Rainey's charges against them. Stark, Strickland, and Scheiner pledged their support of Bullington's statement with their signatures. According to Bullington, Rainey initiated the conflict between himself and the trustees in early 1941 by treating them with an air of condescension. He noted that the University did not even employ a president until 1895, twelve years after the institution opened. The Regents had been around since 1881 and were ultimately responsible for the University, not the president, and could manage the institution without one. Furthermore, Rainey had directed four of his charges at Regents who were no longer on the board, two of whom were dead. Many of Rainey's claims were outright false, including the Regents' objections to the report produced by the Bureau of Municipal Research.[108]

Bullington directed to majority of his rebuttal to the incidents involving the economics faculty and the Dos Passos novel. Addressing the dismissal of the three economics professors in 1942, Bullington stated that the Regents granted a hearing to the three faculty members. During this hearing, the Regents informed them that they had violated Section 6 of the University Rules and Regulations composed by former President H. Y. Benedict. The section stated that a faculty member was free to communicate his opinions both in and out of the classroom, provided that opinion related to his field of expertise and that the faculty members exercised a "generous respect for the rights, feelings, and opinions of others." The three economics professors violated this rule and showed great disrespect to Southern Methodist University President Umphrey Lee and minister George W. Truett. On top of their rudeness, the three refused to apologize for their actions. The Regents did not infringe on the faculty members' academic freedom; rather, the instructors violated the principles of propriety. The Regents did not oppose academic freedom, but they did oppose academic license. These faculty members assumed a license without accepting responsibility for their actions.[109]

In reference to *The Big Money*, Bullington stated that the Regents removed the book because parents complained that it was inappropriate. Once the Regents analyzed the book, they found a wealth of sex, profanity, and blasphemy. Bullington declared *The Big Money* to be obscenity, not literature and urged the "mothers and ministers" of Texas to review the novel.[110]

In addition to responding to Rainey's charges, Bullington introduced two claims against Rainey, both of which related to Rainey's inability to hire suitable faculty. Bullington contended that the U.S.

military put officers through FBI background checks before approving them. Given the current state of the world, Rainey should have placed applicants through an equally rigorous inspection. Bullington referenced an article from the October 12, 1944 edition of the *Dallas Times Herald* that stated that Arthur Goodwyn Billings, a former Socialist candidate for the U.S. Senate from Kansas and UT economics instructor, was headed to prison to serve a sentence for his evasion of the draft following his induction. Rainey allegedly knew that Billings was a conscientious objector, but he kept this information from the Regents. Billings served as an instructor from 1941–1942, and Rainey suggested him as a replacement for one of the three dismissed economics instructors. Billings was inducted in August 1942, and refused to comply, stating he was a conscientious objector. A federal district court declared that he could not use the conscientious objection defense because he was an agnostic. In addition, he stated in court that the German and Japanese atrocities were exaggerated.[111] Bullington cited to the Regent's Rules, Sec. 1, Chapter 2, that stated that the president was responsible for keeping the Regents abreast of information concerning issues related to the administration and welfare of the University, he alleged. Regents heard that there were subversive activities at UT, asked Rainey about it during the summer of 1942, and Rainey replied that such claims were false. All the while, Billings was engaged in subversive activities.[112]

The second charge from the Regents involved a man for whom Rainey had requested approval for hire in October 1944. This man was later indicted for committing "an alleged unspeakable and unmentionable social crime." Bullington elaborated on this episode during his testimony to the Senate Investigating Committee when he accused Rainey of tolerating a homosexual ring at the University.[113]

In addition to Bullington, Regent Strickland volunteered his opinions about Rainey's leadership to the Senate Investigating Committee. Rainey wanted to admit African Americans to the University. When asked his opinions about African Americans attending UT, Strickland stated, "We send them off to schools in other states.... If I were going to criticize him [Rainey] I think I'd criticize his being associated with Nigger-white groups—I'd say he is a little ultra-liberal on the Nigger question." Strickland's language represents the Regents' racist attitudes. In spite of his failure to provide evidence, Strickland also claimed that the economics faculty was teaching communism. The Regents' claim that the economics department was overrun with communists was an old canard from this group. The claim that Rainey supported desegregation at the University of Texas was new and false.[114]

"Era of Tranquility"

The AAUP and the Southern Association of Colleges and Schools would not complete their investigations until the summer of 1945, but UT had to regain order immediately after the scandal unfolded in November 1944. The first step was to appoint a strong, but non-controversial interim president and a well respected and politically connected businessman as chair of the Regents. The Regents met with interim President Theophilus Painter, a noted geneticist in January 1945 to further critique the Rainey incident and plan for the immediate future. Marguerite Fairchild attended as the sole Rainey supporter. Dudley Woodward, the Dallas attorney appointed as chairman on November 15, 1944, began the meeting with an anti-Rainey diatribe. Woodward noted that the Regents had governed the University in a consistent manner from 1881 to 1939 when Rainey assumed his post. To support the claim that Rainey was a poor leader, Woodward presented an anonymous letter from a former Bucknell trustee who noted that Rainey encountered problems while president there because he aligned himself with a small faction of faculty at the expense of others.[115]

Woodward deemed that the content of *The Big Money* was the medium of "sophisticates who find it necessary to follow the gutter into the sewer for an idea." Rainey claimed that the Regents' had inappropriately denied funds from the University Research Foundation. Since these funds came from the Legislature, the Board could not elect to support projects that could put the entire research budget at risk. The Board's discretion regarding these funds was not about academic freedom, but pragmatism. As for Rainey's charge that the Legislature had slashed appropriations, Woodward pointed out that the University possessed fewer students and faculty during this time of war. Rainey charged that the Regents had barred him and other administrators from attending executive session. While this action was unfortunate, Woodward wondered if the Regents made this decision because they could no longer work effectively in Rainey's presence.[116]

Once Woodward delivered his tirade, he set out to repair the damage done to UT's reputation. During their meeting on February 16,

1945, the Regents issued a statement of nine principles. They declared their adherence to what they described as nationally regarded policies and procedures adopted by colleges and universities, although they did not provide specifics. The Regents then committed themselves to an expanded physical plant and faculty to meet the demands of postwar society. The statement went on to stress the importance of research and pledged their support to all faculty research endeavors. Once again, the Regents did not identify specific areas that they intended to support. The Board "unreservedly" defended academic freedom and defined it as "freedom in research, freedom to proclaim and teach the results of such research, freedom to teach what the teacher believes to be true, limited only by the recognized decencies and properties obtaining among normal human beings." Next, Regents affirmed their belief in tenure and invited amendments to the current policies from the faculty, if needed. The University stood ready to accept whatever sanctions might be warranted from external agencies. The statement proclaimed that this was a new "era of tranquility," and that during this period, the Board would be committed to selecting the best man available to serve as permanent president and valued the faculty's assistance in locating this individual.[117]

Probation

The Southern Association of Colleges and Schools appointed a commission that conducted an investigation at UT in January 1945 and released its report on July 22, 1945. After meeting with both pro- and anti-Rainey camps, the Southern Association officials determined that neither side had any interest in compromise. Destructive "bias and prejudice" existed between students, faculty, and staff and between the Regents, faculty, staff, and students. These sentiments had to be removed and replaced with "objective judgment and justice" in order for UT to adhere to the Southern Association's standards.[118]

The commission went on to present their view of proper roles and responsibilities. According to the Texas Constitution, the elected state senators approved the executive-appointed Regents. The Regents' mandate was to represent Texas citizens by establishing and maintaining the "broad policies" of the University. The commission concluded that even if charged with the power, the Regents did not possess the right to micromanage the president or other administrators of the institution, just as the president and administrators did not possess the right to take over a professor's classroom. The Regents violated the principle of "proper sphere[s]" when they eliminated faculty members against the recommendation of faculty and administrators.[119]

The commission noted that various UT groups believed that the new guidelines threatened the institution of tenure, but the accrediting body believed that the new guidelines could be viewed as simply a clarification of the previous tenure rule. With the exception of John Spies, the Regents had not violated the principle of tenure. Tenure was not even an issue in the investigation.[120]

The commission determined that while the Regents had made poor choices in denying funding to certain research projects and the manner in which they dismissed the three economics instructors, no serious violation of academic freedom had occurred. The Regents cut the research funding in defiance of Rainey's recommendations. The Regents claimed that they did not dismiss the three for the expression of their views, but for refusing to apologize for their rude behavior in Dallas. The commission could not prove that the Regents had violated the instructors' right to express their beliefs. University of Kentucky president Herman Donovan went on record as disagreeing with the rest of the commission regarding both the funding and the dismissals. The Southern Association commission found fault with both Rainey and the Regents and placed the University of Texas on probation until it could demonstrate its "full observance of its principles and standards."[121]

Theophilus Painter wrote Woodward in July 1945 to warn him of the impending probation from the Southern Association. Commission chair and Tulane President Rufus Harris assured Painter that the report had portrayed Rainey, Strickland, and Bullington in a negative light. In spite of probation, Painter believed the Southern Association's report stood to help him and Woodward as they led UT into a new era because the report highlighted the institution's many past mistakes and challenges.[122] Speaking for the Regents, Woodward issued a statement on August 5, 1945. He accepted the Southern Association's criticisms of the pre-November 1944 state of affairs at UT, but he resented the probation ruling since much had been done in the subsequent months to rectify the situation at the University.[123]

Students organized and published anonymous literature in support and in opposition to the Southern Association's decision in the summer of 1945. One group published "The Lite: A Menu for Realistic Thought" and denounced Rainey for his failure to lead the University. These students maintained that academic freedom had been protected throughout Rainey's tenure. Another organization issued the "Probation News" and deemed Rainey's dismissal as part of a conspiracy by the Regents to root out liberals.[124] The Common Sense Organization, a student group formed to help remove UT from the Southern Association's probation list, issued a harsh statement on September 10, 1945. Led by future legislator and lieutenant governor Ben Ramsey, Common Sense criticized Painter for hurting the institution with his prostrated stance before the Regents, as well as his racial intolerance, anti-Semitism, and excessive nationalism.[125]

The Rainey Episode in Retrospect

Scholars and journalists have depicted Rainey as a pristine hero who fought a cadre of evil men. While there is no doubt that the Regents behaved badly, Rainey was not without blame for the public nature of his dismissal. Rainey showed no respect for the Regents when he chose to submit his sixteen grievances to the UT faculty and the state media before sitting down with them. Rainey's method of conflict resolution was bound to get him fired, since he had backed the already hostile Regents into a corner. J. R. Parten suggested that Rainey publicized his conflict with the Board as part of a strategy to launch a gubernatorial campaign. Even though Rainey did not run until 1946, he made his conflict with the Regents his primary campaign issue. He endorsed the various issues the Regents objected to: publicly funded social and educational programs, interracial cooperation, and higher taxes. He even went as far as to falsely accuse his opponent and former UT Regent, Beauford Jester, of being a member of the Ku Klux Klan. In the end, Rainey left Texas with a tarnished image and a failed gubernatorial campaign.[126]

While Ronnie Dugger depicted the faculty as solidly behind Rainey, not everyone saw him as a hero. Possibly speaking for the majority of the faculty, historian Walter Webb noted that Rainey was neither a "superman" nor the "real Moses." The faculty banded together in support of Rainey as a response to the Regents' outrageous actions, not because Rainey was a great president.[127]

Regardless of the negative details surrounding Rainey's character and leadership, his dismissal was an important turning point. It took a crisis to kill the germs of political interference that had infected UT since its establishment. The Rainey episode initially proved far more damaging to UT than the Ferguson controversy twenty-seven years before. This time, the meddling resulted in the firing of a president, a censure from the AAUP, and probation from SACS. While the scandal may have looked like the demise of UT, it was, in retrospect, simply the end of an era. Following the embarrassment of national criticism, the new UT Regents, Governor Beauford Jester (1947–1949), and Theophilus Painter made a commitment to make UT a nationally competitive research university. With the exception of some alarming anticommunist laws and a legislative investigation of economist Clarence Ayres in 1951, political interference would slowly decline in the post-Rainey era. Instead of firing Ayres, the Regents defended him to the Legislature.

The more polished Dudley Woodward replaced Orville Bullington and Luther Stark. Woodward shared their politics, but not their style. Dudley Woodward was in many ways Painter's greatest asset. As chair of the Regents (1944–1952), he served as the chief spokesman for the 1947 College Building Amendment and spoke publicly and passionately about the need for more labs and research facilities. Woodward also cared about restoring UT's reputation with its benefactors. Concerned that UT might lose the support of the Benjamin Clayton Foundation for Biochemical Research following the Rainey episode, Woodward attempted a degree of damage control by writing Clayton a letter of reassurance. Woodward proclaimed to this generous benefactor that UT was already regaining respect in the academic world. The new group of Regents had strengthened their commitment to organized research with Theophilus Painter as president: "The attitude…is in fact one of genuine appreciation and enthusiasm…of investigations worthy of the name research…. Much of the Board's attitude with reference to research is no doubt due to Dr. Painter's wholesome influence."[128] In future years, the Regents cared less about controlling the work of the UT faculty and more about increasing UT's share of the Cold War research economy.

Notes

1. Don E. Carleton, *A Breed So Rare: The Life of J.R., Liberal Texas Oil Man, 1896–1992* (Austin: Texas State Historical Association, 1998); Alice Carol Cox, "The Rainey Affair: A History of the Academic Freedom Controversy at the University of Texas, 1938–1946" (Ph.D. diss., University of Denver, 1970); Ronnie Dugger, *Our Invaded Universities: Form, Reform, and New Starts* (New York: W. W. Norton, 1974); George N. Green, *The Establishment in Texas Politics: The Primi-*

164   Perspectives on the History of Higher Education

tive Years, 1938–1957 (Norman: University of Oklahoma Press, 1979); John Gunther, *Inside U.S.A.* (1946; reprint, New York: The New Press, 1997); J. Evetts Haley, *The University of Texas and the Issue* (Amarillo: Miller Printing, 1945); Kimberly Marinucci, "Probing the Nation: Americanism, Public Universities, and the Politics of Academic Freedom, 1918–1946" (Ph.D. diss., State University of New York at Stony Brook, 2001); Homer Price Rainey, *The Tower and the Dom: A Free University Versus Political Control* (Boulder: Pruett Publishing, 1971); Henry Nash Smith, "The Controversy at the University of Texas, 1939–1945: A Documentary History" (Austin: Student Committee for Academic Freedom, University of Texas Students' Association, 1946); Texas Senate, Investigation of the University of Texas by the Senate Investigating Committee, *Hearings*, Forty-ninth Legislature, November 1944, four vols.

2. Patricia Limerick, one of the most prominent contemporary Western historians, considers Texas to be part of the West. For a complete account of Limerick's thesis, see Patricia Nelson Limerick, *Legacy of Conquest: The Unbroken Past of the American West* (New York: Norton, 1987). Southern historians have included Texas in the region in part because Southerners constituted the largest portion of settlers in the Mexican colony beginning in the 1820s. Texas revolutionaries waged war against Mexico for a host of reasons, not the least of which was Mexico's ban on slavery. Once Texas gained independence from Mexico in 1836, the new republic permitted slavery. Texas politicians aligned themselves with political leaders in the Southern states from the time Texas achieved statehood in 1845 and continued to stand with the South when Southern Democrats bolted the party and formed the Dixiecrats in 1948. Following the Civil War, Texans created racially segregated schools and colleges, disfranchised African Americans, and instituted poll taxes.

3. Walter Buenger, "Texas and the South," *Southwestern Historical Quarterly* 103, no.3 (2000): 309–324; Robert Engler, *The Politics of Oil* (Illinois: University of Chicago Press, 1961), 351; V. O. Key, *Southern Politics in State and Nation* (New York: Vintage Books, 1949), 260.

4. Virginia Durr to Maury Maverick Jr., 18 July 1962, Maury Maverick Jr. Papers, Center for American History, The University of Texas at Austin (hereafter cited as UTCAH), Box 3N412, Personal Files: July–August 1962.

5. Daniel J. Elazar, *American Federalism: A View from the States* (New York: Crowell, 1966), 86–103; Dan Nimmo and William Oden, *The Texas Political System* (Englewood Cliffs, N.J.: Prentice-Hall), 197–10, 50–54; David Nevin, *The Texans* (New York: Morrow, 1968), 182–183; Green, *The Establishment in Texas Politics*, 8–10.

6. Green, *The Establishment in Texas Politics*, 3–20.

7. Green, *The Establishment of Texas Politics*, 17, 25; Gunther, *Inside U.S.A.*, 839; Key, *Southern Politics*, 266.

8. Roger A. Griffin, "To Establish a University of the First Class," *Southwestern Historical Quarterly* 86 (October 1982): 135–160, reference on 150.

9. Lewis L. Gould, *Progressives and Prohibitionists: Texas Democrats in the Wilson Era* (Austin: University of Texas Press, 1973); Lewis L. Gould, "The University Becomes Politicized: The War With Jim Ferguson, 1915–1918," *Southwestern Historical Quarterly* 86 (October 1982): 255–276.

10. Article by William Sutton in *Educational Review*, November 1917, 390–409 in William Hogg Papers, UTCAH, Box 2J315, Ferguson Proceedings and Impeachment, vol. 2, July 1917–January 1919 folder, quote from 405.

11. James Ferguson to M. Faber, 25 September 1916, James Ferguson Papers, Texas State Library and Archives Commission (hereafter cited as TSLAC), Box 301–378, letterpress book, quote p. 2.

12. Gould, "The University Becomes Politicized," 276.
13. Norman D. Brown, *Hood, Bonnet, and Little Brown Jug* (College Station, Tex.: Texas A&M University Press, 1984), 161; Eugene Barker to M. B. Porter, 13 July 1923, Eugene Barker Papers, UTCAH, Box 2B129, UT Faculty Records Correspondence, 1923–1954 folder.
14. Brown, *Hood, Bonnet*, 166–167.
15. Carleton, *A Breed So Rare*, 157; "Dr. Muller Resigns to Become Genetics Expert for Russia," *Daily Texan*, 28 April 1936, 1, 4; Federal Bureau of Investigation, Hermann Muller Investigation, conducted April 1947, Bureau File # 116–2927, San Antonio File #116–266, available at the UTCAH.
16. Pope quote from "Benedict Unopposed to Investigation," *Daily Texan*, 10 January 1936, p. 1; Hermann J. Muller, *Out in the Night* (New York: Vanguard Press, 1935); "Muller Predicts Artificial Means for Parenthood," *Daily Texan*, 30 January 1936, p. 1; Carleton, *A Breed So Rare*, 157–158.
17. Carleton, *A Breed So Rare*, 158–159.
18. See Green, *The Establishment in Texas Politics*.
19. Ibid., 14.
20. Ibid., 15; George B. Tindall, *The Emergence of the New South, 1913–1945*, vol. 10, *A History of the South* (Baton Rouge: Louisiana State University Press, 1967), 618–619.
21. Key, *Southern Politics*, 255.
22. Green, *The Establishment in Texas Politics*, 16.
23. Texas held two state conventions during election years. The first occurred in May to select delegates for the national convention and to appoint presidential electors. The second convention occurred in September during which officials announced the results from the primaries and adopted a platform. In 1944, delegates who opposed Roosevelt gained control of the May proceedings and pledged to vote against the Democratic nominees. A third of the convention marched out of the convention and named a new set of delegates to the national convention. By September, Roosevelt supporters regained control of the state party and named a pro-Roosevelt slate. Those in opposition named themselves the Regulars, as in those who still stood for the traditional Democratic values and appeared on the ballot as their own party. These events are described in a number of sources including Green, *The Establishment in Texas Politics*, 45–57.
24. Green, *The Establishment in Texas Politics*, 79.
25. Stanley Schneider, "The Texas Regular Party of 1944," (Master's thesis, University of Chicago, 1948), 53, 97–102, 184; Green, *The Establishment in Texas Politics* 49.
26. *Austin American*, October 6, 1944.
27. Green, *The Establishment in Texas Politics*, 57.
28. SB 359, *Texas Senate Journal*, Regular sess., Forty-fifth Legislature (1937): SB 359 (compelling witnesses to testify before legislative bodies and committees under heavy penalty and denying privileges to refuse), 343, 373, 441, 508, 510, 519; *Texas House Journal*, Regular sess., Forty-seventh Legislature (1941): HB 313 (legal to kill Communists), 412, and HB222 (elimination of Communists from ballot), 293, 3602, 3900, 4012, 4228, 4295.
29. *Texas Senate Journal*, Regular sess., Forty-seventh Legislature (1941): SB 38 (loyalty oath for educators), 69, 124, 126, 131, 489,496, 2464–2465, 2481, 2500 and Senate Resolution 7 (establish little HUAC for Senate), 45–46, 163; Appropriations clause from *Subsection 17, Special Laws of the State of Texas, Forty-sixth Legislature* (1939), 448–449: "in order that the American people may be fully protected from all sources alien and un-American propaganda to the end that the American way of life shall be preserved and that war shall never again take the sons

of American mothers overseas to alien soil and into a holocaust brewed of the hates of the nations; and to this end in order that the youth of America may be protected against unscrupulous or unwise and un-American doctrines and principles, it is hereby further provided that any member of any faculty of any State-supported institution who shall advocate, subscribe to or believe in Communism, or in any form of totalitarian state doctrine, that is, that the individual citizen exists for the benefit and glory of the state, which is the opposite and antithesis of the American ideal and theory that all governments should exist for the benefit and glory of the citizens thereof, shall be discharged from such faculty when found guilty of advocating or encouraging such theories of government by the governing board of such institution." The Texas A&M Board of Directors printed this section in its entirety in its meeting minutes on 30 April 1940 and pledged to carry out their responsibility in controlling such teaching in their college, A&M Board of Directors' Minutes, 30 April 1940, 4.

30. *Texas Senate Journal,* Regular sess., Forty-seventh Legislature (1941): Senate Resolution 7 (establish little HUAC for Senate); *Texas House Journal,* 1st called sess., Forty-seventh Legislature (1941): HSR 12 (establish little HUAC for House), 62, 123, 630.

31. Following the formation of the Dies Committee, several state legislatures established Little Dies committees, including New York, California, and, briefly, Texas. New York established the Rapp-Coudert Committee in 1940 and conducted its most extensive investigation at the City College in New York (CCNY). This investigation lasted from June 1941 into 1942 and resulted in the dismissal of twenty faculty members and eleven resignations. California legislator Jack Tenney organized a committee in 1941, but it did not conduct a thorough investigation of the University of California until after the war. It is possible that Tenney saw no need to pursue communists in the University of California at Berkeley because its regents made it the first university in the nation to restrict membership in the Communist Party in 1940. See Ellen Schrecker, "Academic Freedom: The Historical View," in *Regulating the Intellectuals: Perspectives on Academic Freedom in the 1980s,* ed. by Craig Kaplan and Ellen Schrecker (New York: Praeger, 1983).

32. *Texas House Journal,* Regular sess., Forty-eighth Legislature (1943): HSR 158 (to investigate the *Daily Texan*), 888–889.

33. Ibid., 2876–2889, Rainey's quote on p. 2877.

34. *Smith v. Allwright,* 321 U.S. 649, 64 S. Ct. 757 (1944). A second case, *Sweatt v. Painter,* was decided in 1950, but this case had its roots in the early 1940s. The Supreme Court ruled that the makeshift law school established for blacks in 1946 was inferior to the UT law school and ordered Hermann Sweatt's admission to the white college in Austin. See Amlicar Shabazz, "The Opening of the Southern Mind: The Desegregation of Higher Education in Texas, 1865–1965" (Ph.D. diss., University of Houston, 1996), 74–76; Alan Brinkley, *The End of Reform: New Deal Liberalism in Recession and War* (New York: Vintage, 1995), 143.

35. T. S. Montgomery, *The Senior Colleges for Negroes in Texas: A Study Made at the Direction of the Bi-Racial Conference on Education for Negroes in Texas* (April 1944), 12, 83–84.

36. Bullington to John A. Lomax, 7 January 1944, John A. Lomax Papers, UTCAH, Box 3D154, "The Homer Rainey Controversy" folder.

37. "Higher Education Advantages for Negroes," *Texas Interracial Review* 2 (September 1942).

38. Maury Maverick Sr. to Maverick Jr., Maury Maverick Jr. Papers, UTCAH, Box 3N412, Personal File: 1941–1947, 1953, 1955, 1958 folder.

39. Ellen Schrecker, "Academic Freedom: The Historical View."
40. Walter P. Metzger, *Academic Freedom in the Age of the University* (New York: Columbia University Press, 1955), 202–204; Green, *The Establishment in Texas Politics*, 89.
41. "Higher Learning in Time of Crisis," *Bulletin of The American Association of University Professors* 26 (October 1940), 540–547.
42. Smith Act as quoted in Schrecker, *No Ivory Tower: McCarthyism and the Universities* (New York: Oxford University Press, 1986), 6; Alan Brinkley, *The End of Reform: New Deal Liberalism in Recession and War* (New York: Vintage, 1995), 141.
43. Seth McKay, *W. Lee O'Daniel and Texas Politics, 1938–1942* (Lubbock: Texas Technological College, 1944).
44. Carleton, *A Breed So Rare,* 186–210.
45. Coffman quote in Carleton, *A Breed So Rare,* 195; statements regarding Regents' concerns about Rainey on 195, 210.
46. George N. Green, *Handbook of Texas Online*, s.v. "Homer Price Rainey," http://www.tsha.utexas.edu/handbook/online/articles/view/RR/fra54.html (accessed 17 February 2005).
47. J. Orin Oliphant, *The Rise of Bucknell University* (New York: Appleton-Century-Crofts, 1965), 269–282.
48. University of Texas Board of Regents (hereafter cited as UTBOR) Minutes, 4 February 1939, 79.
49. Carleton, *A Breed So Rare,* 219–220, 223.
50. UTBOR Minutes, 29 July 1939, 277–279, 288–289, 314–317. The Division of Research contained the following: University of Research Institute ($25,000), Bureau of Municipal Research ($8,000), Bureau of Research in the Social Sciences ($17,550), Research in Zoology ($5,000), Research in Anthropology ($6,000), Research in Chemistry ($7,400), Bureau of Business Research ($33,850), Bureau of Economic Geology ($49,890), Bureau of Engineering Research ($14,977), and Bureau of Industrial Chemistry ($40,200); Carleton, *A Breed So Rare*, 220.
51. Roger L. Geiger, *To Advance Knowledge: The Growth of American Research Universities, 1900–1940* (New York: Oxford University Press, 1986), 212–213; Carleton, *A Breed So Rare,* 223.
52. Carleton, *A Breed So Rare,* 223–224, Lawrence quoted on 224.
53. Ibid., 224.
54. Ibid., 224–225, quote from 225.
55. Homer P. Rainey, "The State and Public Education" in *The State and Public Education, Inaugural Address of Homer P. Rainey as President of the University of Texas and the Papers and Discussion Presented at the Educational Conference, 7–9 December 1939*, ed. Arthur Brandon (Austin: University of Texas, 22 May 1940), quote on 8.
56. Rainey, "The State and Public Education," quote on 12.
57. Ibid., 15.
58. Carleton, *A Breed So Rare,* 226, UTBOR Minutes, 15 June 1940, 174.
59. UTBOR Minutes, 7–9 October 1939, 388–389; 13 January 1940, 445–453.
60. UTBOR Minutes, 13 January 1940, 445–453.
61. UTBOR Minutes, 10 April 1940, 49–50; 25 November 1940, 318.
62. Homer P. Rainey, *The Tower and the Dome* (Boulder, Co.: Pruett Publishing Company, 1971), 2–3; Gunther, *Inside U.S.A.*, 839. Gunther argued that the Texas governor had the power to make more governmental appointments than almost any governor in the United States, except perhaps the governor of Oklahoma.

63. Green, *The Establishment in Texas Politics,* 29.
64. "The University of Texas Controversy," pamphlet from J. R. Parten's statement to the Texas Senate Educational Committee, 28 November 1944; "The Tragedy at the University of Texas, a statement before the Senate Investigating Committee," 27 November 1944, by Robert Lee Bobbitt, Alexander C. Ellis Papers, UTCAH, Box 2P45, Rainey Crisis-General folder. Bobbitt was the former state attorney general, former speaker of the Texas House, and then vice president of the UT Ex-Students Association.
65. UTBOR Minutes, 31 May 1940, 71–72.
66. First quote: William M. Thorton, "Senate Okays 2 Wilkieites for Texas U," *Dallas Morning News,* 30 January 1941, section 8–1; Second quote: letter from D. K. Martin to W. Lee O'Daniel, 30 January 1940, W. Lee O'Daniel Papers, TSLAC, Box 2001/138–145, Resignation, UT Regents folder, TSLAC.
67. UTBOR Minutes, 26 July 1941, 18–19, quote on 18.
68. UTBOR Minutes, 29–30 September 1941, 88–90.
69. UTBOR Minutes, 25 October 1941, 112–117.
70. UTBOR Minutes, 22 November 1941, 123–128.
71. UTBOR Minutes, 28 February 1942, 197.
72. UTBOR Minutes, 198–199.
73. UTBOR Minutes, 11 March 1942, 224–225.
74. UTBOR Minutes, 22–23 May 1942, 315–324.
75. UTBOR Minutes, 8 August 1942, 491–492; 25 September 1942, 29.
76. Forty Acres was the amount of land originally designated as the University of Texas.
77. Rainey, *Tower,* 48–49.
78. A fourth individual, Valdemar Carleson, a visiting lecturer on leave from Antioch, joined the UT economists.
79. The National Labor Relations Act, also known as the Wagner Act, established the National Labor Relations Board and established workers' right to collective bargaining. The Fair Labor Standards Act of 1938 provided a national minimum wage and provided for overtime pay.
80. Texas had never been a place that was terribly receptive to labor unions. The American Federation (AFL) was certainly more palatable than its more radical counterpart, the Congress of Industrial Organizations (CIO). In 1941, the legislature passed an anti-union law that had been introduced by Governor O'Daniel. The O'Daniel law criminalized any use of force designed to prevent anyone from working and outlawed labor gatherings in the physical vicinity of any labor dispute. There were additional anti-labor rumblings, especially from the Texas State Manufactures Association, who accused the CIO of pledging its allegiance to the Soviet Union 1941—described more fully in Green, *Establishment in Texas Politics,* 31–32.
81. *Dallas Morning News,* 17 March 1942.
82. Green, *Establishment in Texas Politics,* 61–62. O'Daniel supported the Christian Americans, Vance Muse's anti-labor organization that had published a number of advertisements in the *Dallas Morning News* in which the group criticized unions for stifling war production with repeated strikes.
83. Rainey, *Tower,* 42–43.
84. George Green, Ronnie Dugger, and Homer Rainey each note that D. F. Strickland called for the dismissal of four economics professors during the January 1942 Regents' meeting. Rainey made this claim in his 1971 memoir and in a subsequent interview with Dugger. When Rainey asked him why, Strickland allegedly replied that the Regents did not approve of what these men were teaching. This story is impossible because Strickland was not even appointed until June 1942. Strickland

initiated a discussion on regulations regarding faculty dismissal in January 1943, and it is possible that Rainey confused his facts over the almost thirty years between the events and the publication of his book. It is also possible that Rainey confused January and June. Carleton notes that Strickland passed Rainey a note during the June 1942 meeting calling for the elimination of four economics instructors. See Green, *Establishment in Texas Politics,* 84; Rainey, *Tower,* 7–8; Dugger, *Our Invaded Universities,* 42–43; Carleton, *A Breed So Rare*, 301.

85. James L. Nelson to Stevenson, 20 July 1942, 7 July 1942 resolution by Democratic Club of Tarrant County attached; Resolution by the Austin League of Women Voters, 14 June 1942, addressed to UT Regents and Rainey; Mrs. Alfred Taylor to Stevenson (no date); Stevenson's reply to Taylor, 14 July 1942, Coke Stevenson Papers, TSLAC, Box 4/14–131, UT folder.
86. UTBOR Minutes, 25 September 1942, 34–35.
87. H. Bailey Carroll to Roy Bedichek, 13 February 1943, Roy Bedichek Papers, Box 3Q28, Webb Correspondence folder.
88. UTBOR Minutes, 30 January 1943, 143; 27 March 1943, 216–217.
89. UTBOR Minutes, 25 June 1943, 288.
90. UTBOR Minutes, 25 June 1943, 287–289; 16 July 1943, 329.
91. T. Whitfield Davidson to John H. Bickett, 13 September 1943, Stevenson Papers, Box 4/14–147.
92. Orville Bullington to John Lomax, 24 April 1944, John A. Lomax Papers, UTCAH, Box 3D154, Correspondence with Bullington folder; UT Regents' Minutes, 1 October 1943, 449.
93. Rainey, *Tower*, 43; Green, 86–87; Dugger, *Our Invaded Universities,* 44–47; *Addendum to the General Faculty Minutes, April 1, 1946, Report of the Faculty Council,* Ruth A. Allen Papers, UTCAH, Box 3G205, General Faculty Minutes folder, 1944–1946, 3396–4019.
94. UTBOR Minutes, 27 June 1942, 345, 357–359. Postponed projects are as follows: (1) Project #66, first approved by the Regents on 26 July 1941, C. A. Timm of the government department, for continuation of a social history project on the drainage basin of the Rio Grande (already funded, in part, by Carnegie Endowment for International Peace); (2) Project #73, first approved by the Regents on 22 November 1941, Mody Boatright and Harry Ransom of the English department, for continuation of a study of the impact of oil upon the folk culture of Texas; (3) #95, C.W. Reimuth of the classics department, for preparation of a dictionary of technical terms derived from Greek and used in specialized fields of science.
95. UTBOR Minutes, 27 June 1942, 345, 357–359. The Regents' objections to these programs pose more questions than answers, as there is no unifying theme in these proposals: (1) Project #92, submitted by D. L. Clark of the English department, to prepare a biography on the life of eighteenth-century horror novelist Charles Brockton Brown; (2) Project #3, submitted by C. M. Rosenquist of the sociology department, supplemental funds to produce the next issue of a faculty journal entitled *Southwestern Social Science Quarterly*; (3) Project #40, submitted by G. W. Stumberg of the law school, to extend a project first approved by the Regents in August 1940 on the phases of criminal law or criminal proceedings that may be in need of reform; (4) Project #65, submitted by Charles McCormick, dean of the law school, to continue a program first approved by the Regents in July 1941, to produce additional issues of the *Texas Law Review,* so as to increase publication opportunities for law school faculty; (5) Project #72, submitted by Robert Slayton of the law school, to extended a program first approved by the Regents in October 1941, to assess the Texas market for legal services; (6) Project #79, submitted by H. E. Moore of sociology, to continue a project first approved by the Regents in February 1942, to study war

booms in three Texas towns; and (7) Project #93, submitted by J. H. Frederick of the business administration school, to study the origins and current status of air transportation in Latin America.

96. Rainey, *Tower*, 47–48; Postponed projects #73 (see UTBOR Minutes 23 October 1942, 552–556) and #95 were later approved, as were rejected projects #72 and #92 renumbered #110 (see UTBOD 1–2 Minutes October 1943, 449, 457, 471–478).
97. "Communist murders" Orville Bullington's term. See Bullington's statement printed in UT General Faculty Meeting Minutes, 14 November 1944, 2851; Rainey, *Tower,* 48; Guenther, *Inside U.S.A.,* 856.
98. *Dallas Morning News*, 10 October 194; *Austin American,* 14 October 1944.
99. Rainey, *Tower,* 39–54.
100. Rainey, *Tower,* 56–57, Strickland reference from *Newsweek*, 13 November 1944, 84; Alice Cox, "The Rainey Affair," , 93.
101. Quote taken from Cox, "The Rainey Affair," 94–95, statement can be found in Rainey's testimony before the Senate Investigating Committee, Senate Proceedings, I, p. 114.
102. Cox, "The Rainey Affair," 92–98; Carleton, *A Breed So Rare*, 306–307.
103. While W. Lee O'Daniel was flamboyant, John Gunther describes Coke Stevenson as a "cool customer" who avoided conflict and worked towards compromise. Stevenson could slither through any hole or wedge through any crack to escape controversy (Gunther, *Inside U.S.A.,* quote on 840). When possible, Stevenson would allow divisive bills to pass without his signature such as in 1943 when he abstained from signing the Manford bill that placed a set of strict regulations on labor unions (Green, *The Establishment in Texas Politics,* 81).
104. Quote appears on page 87 of Green's *The Establishment in Texas Politics,* from a letter from Stevenson to Regent K. H. Aynesworth, 23 March 1943, full citation found on page 255, note 22.
105. Rainey, *Tower,* 58; Green, *The Establishment in Texas Politics,* 87; Gunther, *Inside U.S.A.*, 858; "Texas Ousts University Head," *New York Times*, 3 November 1944, p. 38; "Students Continue Protest," *New York Times,* 4 November 1944, p. 17.
106. *Dallas Morning News,* 26 January 1941, 12–1.
107. Bernard DeVoto, "The Easy Chair," *New Republic,* 191 (August 1945): 136–137.
108. Orville Bullington's "Reasons for Vote," printed on pages 2848–2858 in the minutes of the UT General Faculty, 14 November 1944, Ruth Allen Papers, UTCAH, Box 3G205, General Faculty Minutes folder, 1944–1946.
109. Bullington, "Reasons for Vote," 2848–2858.
110. Ibid., in addition, Bullington's opinions about *The Big Money* are revealed in a series of letters he wrote to his friend and folklorist John Lomax dated 12/17/42 and 1/25/43, in John A. Lomax Papers, UTCAH, Box 3D154, Correspondence with Orville Bullington folder.
111. *Ex parte* Billings, D. Kansas 46 F. Supp. 663 (1942).
112. Bullington, "Reasons for Vote," 2848–2858.
113. According to Rainey, the Regents interviewed this man after he had been arrested for engaging in homosexual activity. After two hours of questioning, Bullington and Regent Bickett concluded that the man was not a homosexual and innocent of the charges. Two weeks later, the man confessed before a grand jury in Austin. Rainey, *Tower,* 91.
114. *An Educational Crisis: A Summary of Testimony Before a Senate Committee Investigating the University of Texas Controversy,* 15–28 November 1944, Strickland quote on p. 2; Bullington to Lomax, 2 September 1945, John Lomax Papers, UTCAH, Box 3D154, Correspondence with Bullington folder.

115. UTBOR Minutes, 25–26 January 1945, 31–34.
116. UTBOR Minutes, 43–46.
117. UTBOR Minutes, 16 February 1945, 107–108.
118. UTBOR Minutes, 28 September 1945, 404–405, Southern Association representatives: President Herman L. Donovan, University of Kentucky (chair), Dean M.C. Huntley, University of Alabama, President Theodore H. Jack, Randolph Macon Woman's College, Dean W. W. Pierson, University of North Carolina, President Rufus C. Harris, Tulane (ex officio, chairman of the Executive Council of the Commission of Colleges and Secondary Schools).
119. UTBOR Minutes, 28 September 1945, 405.
120. Ibid., 406.
121. Ibid., 407–408.
122. Painter to Woodward, Dudley Woodward Papers, UTCAH, Box 2Q125, UT Southern Association folder.
123. UTBOR Minutes, 5 August 1949, 408–409.
124. "Lite: A Menu for Realistic Thought," 5 August 1945; "Probation News," 30 July 1945, vol. 1, no. 1, Dudley Woodward Papers, UTCAH, Box 2Q125, UT-Southern Association folder.
125. "Resolution Adopted by Members of Common Sense Organization," 10 September 1945, Theophilus Painter Papers, UTCAH, Box 2.325/M88C, Speeches 1944 folder.
126. Carleton, *A Breed So Rare*, 305; Cox, "The Rainey Affair," 135–136; Green, 96.
127. Walter Webb to Roy Bedichek, 13 March 1945, Roy Bedichek Papers, UTCAH, Box 3Q28, Webb Correspondence folder.
128. Dudley Woodward to Benjamin Clayton, 21 July 1945, Theophilus Painter Papers, UTCAH, Box 2.325/M88C, Speeches 1944 folder.

A Not-So-Systematic Effort to Study Art: Albert Barnes and Lincoln University

Edward Epstein and Marybeth Gasman

This study explores historically black Lincoln University's relationship with the famed Barnes Foundation. The authors explore the extent to which Albert Barnes's choice to place his Foundation under the control of African Americans was an outgrowth of his beliefs about the potential black people offered in the area of art and culture. Conversely, the authors examine the efforts made by Lincoln University to use Barnes's resources. In light of recent court decisions that effectively nullified Barnes's wishes regarding the collection and transferred power from Lincoln University to a cadre of large philanthropic foundations, the study asks whether or not the institution in its current form offers greater potential to include African Americans in the cultural mainstream.

As a rule, art is housed in museums controlled by wealthy and powerful individuals. In the quiet suburb of Lower Merion, just west of Philadelphia, there is a huge exception to this rule: Albert Barnes's magnificent collection of early modern masterpieces, which is controlled by the small and sometimes struggling, historically black, Lincoln University. What led to this arrangement and what are its consequences for the education of African Americans?

Since Barnes's untimely death in 1951, the Barnes Foundation, which houses his collection, has been mired in controversy.[1] From the time he chartered his foundation in 1922, Barnes tightly controlled access to the artworks. The institution was not a museum but a house of study, Barnes insisted, and therefore, visitors were admitted by invitation only and viewed the collection under the tutelage of Barnes and his staff. To this day, guests of the Barnes Foundation must make appointments weeks in advance of their pilgrimage (twenty-five minutes by train from Philadelphia) to the stately French-style mansion that houses the collection.

Perspectives on the History of Higher Education 24 (2005): 173-190.
©2005. ISBN: 1-4128-0517-1

The apparent guardedness of the Barnes Foundation towards its audiences seems out of place in a city with so many rich cultural offerings. However, during his lifetime, Barnes made enemies of the Philadelphia cultural stewards, and he stipulated in his Foundation's by-laws that, "no Trustee shall be a member of the faculty or Board of Trustees or Directors of the University of Pennsylvania, Temple University, Bryn Mawr, Haverford or Swarthmore Colleges, or Pennsylvania Academy of the Fine Arts."[2] Upon his death, Barnes placed the Foundation under the direction of associates who shared his non-traditional ideas about art.[3] After the tenure of the Barnes insiders expired, the Foundation's indenture stipulated that the majority of its trustees would be appointed by Lincoln University, a black college outside of Philadelphia. During the 1950s and 60s the Pennsylvania attorney general made an unsuccessful attempt to dislodge the collection from its caretakers, citing the Foundation's irregular and seemingly exclusionary policies toward visitors.[4] During the period from Barnes's death to the point at which Lincoln-appointed trustees took over, the Foundation experienced continued financial decline.[5] Further financial mismanagement marred the tenure of Lincoln-appointed trustee Richard Glanton. A recent court decision has made it almost inevitable that Dr. Barnes's treasured art collection, long protected by an odd combination of educational vision and personal vendetta, will be moved against his wishes to a place where it will be more accessible to the public. The likely home would be on Benjamin Franklin Parkway in the heart of Philadelphia's museum district—joining a truly world class block of cultural establishments and adding to an important tourist attraction.[6]

But in this current controversy, we argue, the racial question is more critical. The recently approved changes to the Barnes Foundation's by-laws would expand the number of board members from five to fifteen, with the additional members appointed not by Lincoln but by large foundation donors such as Annenberg, Pew, and Lenfest.[7] A change like this would effectively nullify Lincoln's control of the Foundation. This article asks whether Barnes's decision to place the board under Lincoln's control was merely an act of spite against his personal enemies or a genuine part of his complex educational philosophy—an attempt, in effect, to embed a different perspective on art in the governance of the institution and ensure that African Americans had a direct connection to this outstanding cultural resource.

Previous scholars have described the Barnes Foundation's educational program as being organized on John Dewey's principle of "art as experience."[8] Barnes was an admirer of the great Pragmatist philosopher and educator, and his writings certainly show Dewey's influence.[9] However, it would be an oversimplification to claim that Dewey provided the blueprint for Barnes's educational efforts. The relationship between the two men was much more of a two-way street, with Barnes providing the inspiration for many of Dewey's writings, including the text *Art as Experience*.[10] More accurately, the guiding principles of the Barnes Foundation were an amalgamation of ideas the millionaire industrialist had developed over the years, some through academic pursuits, some through collecting art, and some through running the factory that made him his millions. Among them was an abiding interest in the culture of Africans and African Americans—an interest he claimed went back to his childhood. This led him to amass an outstanding collection of African tribal art, to write books on the subject, to offer financial support to African American artists, and on numerous occasions, to publicly demand that blacks be treated as equals.[11]

If African American culture was on Barnes's mind when he chartered his foundation, we argue that it should be part of the debate over the Foundation's future. The nonprofit community is greatly concerned that Barnes's wishes have been overturned, creating a precedent for large concentrations of wealth and power to override donor intent.[12] Why is this important? Of what significance is it to the greater good whether society honors the wishes of the millionaire Barnes or the billionaire foundations (Pew, Lenfest, and Annenberg)? In this instance, we believe the debate over nonprofit law touches larger questions of race, culture, and society. For if Barnes really intended that a small black college control his art collection, his actions were in a sense empowering, and those of the large foundations debilitating: in their attempt to build a cultural Mecca in Philadelphia, these prominent donors overlooked a core part of Barnes's perspective. The question raised here, then, is twofold. First, to what extent was Dr. Barnes's choice to place his Foundation under the control of African Americans an outgrowth of his beliefs about the potential black people offered in the area of art and culture? Second, in the years after Barnes's death, what efforts were made by Lincoln University—in whose hands the collection would ultimately rest—to utilize Barnes's resources?

To examine these questions, we reviewed course catalogs, syllabi, letters, and newspapers in the Lincoln University archives as well as publications by the Barnes Foundation (housed in the University of Pennsylvania School of Design Library). We also reviewed materials previously written on the Barnes Foundation—including scholarly research, general readership texts, and journalistic accounts. Lastly, we read the original works of both John Dewey and Albert Barnes to understand their philosophy of art education.

Albert C. Barnes: Industrialist and Collector

Born in 1872, the son of a butcher, Albert C. Barnes grew up in a working class neighborhood in Philadelphia. As a child he was interested in art but ultimately decided to pursue a career in science and medicine. His talents in these areas helped him to attain a medical degree in 1892 from the University of Pennsylvania and additional training at the University of Heidelberg in Germany in 1900. It was at this time that he concocted (along with German chemist Hermann Hille) the formula for a silver-based compound called Argyrol—that prevented, among other things, infant blindness. By manufacturing this compound, which required little space and only a handful of employees, Barnes was able to amass a huge fortune by the end of the first decade of the twentieth century.[13]

The newly wealthy inventor soon found that he had too much time on his hands. Rebuffed by the foxhunting crowd in the Philadelphia suburbs where he lived (his street-bred manners were much too coarse for them), Barnes decided in 1912 to devote himself to collecting modern art. Drawing on his hitherto undeveloped visual capabilities (along with his business acumen), he was able to acquire a first-rate collection of Impressionist, Post-Impressionist, and early Modern masterpieces in a brief time span. Beginning in the early 1920s, he would add to that a significant collection of African sculptures. At the same time he began collecting art, Barnes was developing an interest in Progressive educational philosophies. An ardent admirer of the Pragmatist philosopher William James, he believed it possible—and he attributed his own success to this—to apply a kind of scientific method to the resolution of all sorts of mysteries, from the understanding of a painting to how to win in the boxing ring.[14] He thought that, presented in the proper setting and in a way that was geared toward the learner, education could help any individual achieve his or her full potential. According to Barnes:

> Education is the complete and harmonious development of all the capacities with which an individual is endowed at birth, a development which requires, not coercion or standardization, but guidance of the interests of every individual towards a form that shall be uniquely characteristic of him.[15]

In 1915, Barnes decided to put his theories into practice at the Argyrol factory. He instituted a daily program of study that introduced workers—some without high school diplomas—to the philosophy of William James, the aesthetics of George Santayana, and the appreciation of Barnes's burgeoning collection of early modern masterpieces, including works by Matisse, Cezanne, Picasso, among others. The goal, according to Barnes's longtime employee and study leader Mary Mullen, was to "present knowledge stripped of its academic trappings, in a form relevant to actual problems."[16] This daily experiment in education would provide the blueprint for the Barnes Foundation, when it was chartered as an educational institution in 1922.[17] Although the education of the masses seemed a noble goal, one might ask whether in this guise—the presentation of erudite texts to an audience that could barely read—the experiment had more to do with Barnes's desire to indoctrinate his subordinates and create a showcase for his ideas.

While professing a faith in Pragmatic education, Barnes expressed disdain for more traditional academicism, especially where it was connected to art. It was this view that led to some of his famous battles with established educational institutions, notably the University of Pennsylvania and the Philadelphia public school system.[18] His failed attempts to develop partnerships with these institutions resulted in part from his brash dismissal of their conservative attitudes, but also from his unwillingness to compromise on logistical and leadership decisions. Moreover, he seemed to think that the wrong kind of erudition could muddle and confuse the creation of art—and he cited this as a reason that African art had exceeded its European counterpart in its understanding of three-dimensional form. In his 1925 volume, *The Art in Painting* (and in an essay appearing in the 1929 collection *Art and Education*), Barnes made the following comparison of African and Greek sculpture:

> In the early periods of Greek sculpture figures were conceived as combinations of back, front, and side bas-reliefs. Design was too often encumbered by representation, so that the arrangement of masses—head, trunk, and limbs—which would have made the most effective esthetic ensemble, is rarely found. Literature, in other words, stood in the way of plastic form. With Negro sculpture, the literary motive is submerged in the artist's distribution of masses in accord with the requirements of a truly sculptural design.

> There is no suggestion of bas-relief: the figures are three-dimensional through and through. Freedom from the adventitious or meaningless gives Negro art a sculptural quality purer than that of the best Greek work or of Renaissance sculpture, which is Greek in another guise.[19]

Here Barnes points to the "freedom" in "Negro" art but also the tendentious aspect of some Greek art ("encumbered by representation") that he feels prevents it from attaining a fully sculptural quality.

The notion that African artists showed a unique gift for the manipulation of pure form was more fully developed in *Primitive Negro Sculpture*, one of the first volumes devoted entirely to that subject. Although the book listed Paris art dealer Paul Guillaume and aesthetic philosopher Thomas Munro as its authors, it was truly a Barnes affair. These two individuals were both closely affiliated with Barnes (Guillaume advised him in amassing his collection of African art, and Munro was an instructor at the Barnes Foundation). Moreover, much of the art cited and reproduced in the book was from the Barnes collection, and it is widely believed that Barnes wrote large portions of the text.[20]

On the very first page of the book, the authors put forth the notion that African art had advanced beyond European. Describing the discovery of African sculpture by modern European artists in the first decade of the twentieth century, they said,

> the small wooden figures, carved many centuries ago by unknown artists of the jungle, were superior in many ways to the finished products of the academies. These figures were not mere childish attempts to make our kind of statue; they were successful attempts to make an entirely different kind of statue. Where they seemed to be misshapen, badly proportioned, they were really fashioned with consummate skill to achieve effects that Europeans had not been able to see or appreciate. Instead of being the beginnings of art, valuable only as historical relics, they were perhaps a stage in advance of European evolution, and valuable as ideals.[21]

The book went on to disparage all previous writings on the subject, and declare (in a rather self-serving manner) its intent to take a more objective look at the subject. It aimed its fiercest barbs at art critics, who it accused of "premature and over confident generalizations."[22] In typical Barnes fashion, the prose was overflowing with contempt for these high society arbiters of culture:

> The manner is easy, journalistic, sprinkled with scientific phrases, but enlivened with anecdotes that reveal his [the art critic's] personal acquaintance with celebrities, and his knowledge of the lives of minor artists of the past. He is inclined to be blasé, with an air of having outgrown callow enthusiasms, but of possessing an exquisitely rarefied

sensitivity to beauties which the vulgar can never feel. His comment on Negro art will consist of a little gossip of art circles, a few generalities expressed in vague technical jargon, a few dogmatic appraisals and much airing of personal preferences.[23]

The feeling expressed by the book, then, was one part zealous admiration for African art, one part unmitigated contempt for the cultural establishment.

A problematic aspect of the book was its claim that the genius expressed by African sculpture belonged to the distant past, and that centuries of oppression had sucked the life out of more recent creative efforts by blacks. In a section entitled "The Negro Mind," the book asserted the basic proposition that any lack of accomplishment on the part of blacks within white society was the result of centuries of slavery and exploitation.

Thus, the question that emerges, in the reading of Barnes's ideas about African artists, is whether he regarded them with genuine admiration and respect or as just a useful ally in his quarrel with polite society. He believed (perhaps as a consequence of having been marginalized himself) that all that was pure and true lay outside the boundaries of the establishment. African art, one might conclude, was great in Barnes's mind because it was outside of the European mainstream; it ceased to be great as soon as it mixed with white culture.

But regardless of the position Barnes took in *Primitive Negro Sculpture*, the fact is, Barnes appreciated much in black culture that was not isolated from European civilization. In delivering a 1936 speech to his high school alma mater, Philadelphia Central High, he publicly stated that his curiosity about blacks began as a result of a childhood experience at a revival meeting:

> My experience with the Negro began when I was eight years old. It was at a camp-meeting in Mercantville, New Jersey, and the impression was so vivid and so deep that it has influenced my whole life.... I became an addict to Negro camp-meetings, baptizings, revivals, and to seeking the company of Negroes who, as I soon discovered, carried out in their daily lives the poetry, music, dance, and drama which, when exercised by a group, give the camp-meeting its colorful, rhythmic, vivid, and compelling charm.[24]

Perhaps as a result of his camp-meeting experiences, the singing of spirituals would become a regular feature at Barnes Foundation events, alongside of European orchestral music. Much of Barnes's effort as an adult would be dedicated to promoting the work of then unrecognized African American artists; Barnes is counted among the few white promoters of the Harlem Renaissance. He attended a well-known 1924 dinner at New York's Civic Club in which black writers mingled with white publishers—an event that boosted the careers of Langston Hughes and Zora Neale Hurston, among others.[25] He and his Foundation staff were regular contributors to *Opportunity* magazine, which published the works of these Harlem Renaissance luminaries, and whose editor, Charles S. Johnson, was responsible for organizing the Civic Club dinner.[26] And his Foundation offered scholarship support to emerging black artists wishing to study there, including painters Aaron Douglas and Claude Clark and writer and artist Gwendolyn Bennett.[27]

While promoting the work of contemporary black artists, Barnes actively opposed policies that discriminated against them. In one incident during the late 1940s, scholarship recipient Claude Clark was invited to exhibit his work at his former high school in Philadelphia. In a typically racist presumption, however, the principal doubted Clark's assertion that a millionaire white collector like Barnes would attend the opening. In response, Barnes and his entire Foundation staff crowded into the principal's office on the day of the reception, then marched with Clark into the auditorium to greet the assembly of students. Another incident enlisted a 1949 juried art exhibition at the University of Alabama, which accepted entries from students at the all-black Talladega College, but did not permit them to attend the opening. In protest, Barnes used a well-organized letter writing campaign that involved John Dewey, artists Max Weber and Rockwell Kent, and political figure Harold Ickes to encourage keynote speakers Thomas Munro (the former Barnes Foundation instructor) and Henry Francis Taylor (of the Metropolitan Museum of Art) to boycott the event.[28] Together these actions by Barnes in support of contemporary black artists suggest more than a superficial appreciation of the contributions of blacks, and one that extended beyond the notion of a pure African art that predated European civilization.

Complicating the picture further was the fact that Barnes was always willing to defend an outcast as long as he or she pledged complete loyalty. Barnes surrounded himself with a diverse group of artists and intellectuals who, although controversial at the time, are now part of the pantheon of great figures of the twentieth century. These included philosopher Bertrand Russell, who was given a Barnes Foundation appointment when he was barred from teaching at the City College of New York in 1943 for his "libertarian opinions about sexual morals, education, and war."[29] Soon dismissed from the Barnes Foundation as well (having incurred the wrath of his patron), Russell said of Barnes, "he enjoys the company of Negroes and dogs because he considers neither his equal."[30] In this view, Barnes's embrace of the outsider was borne of profound insecurity. It was the behavior of a man who, having been given the cold shoulder by polite society, surrounded himself with others in a similar situation—partly because he could understand them and partly because they depended on him.

Power in the Hands of Lincoln University

Lincoln University in Pennsylvania was established in 1854 as Ashmun Institute,[31] "the first institution found anywhere in the world to provide a higher education in the arts and sciences for male youth of African descent."[32] The black college was located in southern Chester County, near Oxford, Pennsylvania—approximately forty-five miles southwest of Philadelphia and thirty miles west of Lower Merion, the home of the Barnes Foundation. The Foundation's association with Lincoln University is the byproduct of a friendship between Lincoln's eighth president Horace Mann Bond and Albert Barnes.[33] The relationship began with Bond asking Barnes to make a donation to Lincoln in 1950. Failing to gain Barnes's financial support, the college president asked him to teach a class at the University. The art collector declined but he began to develop a warm relationship with Bond, which resulted in another arrangement between the two institutions. In this partnership, Barnes provided a lecturer to teach a small group of Lincoln students at the Foundation's gallery. Excited by the collaboration with Lincoln, the millionaire wrote to Bond saying that, "when given the proper opportunity, the Negro demonstrates that his intellectual capacity is at least equal to that of the white man" and "his endowment of aesthetic appreciation is even greater than that of the average white man."[34]

Horace Mann Bond never succeeded in obtaining gifts from Barnes; however, the millionaire amended the Foundation's by-laws to give Lincoln the authority to select trustees following his death and that of his wife.[35] In typical Barnes fashion, the collector was unwilling to give a penny of his money for use at another's discretion. But he was willing to share his assets in ways that showcased his ideas and supported those who had pledged loyalty to him—more so if there was a chance to show spite for the establishment in the process. Thus, what seemed like an enormously generous act—the apparent bequest of an unrivaled art collection—was ill-conceived in ways that the Barnes Foundation and Lincoln University staff could never have imaged at the time. Correspondence between Barnes and the Lincoln University dean showed that the collaboration was off to a rocky start; however, Barnes's untimely 1951 death in a car accident eliminated any chance for a meaningful alliance to evolve.

Art in the Curriculum

From the beginning the attempt to place Barnes Foundation resources at the disposal of the Lincoln University community was thwarted by Albert Barnes's authoritarian tendencies. Rather than consulting Horace Mann Bond and the Lincoln faculty about the best way to proceed, the millionaire collector looked upon the Lincoln relationship as another means for spreading Barnes Foundation gospel. Barnes simply grafted his existing curriculum onto the Lincoln course catalog.

The 1950–51 catalog boasted a separate section labeled "the Barnes Foundation courses in art," which included a two-page explanation, obviously written by Barnes Foundation staff.[36] The content of this explanation included typical Barnes rhetoric, Deweyan "art as experience" philosophy, and a not-so-subtle rebuke of society ladies who take art classes:

> The appreciation of works of art requires organized effort and systematic study.... Art is not a phase of life apart from the workaday world, to which one may turn in moments of leisure, or perhaps in the name of "culture" or in a spirit of worship.... The Barnes Foundation is not a public gallery. It is an educational institution with a program for systematic work, organized into classes and conducted by a staff of experienced teachers.[37]

After this explanation, the catalog listed two one-year courses held at the Barnes Foundation, each of which was worth six credits. Jon Longaker, a Barnes Foundation staff member, was the instructor during the first year that these courses were offered.[38] Clearly, the manner in which this material was inserted into Lincoln's curriculum offered no opportunity for input from the black college's faculty. Instead, it burdened the university with Barnes's personal neuroses and unresolved conflicts.

Proceeding in this manner, the Barnes Foundation was repeating a pattern of failed collaboration that the collector himself had established years earlier. As mentioned, Barnes had previously attempted to forge a similar alliance with the University of Pennsylvania. The potential partnership failed because Barnes refused to compromise. In Barnes's mind, it was the responsibility of students and faculty at the institution with which he was working to adjust its worldview to accommodate the Barnes Foundation approach.[39]

Through the 1950s the Barnes Foundation-Lincoln teaching collaboration faded away uneventfully. The Barnes course continued to appear in the catalog up to 1958, but beginning in 1955, the classes were offered with no credit.[40] A letter to Horace Mann Bond from college dean J. Newton Hill, dated February 16, 1954, explained some of the logistical difficulties in making the Barnes partnership work—the lack of transportation, but above all the fact that only a small number of students (enough to fill a station wagon) were interested in the program. According to Dean Hill,

> It appears to me that the success of our entire arrangement for this sort of extension study can be justified only when transportation difficulties have been decreased. I can conceive of no satisfactory arrangement for a successful solution to our problem short of the purchase of a modestly priced station wagon capable of transporting at least six students in comfort....[41]

Although the letter states that Barnes Foundation chair and educational program director Violette de Mazia was "entirely favorable to a new approach in the study of art and in the arrangements to that study as a part of [the] project 'New Program' at Lincoln University," there is no evidence that the Barnes Foundation director ever offered to purchase a vehicle like the one described in Dean Hill's letter.[42] Had Albert Barnes been alive, he may have—just as he did countless other times—provided transportation for those he deemed worthy of seeing his collection.[43]

In addition to the logistical problems, an essential ingredient needed to sustain any program of this type was missing: an established interest within the Lincoln community in the study of visual art. At the time the partnership began, Lincoln had neither art courses nor a faculty member in that area. With Barnes being perhaps the only person involved with a vision for Lincoln's use of the collection (Barnes associates such as Violette de Mazia apparently did not share this vision), the collector's death made the collapse of the curriculum inevitable. After 1958, no reference to Barnes Foundation classes appears in the Lincoln University course catalogs.

It is instructive to compare the Lincoln-Barnes collaboration with another black college art program from the same time—Fisk University in Nashville, Tennessee, received an infusion of modern art in 1949 when Georgia O'Keeffe donated her late husband Alfred Stieglitz's major collection (also including works of Picasso, Cezanne, and Matisse). This collection continues to be housed at the Fisk campus, and although at times its use has lapsed, it is a focal point of the college and art department curriculum. Besides the obvious factor that the Stieglitz collection is located on the campus itself, not thirty miles away, the Fisk arrangement has been more successful because the impetus for its acquisition and use was largely from within the school itself. Fisk's president, Charles S. Johnson, who was mentioned earlier as the organizer of the famed 1924 Civic Club dinner, was the conduit for bringing the collection to the campus. When installed, it found a home in an already established art department led by Harlem Renaissance painter Aaron Douglas (who happened to be a beneficiary of the Barnes Foundation fellowship program).[44] Moreover, the campus curriculum in which this art department was situated included a wide array of artistic and cultural experiences, many of which were led by President Johnson's former Harlem Renaissance colleagues, including writer Arna Bontemps and poet Langston Hughes. By comparison to the Fisk-O'Keeffe arrangement, the Barnes-Lincoln collaboration seems much more like an add-on to the curriculum than a fully integrated campus program.

Conclusion

Critics of the Barnes Foundation frequently claim that the millionaire's decision to put the control of the Barnes collection in the hands of Lincoln University was primarily an act of spite.[45] A self-made man, Barnes was forever in opposition to the established elites who refused him entry into their social circles. Barnes's spite explained his incessant battles with the town fathers in Lower Merion, the Philadelphia museum crowd, and the university community—and according to critics, his continual threats to invite the "Negro" into these circles.[46] The difference with Lincoln University is that this time he made good on his threat. To those who would dismantle the Barnes Foundation, the Lincoln partnership was just another eccentric decision on the part of Barnes—a decision whose lack of foresight is borne out by Lincoln University's failure to capitalize on its connection to the Foundation.

A close examination of Barnes's life and an understanding of historically black colleges show that these claims, although substantive, do not fully explain the situation. Contrary to the words of his critics, Barnes supported African Americans not merely "as a weapon"; his kinship with blacks and their art began when he was a child and extended to a vast array of experiences, including music, sculpture, and literature. His admiration for black art included the works of contemporary African Americans as well as "tribesmen" from previous centuries.[47] According to Roy Sieber, the book *Primitive Negro Sculpture*—penned by Guillaume and Munro, but really expressing Barnes's ideas—was groundbreaking in its appreciation of African creative genius: "*Primitive Negro Sculpture* accords the African artists creative agency, thereby refuting modernist criticism of its time, which saw this work as a product of pure instinct."[48] Barnes's appreciation for art by blacks placed him in the center of the Harlem Renaissance social milieu—as shown by the inclusion of his chapter in Alain Locke's *The New Negro* and his invitation to Charles S. Johnson's Civic Club dinner.[49] Finally, when directed against racist forces, Barnes's tendency to make a public nuisance of himself was an effective tool for protest. Although self-serving on some level, Barnes's refusal to tolerate racism at the University of Alabama's art exhibition, for example, was not meaningless.

Although it is accurate to say that Lincoln University has not taken full advantage of its ties to the Barnes collection, it would be unfair to say that the black college has mismanaged the Foundation. Throughout their history, black colleges have been an easy target for malicious accusations that are not grounded in an understanding of the culture or inner workings of these institutions.[50] Lincoln University-appointed attorney Richard Glanton has been at the center of the Barnes controversy. An ambitious African American selected to represent Lincoln on the Barnes Foundation board in the late 1980s, Glanton attempted to treat the collection in much the same way many prominent white-run museums have treated theirs—as a "cash cow." For example, he organized a high-profile world tour for the Barnes collection, he attempted to sell off paintings to raise money for the endowment, and he sold the reproduction rights for items in the collection to publishing companies—all of which were forbidden or discouraged by the Foundation's by-laws.[51] Most notorious among Glanton's efforts was his attempt to triple the number of visitors to the collection by adding a new parking lot. When nearby residents protested, Glanton responded by filing a race discrimination lawsuit against the town of Merion. After years of litigation, the Foundation was left with no parking lot and $6 million in legal fees. Glanton's attempts at promoting Barnes's resources did not net nearly the amount of cash he expected they would, and as a result the foundation was pushed to the brink of bankruptcy. However, the high-powered lawyer was neither a Lincoln University faculty member nor administrator. His actions were not those of the Lincoln art department and were not undertaken as part of the campus curriculum. Moreover, the fact that Barnes's endowment has been squandered is as much the fault of the ill-advised investment strategies of the white trustees who ran the collection immediately after Barnes's death as it is of Glanton and other African American Lincoln University-appointed trustees.

Recent debate about the future of the Barnes Foundation produced a storm of righteous indignation. While one side recoiled in horror at the effort to undo a deceased man's wishes, the other shouted with equal vehemence about the beleaguered institution's inability to maintain the delicate treasures in his collection.[52] The Barnes Foundation board itself led the charge to reinvent itself as a mainstream institution and relocate to Philadelphia. The core of its argument was that without such a change the institution would soon disintegrate. And the court that decided the Foundation's future seemed to agree. In an opinion on the decree to amend the Foundation's by-laws, Judge Stanley Ott found "...that expanding the size of the Board of Trustees [hence nullifying Lincoln's control] was appropriate in today's sophisticated world of charitable fundraising," and moreover,

> that the Foundation was on the brink of financial collapse, and that the provision in Dr. Barnes' indenture mandating that the gallery be maintained in Merion was not sacrosanct...provided we were convinced the move to Philadelphia represented the least drastic modification of the indenture that would accomplish the donor's desired ends.[53]

Those in the nonprofit community have complained that the legal reasoning here is circuitous and fails to honor donor intent.[54] The changes requested represent "the least drastic modification" of Barnes's indenture because without them the large foundations will withhold their infusion of cash.[55] Without their support, the Barnes Foundation will not succeed as the mainstream institution the donors (and not Dr. Barnes) want it to become. In spite of its profession of good faith toward Barnes's will, the current Foundation's efforts (in tandem with those of the governor, the mayor, and three of the area's largest philanthropic foundations) to locate the Barnes collection in Philadelphia's throbbing artery of culture are a little bit unseemly. For truly, was not Barnes's goal in setting up the Foundation to create a sort of "un-museum"—a temple of quiet, a testament to the donor's often quirky but sometimes prescient choices, and a place distant from precisely the "sophisticated world of charitable fund raising"—to which the judge referred? The Barnes Foundation is definitely rough around the edges, and intentionally so: it is the art collection equivalent of the "independent label" in filmmaking or music recording.

And one aspect of Barnes's independence is its affiliation with a historically black college. Why is this intolerable to so many people? That Barnes burdened Lincoln with his trail of soured relationships is regrettable; that he gave the black university control of his collection is not. Had it been successful, this partnership could have translated Barnes's enthusiasm for black culture into a working laboratory for an African-centered approach to the appreciation of art. This effort might have united the study of African tribal art, the modern European art that it inspired, and contemporary work by black artists. Such an institution might have resembled the center for the study of black culture that Barnes threatened to create in 1927 in response to a dispute with the Lower Merion town fathers over real estate. Although cited as another example of Barnes's contempt for his neighbors, this proposal had in it all of the ingredients of his educational philosophy and long-running interest in black art:

> In order to make the native qualities of the Negro contributory to a richer and more intelligent civilization in America, plans are being prepared to have the Barnes Foundation property serve as a national center for the development, by scientific educational methods of the rare, artistic, and mental endowments of the Negro.[56]

Thus, the Barnes Foundation might have become, like the black college that controlled it, a uniquely African-centered institution. This lost potential for the creation of such an institution—more than lost admission receipts—should be on the minds of those who undertake to rebuild the Foundation in the upcoming years.

Notes

1. Barnes's life was cut short in 1951 when his car was hit by a truck at an intersection in suburban Philadelphia.
2. By-Laws of the Barnes Foundation, 1950, Article IX, p. 7.
3. Barnes surrounded himself with a closely knit group of disciples—some were university-trained art historians and philosophers and others were employees of his factory in whom he instilled a mix of ideas stemming from Pragmatist philosophy

and including a unique appreciation of modern art. Perhaps his closest associate was Violette de Mazia, an émigré from Paris who showed up in a Barnes Foundation class in 1925 and formed a life-long relationship with the millionaire. De Mazia headed the educational program at the Foundation and after Barnes's death became the chair of its board of trustees. She maintained a tight grip, not only over the Foundation's educational policies, but its funding as well, until her death in 1989. Other members of the Barnes staff included Dewey protégé Thomas Munro, Princeton-trained Laurance Buermeyer, French art dealer Paul Guillaume, and former secretary from Barnes's Argyrol factory, Mary Mullen.

4. John Anderson, *Art Held Hostage: The Battle Over the Barnes Collection* (New York: W. W. Norton, 2003), 52–54.

5. Barnes was an astute financial manager, having prospered during the Depression by maintaining investments in government bonds during the time that the stock market was in decline. His successor, Violette de Mazia, made the mistake of replicating Barnes's financial strategy during a time when the stock market soared and bond returns were flat. The result of this was that the Barnes endowment lost money during the years following his death: Howard Greenfield, *The Devil and Dr. Barnes* (New York: Penguin Books, 1987).

6. Kendra Hamilton, "A Battle of Wills," *Black Issues in Higher Education* 20, no. 11 (17 July 2003); Richard Feigen, "Barnes Betrayed," *Art Newspaper* 13 (13 January 2003); Lucinda Fleeson, "Opening the Barnes Door: How America's Most Paranoid Art Museum Got That Way and How, Under New Management Dramatic Changes Are on the Way," *Philadelphia Inquirer*, 1991 reprint; Michael Rubencam, "Barnes President Says Donors Unwilling to Give," Associated Press, 8 December 2003; Carol Vogel, "Only a Move Will Prevent Bankruptcy Barnes Says," *New York Times*, 9 December 2003; John Hurdle, "Court to Way Fate of Famed U.S. Art Collection," Reuters, 23 November 2003; John Pulley, "Barnes Collection Seeks to Cut Lincoln University's Role," *Chronicle of Higher Education* 49, no. 10, (1 November 2002); Robert Hughes and Daniel S. Levy, "Opening the Barnes door," *Time Magazine* 141, no. 19 (10 May 1993); Ernest Beck, "The Barnes Battle Continues," *Art News* 102, no. 1 (January 2003); Ralph Blumenthal, "Audit Sharply Criticizes Art Institution's Dealings," *New York Times*, 2 July 2003; Acel Moore, "Barnes: Ego Fest, Not Race," *Philadelphia Inquirer*, 10 June 2003; Patricia Horne, "Barnes Relocation Campaign is Shaking," *Philadelphia Inquirer*, 8 June 2003; Edward J. Sozanski, "For Barnes' Disciples, a Schism over Dogma," *Philadelphia Inquirer*, 18 July 2004; John Hurdle, "Barnes Museum Can Move to Downtown Philly," *ABC News*, 13 December 2004; Hedy Weiss, "Passion, Rules, Art, Race Collide in 'Collection'" *Chicago Sun-Times*, 1 February 2005; "Barnes Foundation Appoints Five to Newly Expanded Board of Trustees," Associated Press, 21 January 2005; Julia M. Klien, "Barnes's Long Road to Philadelphia, *Herald Tribune*, 22 January 2005.

7. Opinion of Judge Stanley Ott in Decree Sur Second Amended Petition to Amend Charter and Bylaws, The Court of Common Pleas of Montgomery County, Pennsylvania, Orphans Court Division, No. 58,788, 13 December 2004, transcript.

8. Newman Robert Glass, "Theory and Practice in the Experience of Art: John Dewey and the Barnes Foundation," *Journal of Aesthetic Education* 31, no.3 (Fall 1997): 91–105; Roy Sieber, "Defining African Art: Primitive Negro Sculpture and the Aesthetic Philosophy of Albert Barnes," *African Arts* (Spring 2003): 40–51.

9. Jeremy Braddock, "Neurotic Cities: Barnes in Philadelphia," *Art Journal* (Winter 2004).

10. John Dewey, *Art as Experience* (New York: Perigee Books, 1934). In the preface to this book, Dewey wrote, "My greatest indebtedness is to Dr. A. C. Barnes. The

chapters have been gone over one by one with him and yet what I owe to his comments and suggestions on this account is but a small measure of my debt. I have had the benefit of conversations with him through a period of years, many of which occurred in the presence of the unrivaled collection of pictures he has assembled. The influence of these conversations together with that of his books has been a chief factor in shaping my own thinking about the philosophy of esthetics" (p. viii). In addition the book is dedicated "Albert C. Barnes, in gratitude" (p. vi).

11. Vincent Jubilee, "The Barnes Foundation: Pioneer Patron of Black Artists," *Journal of Negro Education* 51, no. 1 (Winter 1982): 43–46.
12. According to the Don Kramer of the *NonProfit Times*, "Although [the court's] opinion is actual legal precedent in only one county in Pennsylvania, it helps determine the general climate for challenges to restrictions placed on charitable gifts for donors throughout the country. It may also suggest to 'alpha donors' [large donors] that they can sway court opinions by withholding funding unless the court agrees to the alpha donors' conditions." See Don Kramer, "Court Allows Barnes Foundation to Move Collection to Philadelphia," *NonProfit Times*, 16 December 2004–15 January 2005 (www.nonprofittimes.com).
13. Greenfield, *The Devil and Dr. Barnes*.
14. Ibid., 25
15. Ibid., 24
16. Ibid., 56
17. Ibid.
18. Barnes's disagreements with the University of Pennsylvania began in 1924 when he tried to organize a joint class between the Barnes Foundation and the University and was greeted with a barrage of ridicule from conservatives in all corners of Philadelphia's art establishment. Barnes received a similar rebuff when he tried to make his collections available to the Philadelphia public school system at the same time. Barnes's subsequent attempts at collaboration with Penn also failed but this was as much the fault of Barnes's intransigence and desire for control as lack of interest by the University. See Greenfield, *The Devil and Dr. Barnes*.
19. Albert Barnes, *The Art in Painting* (New York: Harcourt, Brace, 1925), 354; see also Albert Barnes, *Art and Education* (Philadelphia: The Barnes Foundation Press, 1929).
20. Sieber, "Defining African Art."
21. Paul Guillaume and Thomas Munro, *Primitive Negro Sculpture* (New York: Harcourt, Brace, 1926), 1
22. Ibid., 6.
23. Ibid., 6.
24. Gilbert M. Cantor, *The Barnes Foundation: Reality vs. Myth* (Philadelphia: Chilton, 1963), 78.
25. David Levering Lewis, *When Harlem Was in Vogue* (New York: Oxford University Press, 1979).
26. Patrick J. Gilpin and Marybeth Gasman, *Charles S. Johnson: Leadership beyond the Veil in the Age of Jim Crow* (New York: State University of New York, 2003).
27. Jubilee, "The Barnes Foundation."
28. Ibid., 47
29. Bertrand Russell Archive, McMaster University, Canada.
30. Greenfield, *Devil and Doctor Barnes*, 281.
31. William D. Johnson, "Lincoln University," University of Pennsylvania Rare Documents Collection, 1867.
32. Horace Mann Bond, *Education for Freedmen: A History of Lincoln University* (New Jersey: Princeton University Press, 1976), 23.

33. Wayne J. Urban, *Black Scholar: Horace Mann Bond* (Athens: The University of Georgia, 1992).
34. Greenfield, *Devil and Dr. Barnes*, 281.
35. Greenfield, *Devil and Dr. Barnes*; Urban, *Black Scholar*.
36. Lincoln University bulletin, January 1951, Lincoln University Archives, Lincoln, Pa. (p. 31).
37. Lincoln University bulletin, 1950–51, Lincoln University Archives (p. 32–33).
38. Lincoln University bulletin, 1950–51, Lincoln University Archives.
39. Greenfield, *Devil and Dr. Barnes*.
40. Lincoln University bulletin, 1955–56, Lincoln University Archives.
41. J. Newton Hill to Horace Mann Bond, 16 February 1954, Horace Mann Bond Papers, Lincoln University Archives.
42. J. Newton Hill to Horace Mann Bond, 16 February 1954.
43. Greenfield, *Devil and Dr. Barnes*.
44. Marybeth Gasman and Edward Epstein, "Modern Art in the Old South: The Role of the Arts in Fisk University's Campus Curriculum," *Educational Researcher* 31, no. 2 (March 2002): 13–20.
45. Greenfield, *Devil and Dr. Barnes*.
46. Greenfield, *Devil and Dr. Barnes*; Anderson, *Battle Over the Barnes Collection*; William Schack, *Art and Argyrol: The Life and Career of Dr. Albert Barnes* (New York: Thomas Yosloff, 1960).
47. Cantor, *The Barnes Foundation*, 77.
48. Sieber, *Defining African Art*, 51.
49. Alain Locke, *The New Negro* (New York: Simon & Schuster, 1925).
50. See for example, Christopher Jencks and David Riesman, "Negroes and their Colleges," *The Academic Revolution* (Illinois: The University of Chicago Press, 1968), 406–479.
51. By-Laws of the Barnes Foundation, 1951.
52. Opinion of Judge Stanley Ott in Decree Sur Second Amended Petition to Amend Charter and Bylaws, The Court of Common Pleas of Montgomery County, Pennsylvania, Orphans Court Division, No. 58,788, 13 December 2004, transcript; Barnes Watch, "The Vultures Return" (www.barneswatch.org, 1994).
53. Opinion of Judge Stanley Ott, 1.
54. Don Kramer, "Court Allows Barnes Foundation to Move Collection to Philadelphia," *NonProfit Times*, 16 December 2004–15 January 2005 (www.nonprofittimes.com).
55. Opinion of Judge Stanley Ott, 1.
56. Greenfield, *The Devil and Dr. Barnes*, 136.

Selected Recent Dissertations in the History of Higher Education

The dissertations listed here are selected from titles supplied by Proquest. Copies of most titles can be ordered by calling 800-521-3042 or via the World Wide Web at www.umi.com. The abstracts have been abridged (with apologies to the authors) to convey the general thrust of the study. Since these titles were compiled from a key word search, some relevant titles may have been overlooked. To achieve more complete coverage, I invite readers to encourage recipients of doctorates in the history of higher education to send *Perspectives on the History of Higher Education* an abstract of their dissertations for possible inclusion in this section.

R.G.

Avery, Vida L. *A Fateful Hour in Black Higher Education: The Creation of the Atlanta University System*. Georgia State University, Ph.D., 2003, 308 pp.

Order No. 3110121

The affiliation of Atlanta University, Morehouse College, and Spelman College was a monumental event in 1929; yet the story of the creation of the Atlanta University System has not been told. John Hope, the first black president of Morehouse College and Atlanta University, was simultaneously president of both institutions. After considering the historiography of philanthropists' involvement in black higher education and their relationship with black college leaders, this dissertation recounts the circumstances surrounding the affiliation in 1929. This dissertation illustrates how one black college president established a relationship with philanthropists, particularly with members of the General Education Board, that went beyond the simple categories of benefactor and recipient. This dissertation also illustrates how philanthropists' positive involvement in black higher education produced a unique higher educational center for blacks.

Bacon, Patricia Rowland. *White Town/Black Gown: The Role of Kentucky State College in the Desegregation of Frankfort, Kentucky, 1940–1962.* University of Kentucky, Ph.D., 2004, 182 pp.

Order No. 3133588

Kentucky State University is a historically black school located in Frankfort, the predominately white capital of Kentucky. From 1940 through 1962, as the Civil Rights Movement gained momentum, the school, known during most of that period as Kentucky State College, played a significant role in the desegregation of public accommodations within the Frankfort community. Working under the constraints of "separate but equal" and skillfully using techniques of negotiation, President Rufus B. Atwood and a dedicated faculty built Kentucky State College from hardly more than a high school in 1929 into a fully accredited four-year college by 1939. Atwood's leadership style and gradualist approach to civil rights was not acceptable to some younger faculty and students who, through affiliation with the Congress of Racial Equality, brought a portion of the campus community into direct confrontation with the white Frankfort community. In Frankfort, where black citizens had achieved and held the right to vote since the late 1800s, voting was not an issue. Neither did the college become involved in desegregation of the local public schools. Battles for equal access centered on public accommodation, especially the integration of recreational facilities and eating establishments. Intergenerational conflict on campus regarding restrictive policies governing student conduct became intertwined with the movement for civil rights, resulting in the burning of the school gymnasium, the expulsion of twelve students, and the firing of two faculty members. Campus turmoil delayed somewhat the push toward integration, but under the leadership of the National Association for the Advancement of Colored People, with a Kentucky State College faculty member as president, protest efforts ultimately resumed. By 1962, at least token integration of public accommodations in the Frankfort community had been achieved.

Bouman, Jeffrey P. *Nonsectarian, Not Secular: Students' Curricular and Co-Curricular Experience with Christian Faith at Brown University, the University of Michigan, and Cornell University, 1850–1920.* University of Michigan, Ph.D., 2004, 358 pp.

Order No. 3138117

Research examining the relationship between Christianity and American higher education between 1850 and 1920 has tended to overlook the experiences of students, focusing instead on an institutional posture toward religion. Historians have often conflated the evolution from an evangelical Protestant conception of knowledge, to the scientific, positivistic notion of knowledge with the secularization of the university. However, rather than a quick removal of religion from the university, this era produced secularization, only after many years of pan-Protestant nonsectarianism. This dissertation examines curricular shifts and student religious experiences. Faculty members in this period remained religious, but were increasingly unlikely to include religious beliefs in course curricula. This failure led to the relegation of religious ideas to the periphery of the academic curriculum, but this marginalization of religious thought did not mean that religion became unimportant in the minds of presidents, in the mission of the university, or in the lives of students and faculty. For students in particular, religion often remained central. Students at Brown, Cornell, and Michigan during this period experienced the confluence of religious faith and higher education in multiple ways that provide a greater understanding of the intersection between faith and knowledge during the rise of the American university. Student activities became more overtly religious between 1870 and 1910, with the Progressive Era impulse toward social service, and the evangelical tendency toward "mission" serving as the best evidence for this important shift.

Breaux, Richard Melvin. *"We Must Fight Race Prejudice Even More Vigorously in the North": Black Higher Education in America's Heartland, 1900–1940*. The University of Iowa, Ph.D., 2003, 506 pp.
Order No. 3097521

This study examines the collegiate experiences of black students at four predominantly white state universities in the western Midwest from 1900 to 1940. It explores how black students, inspired by an emerging and changing New Negro consciousness, or "New Negroism," empowered themselves both because of, and despite racism at the University of Kansas, the University of Iowa, the University of Minnesota, and the University of Nebraska. This study hopes to fill gaps in the existing literature on blacks at predominantly white colleges in the first four decades of the twentieth century. This study begins with an overview of black students' experiences at these four universities before 1900, it then explores how black college students fit into the political milieu that characterized the black political scene in the early twentieth century. It also explores the cultural significance of black Greek-letters organizations and sports. Finally, this work interrogates black students' intellectual and academic experiences in the context of larger social movements such as the New Negro arts and letters movement in the 1920s and 1930s and the Chicago arts movement in the 1930s and 1940s. It concludes with the argument that black students at white colleges between 1900 and 1940 did not passively accept racism; but rather these students used the resources provided by local black communities to fight racism and empower themselves in the face of white supremacy.

Brown, Mary Jude. *Souls in the Balance: The "Heresy Affair" at the University of Dayton, 1960–1967*. The University of Dayton, Ph.D., 2003, 368 pp.

Order No. 3108843

This dissertation examines the "Heresy Affair" at the University of Dayton, a series of events predominantly in the philosophy department that occurred when tensions between the Thomists and proponents of new philosophies reached crisis stage in fall 1966. The "Affair" culminated in a letter written by an assistant professor at Dayton to the Cincinnati archbishop, Karl J. Alter. In the letter, the professor cited a number of instances where "erroneous teachings" were "endorsed" or "openly advocated" by four faculty members. Concerned about the pastoral impact on the University of Dayton community, the professor asked the archbishop to conduct an investigation. This study uses theological and historical analysis to explore the theological, philosophical, and educational assumptions that underlie and are expressed in the positions espoused in the "Heresy Affair." As a case study, this dissertation shows how one particular American Catholic university struggled to achieve academic legitimacy. In telling the story of the "Heresy Affair" at the University of Dayton, the dissertation illuminates the tensions within the Catholic Church and between American and Catholic as applied to higher education.

Burley, Virginia R. *The Emergence of the Academic Department at the University of California: A Historical Study*. The Claremont Graduate University, Ph.D., 2004, 355 pp.

Order No. 3133218

This study explores the historical emergence of the academic department at the end of the nineteenth century. It particularly examines the role played by academic departments in establishing faculty influence within the emerging university structure, the function of the department as an organizational unit in the modern university, and the ways in which the department helped to establish a dimension of power for the faculty. Seeking to distinguish the forms of faculty power established through the department and the senate, the study examines historical data from the University of California during the first five decades of its existence. The study attempts to explore the complex institutional dynamics giving rise to academic departments as this University sought to establish itself as a top-tier institution. Departments emerged as dynamic structures responsive to the multiple demands facing the University from both external constituencies and the academic disciplines. The organization of departments was based predominantly on the efforts of the faculty who functioned as primary sources of information and consultation in the development of a university of national standing. The informal communication between the faculty and administration established a significant basis for critical institutional decisions on facilities, staffing, new directions, and emerging disciplines. Firmly rooted in disciplinary expertise, a deeply engaged faculty assumed an essential role at the department level in guiding the institution. Exploring the complex contributions of the faculty reveals a significant generative power distinguishable from the regulatory power of the academic senate. Largely underplayed or ignored in higher education history, the academic department is revealed as the chief avenue for faculty participation in complex governance systems.

Chen, John Shujie. *Catholic Higher Education in China: The Rise and Fall of Fu Ren University in Beijing.* Boston College, Ph.D., 2003, 365 pp.

Order No. 3103210

This dissertation tells a more complete story of the rise and fall of Fu Ren University (1925–1952) and provides an analysis of a key Catholic higher education institution in China. The theme of the discussion is to show the unique nature of Fu Ren University as both Western Catholic and Chinese. Fu Ren played significant roles in both the Catholic Church and Chinese higher education. Fu Ren University was the only private university in China initiated by Chinese and sponsored by non-Chinese. Two famous Chinese Catholic scholars petitioned the Pope in Rome to send "learned men, meek and humble of heart" from different nationalities to establish a Catholic university in Beijing to study Chinese literature and to introduce Western sciences. Under the leadership of both American Cassinese-Benedictines and the Divine Word Fathers, as well as the Chinese university president, Fu Ren University achieved its goal to be a prestigious university in China in spite of political turmoil and war. Within its twenty-seven years of existence, Fu Ren University went through four different governments: Warlord, Nationalist, Japanese, and Communist. It developed from a small preparatory academy to a university with six colleges and many graduate programs. The dual nature of Fu Ren University as Catholic and Chinese is demonstrated in the conclusion's analysis of (1) the petition and mission of the university, (2) Rome and Benedictine's interests, (3) curriculum development, (4) faculty, and (5) political entanglements. Fu Ren University indeed marked a new beginning for the Catholic Church mission in China.

Elias, Megan J. *Stir It Up: Home Economics in Higher Education, 1900–1945*. City University of New York, Ph.D., 2003, 251 pp.

Order No. 3103106

At the end of the nineteenth century, home economics emerged as an academic discipline in higher education. Theorists of the movement advocated a changed vision of society based in new ideas about the domestic environment. Home economists professionalized a body of knowledge and practice that had hitherto been considered private and natural. Leaders of the movement incorporated new ideas of scientific management and vocational education into their discipline. The predominantly female leaders of the movement gathered a rich assortment of disciplines under one roof. Social science and hard science, urban planning, and clothing design, as well as courses that prefigured women's study curricula found a place within home economics. Focusing on the movement between the years 1900 and 1945, this dissertation describes how founders of home economics conceptualized their discipline, how they secured cultural and academic authority for it and themselves, and to what extent the movement they created was successful in its goals.

Griffin, Peter James. *A History of the Illinois Industrial University/ University of Illinois Band, 1867–1908.* University of Illinois at Urbana-Champaign, Ed.D., 2004, 218 pp.

Order No. 3130925

This study provides a comprehensive history of the band program at the Illinois Industrial University/University of Illinois between the years 1867 and 1908. In 1885 the University changed its name to the University of Illinois from the Illinois Industrial University. The University has been a leader in the field of bands, band music, and music education for well over a century. The history of its band program during the first forty years of its existence is presented with great detail in the following four areas: (1) the leadership of the band during this time frame, (2) the role of the band, (3) the personnel of the band, and (4) the repertoire of the band. Specific attention is given to correcting discrepancies between known sources and filling gaps of missing information that previously existed.

Harrington, Nan Katharine. *Student Activism and University Reform in England, France, and Germany, 1960's–1970's.* The University of Texas at Austin, Ph.D., 2003, 322 pp.

Order No. 3116322

University reform has become one of the most important issues of the past three decades. Initiated in the turbulent 1960s as a response to demands for change, the governments of England, France, and Germany sought to provide change to their centuries-old systems of higher education, largely through politically expedient measures of reform. This study seeks to answer the question: With the passage of time, how effective were student demands for reform? Research indicated that student activism was neither the sole, nor the prime, impetus for higher educational reform in the Sixties, but rather served a supplementary role, that of illustrating the exigency for legislative action. Students of the Sixties, however, changed the perception of the student role within the family, the university, and society; brought educational issues to the public consciousness; advanced the issue of accountability in academia; and earned students the acknowledgement of being a viable social force.

John, Barbara Bastendorf. *Educating Pennsylvania Germans: Franklin College in the Early Republic.* The Pennsylvania State University, Ph.D., 2003, 233 pp.

Order No. 3096989

Franklin College, founded in 1787 in Lancaster, Pennsylvania, was the first college for Germans in America and seemed initially to enjoy the support of the most powerful currents in late eighteenth-century American society: religion and politics. However, within three years, the religious and political divisions and loyalties among the various constituencies associated with the institution affected its success, and the fledgling institution failed. The founders of Franklin College were leading clergymen in the Lutheran and German Reformed churches in America. The trustees were among the most prominent politicians, businessmen, and professionals in America and included four signers of the Declaration of Independence, two future governors of Pennsylvania, and two future United States senators. In the eighteenth century, Lancaster County was the center of the German population in Pennsylvania—a population that held fast to a strong ethnic identity shaped by religion and language: Lutheran, German Reformed, Mennonite, German Baptist, Moravian, and Seventh Day Baptist. The Pennsylvania Germans held varying and, in some cases, contradictory views of education. The men who signed the petition to the Pennsylvania Assembly for the establishment of the college and the trustees of the institution had diverse religious and political affiliations and had personal agendas, grounded either in their religious convictions or political pragmatism, which were inimical to the success of the new institution. The clerics' vision and the politicians' aim for the provision of higher education to the Pennsylvania Germans were different. If the clerics and politicians hoped that religion would serve as the cement that held Franklin College together, they were wrong. The failure of Franklin College was rooted in the founding alliance, the religious and political issues associated with the alliance, and the attitudes of many Pennsylvania Germans regarding education, especially higher education. Franklin College was the first college founded in America affiliated with more than one religious denomination—an attempt at ecumenism before the movement toward ecumenism became part of the fabric of the American experience.

Jones, Stephen Alan. *The Revolution Will Not Be Televised: Black Studies and the Transformation of American Higher Education, 1967–1972*. Michigan State University, Ph.D., 2003, 301 pp.

Order No. 3100440

This dissertation examines the emergence of the Black Studies movement in the late 1960s and explores the impact that movement had on American higher education. It seeks to place the Black Studies movement in the context of the long history of higher education in the United States and explore how the movement was influenced by, and in turn influenced, the patterns of institutional change. It argues that the depth and significance of the movement's impact was obscured by the intensity and political nature of the turmoil that surrounded the creation of Black Studies programs. It also argues that while the turmoil of protest and confrontation and the clamoring rhetoric of political revolution captured the attention of the news media and the American public, the Black Studies movement actually led a less obvious, "untelevised" revolution in awareness that changed the patterns of intellectual activity in academia.

Lockwood, Nadine Sherri. *Bennett College for Women, 1926–1966*. State University of New York at Buffalo, Ph.D., 2004, 330 pp.

Order No. 3125735

Bennett College for Women, located in Greensboro, North Carolina, is one of two remaining institutions of higher education (Spelman College in Atlanta, Georgia, founded in 1881, is the other) for African American women. Unlike Spelman College, Bennett College was originally founded in 1873 as a coeducational institution. In 1926, the Methodist Episcopal Church reorganized the institution as a college for African American women. Educational historians, as well as black and women's history scholars, have largely ignored this history. This research documents the changes in educational philosophies and practices of Bennett College for Women from 1926 to 1966. Traditionally, the academic and student life curricula at Bennett College were designed to promote social justice for its students. Throughout the history of Bennett College, much emphasis has been placed upon "service," that is, race uplift or service to one's people. Young African American women prepared for service in their church community, homes, local community, as well as society at large. The research illustrates how Bennett College for Women graduates were prepared for "service" while undergraduate students.

Miller, Elisa. *In the Name of the Home: Women, Domestic Science, and American Higher Education, 1865–1930.* University of Illinois at Urbana-Champaign, Ph.D., 2004, 331 pp.

Order No. 3130983

This dissertation examines the development of domestic science as an academic field for American women at the turn of the century. In this period, domestic science transcended the private sphere and emerged as an ideology of political and public domesticity in response to the anxieties engendered by the massive transformations of the Progressive Era. The field became a way to contain or moderate the processes of modernity, including immigration, urbanization, and industrialization. In this context, domestic science was viewed as a solution to a wide range of social problems, from racial tensions and labor strife to "race suicide" and the decline in rural populations. These social problems centered on issues of race, class, ethnicity, and region. The author examined four educational institutions to explore the influence of these variables on the history of domestic science. These schools included Hampton Institute, Teachers College, the University of Illinois, and Vassar College. These institutions reveal how race, region, ethnicity, and class shaped the formation of the field and created disparate sets of obstacles and opportunities for American women. For white, middle-class women, domestic science emphasized the value of modernization and science to progress. In contrast, for Native American, African American, white working-class, and immigrant women, domestic science centered around Christianity, civilization, citizenship, and domestic service. Domestic science in this period was wrought with contradictions, with women pursuing disparate, and often incompatible, objectives. These women employed a variety of tactics in order to establish, resist, and reconfigure the ideology and practice of domestic science. Although some women viewed domestic science as a form of social control, for others it provided a feminized sphere in which to pursue career, family, and reform goals.

Mngomezulu, Bhekithemba Richard. *A Political History of Higher Education in East Africa: The Rise and Fall of the University of East Africa, 1937–1970.* Rice University, Ph.D. 2004, 490 pp.

Order No. 3122509

From the 1920s Britain started formulating educational policies for its African colonies as part of the overall imperial policy and in response to African agitation for higher education. In 1937, the publication of the De la Warr Commission Report set in motion a long drawn-out process of establishing the federal University of East Africa. Subsequently, territorial and inter-territorial tensions regarding the nature and function of the envisaged regional University emerged and continued up to independence. After independence, the spirit of nationalism and the divergent policies followed by East African nation-states exacerbated the tensions regarding the anticipated University. When the University was inaugurated in June 1963, these tensions made it inevitable that the University would split. In a sense, the University of East Africa was a stillborn entity. This study explores the tensions within the history of the University of East Africa with the view to establishing why it was established and why it disintegrated in 1970. The study analyzes these tensions at four levels: (1) the tensions that emerged between the British authorities and East African constituencies when the idea of a regional University was conceived during the colonial period; (2) the tensions between the British government and its Governors and Directors of Education in East Africa during the 1920s and 1930s; (3) inter-territorial tensions in East Africa before and after independence; and (4) sustained tensions within each territory.

Mucher, Stephen Shepherd. *Subject Matter and Method in the Preparation of High School Teachers: Pedagogy and Teacher Education at the University of Michigan, 1871–1921.* University of Michigan, Ph.D., 2003, 350 pp.

Order No. 3106129

Many histories of teacher education describe enduring conflict between university faculty in the arts and sciences and their colleagues in education departments. This case study of the University of Michigan, an institution that played a unique and pioneering role in the education of teachers, indicates that such conflict was rare in the nineteenth century. Historical evidence points to considerable collaboration between faculty in the subject matter disciplines and the professors appointed to give instruction in the Sciences and Art of Teaching. Well before it established the nation's first permanent Chair of Pedagogy in 1879, the University offered lectures on the principles of teaching and instituted a special Teachers Course. An emerging agreement over how to best prepare teachers was profoundly influenced by the Diploma System for college admissions wherein professors made annual accreditation visits to area high schools. These visits focused intently on teaching practices and reinforced for the faculty the belief that well-prepared teachers possessed a uniquely deep understanding of the subject matter they taught. By the 1890s, faculty members from a variety of fields at both the University and at the Michigan State Normal School in Ypsilanti had helped create the Michigan Schoolmasters Club and the North Central Association of Schools and Colleges to further strengthen the consensus on teacher preparation. This consensus, however, gave way to conflict in the early twentieth century. Growing high school enrollments and a changing secondary curriculum helped redefine the type of teacher that administrative progressives recruited for modern classrooms. Similarly, a new generation of university-based teacher educators drew clear distinctions between subject matter and method, campaigned for increased departmental autonomy, introduced an increasingly technical conception of method, and effectively lobbied outside professional organizations to endorse these sharp new divisions. The product of these efforts was the modern multipurpose school of education. One result of this institutional evolution was the disappearance of rich conversations about what teachers needed to know about their subject matter disciplines and how this knowledge related to the instructional methods offered by education professors. This separation of subject matter and method continues to plague teacher preparation today.

Pruitt, Samory. *A Reflection of Student Desegregation at the University of Alabama as Seen Through the Eyes of Some Pioneering African-American Students: 1956–1976.* The University of Alabama, Ph.D., 2003, 606 pp.

Order No. 3115070

The University of Alabama admitted its first African American student, Autherine Lucy, in 1956, 125 years after its founding. This event was a pivotal point in the history of the University, the state, and the nation because it focused attention on the growing discussion about race and equality for all citizens. The violence surrounding the enrollment of Autherine Lucy in the 1950s, followed by the infamous "Stand in the School House Door" by Governor Wallace in the 1960s, placed the University of Alabama in the debate about race relations in America. The state became the venue challenging the United States' commitment toward equality of opportunity for all of its citizens, including quality and excellence in higher education. The students involved in this desegregation were "pioneers" whose courage and sacrifice ultimately forced a constitutional crisis on states' rights to sovereignty versus the responsibility of the federal government to intervene in protecting its citizens' rights. Historically, African American contributions to the American way of life have been marginalized. This historical study was intended to help address this deficit. It documents the history of desegregation at the University and gives "voice" and narration to the experiences and contributions of the African American students who "pioneered" there from 1956 through 1976. Oral narrative history interviews with them detail the emotional and intellectual orientation of these students as well as a clearer narration of their personal aspirations, courage, and commitment to achieve. By successfully challenging and dismantling previously established racial barriers and stereotypes in the state that was the focal point of the national Civil Rights Movement, they have contributed significantly to the history and the development of the University of Alabama and the nation.

Richardson, Susan R. *Oil, Power, and Universities: Political Struggle and Academic Advancement at the University of Texas and Texas A&M University, 1876-1965.* Pennsylvania State University, Ph.D., 2005, 430 pp.

Order No. NA

This study traces the development of the University of Texas (UT) and Texas A&M (A&M) from their establishment in the 1870s and 1880s to the gradual collapse of desegregation and oppressive governmental control in the early 1960s. UT and A&M did not begin to become competitive with public universities nationally until after the elimination of segregation and excessive government control in the late 1950s and early 1960s. Throughout the period under study, UT and Texas A&M were hampered by low state appropriations, hostility towards higher education within the state government, battles to gain control over the Permanent University Fund (PUF), segregation, and paranoia rooted in racism and anticommunism. These conditions inhibited research activity and the improvement of academic standards, limited access to higher education for Texans, and compromised academic freedom. In addition, debates at A&M regarding the legitimacy and practicality of an all-male student body (until 1963) and compulsory military training (abolished for the final time in 1965) overshadowed the institution's academic and research aspirations. The thesis analyzes the impact of state government on higher education in Texas. To a lesser extent, the study describes the development of UT and A&M in relation to higher education in the United States between the 1880s and 1960s. Primary sources were consulted at the Texas State Library and Archives Commission (TSLAC) in Austin, the University of Texas Center for American History.

Thomas, Auden D. *From Vision to Action: Jill Conway at Smith College*. Indiana University, Ph.D., 2004, 289 pp.

Order No. 3133868

This historical study examines how Jill Ker Conway articulated and enacted her commitment to women's equality as Smith College's first woman president (1975–1985). Conway's desire to improve the social, economic, and intellectual conditions of women's lives informed her presidency of the elite women's college during a tenure that coincided with the height of the modern women's movement. Her actions, not always welcomed at Smith, brought the self-identified feminist into dynamic association with an institution in need of modernization. She consciously used her presidency to shape the College's policies, practices, and culture toward active support of the women students it educated, and to advance women's equality and opportunity beyond the College itself. In this study, her feminist vision, voice, and actions are refracted through the lens of her Smith College presidency to reveal a portrait of a woman who simultaneously advanced the cause of a selective liberal arts women's college and advocated broader social change for women. This study considers three aspects of Conway's presidency that illuminate her vision for women's education and their careers after college: (1) programmatic and policy emphases at Smith College; (2) fundraising efforts in support of women focused initiatives at the College; and (3) her national advocacy to strengthen women's colleges and higher education policy affecting women. The research addresses the following questions: How did Conway articulate her aspirations for women's formal education and social equality? How did she enact these aspirations into campus programs and policies during her tenure as president of a women's college? What sorts of efforts did she direct at external agencies beyond higher education—corporations, foundations, and government agencies—to secure support for Smith and to improve women's social status? How did she use the platform provided by her college presidency to help shape the national agenda for women's higher education? By the concluding years of her presidency Conway had met with resounding success on some fronts but only moderate gains on others. Through it all, however, the thread of her vision for women's equality and opportunity was evident in her words and actions.

Thurston, Anne Elizabeth. *Endangered Daughter: A Life and Death Struggle of a Southern Women's College. A Case Study of Peace College, 1950–1962*. University of Kentucky, Ph.D., 2003, 265 pp.
Order No. 3097395

In the 1950s and 1960s, small, private women's colleges were typified as invisible colleges headed for extinction because of declining enrollments, financial problems, and competition from coeducational institutions. By connecting the history of higher education with the history of invisible colleges and southern women's colleges, this case study documents Peace College's struggle to gain organizational autonomy from the North Carolina Synod in order to survive. This study uses the theoretical frameworks of organizational saga from Burton Clark (1972), and invisible colleges from Astin and Lee (1972). It attempts to understand how and why Peace College was able to successfully resist closure and remain a women's college during a time when the Synod of North Carolina wanted to consolidate several of its smaller two-year institutions in order to create a four-year coeducational institution. Peace College provides a significant microcosm of the various kinds of problems many small, church-affiliated colleges faced over the last century concerning identity and survival. While Clark's theory of organizational saga was applied specifically to four-year institutions, this study shows organizational saga theory can be applied to a broader range of institutions. In addition, this study demonstrates how strong organizational character is found among invisible colleges. The most important aspect of Clark's theory is his assertion that the central ingredient in building a college of distinction is the institution's belief in itself, its mission, and its organizational character. This study of Peace College's struggle to gain autonomy from the Presbyterian Synod demonstrates the strength of its organizational character through a nucleus of leadership who determined that Peace College belonged in the educational community of North Carolina, despite the Synod's belief the institution had outlived its usefulness.

Underhill, Robin Whyte. *Founding Colleges to Protect a Protestant Heritage: Promotional Rationales for Stone-Campbell Schools, 1900–1940*. Case Western Reserve University, Ph.D., 2003, 288 pp.

Order No. 3097370

At the turn of the twentieth century, pluralism and a new intellectual climate threatened the cultural reign of American Protestantism. American Protestants invested greatly in institutions of higher education that they believed would protect and advance their values. This study reveals three concerns that Stone-Campbell leaders hoped to resolve with postsecondary education. These concerns paralleled main divisions within the Stone-Campbell movement: moral leadership for the country, safe education for one's children, and a loyal ministerial workforce for the Church. The often accepted sacred to secular declension model does not fully describe the history of American higher education. While some colleges certainly did move toward the secular, new colleges devoted to Christian purposes have continued to be founded throughout U.S. history. The standard accounts fail to note the evangelical response and reaction of Stone-Campbell leaders and others. Three denominational strands represent the legacy of Barton Stone and Thomas and Alexander Campbell: The Churches of Christ, the Christian Church (Disciples of Christ), and the Christian Churches/Churches of Christ. Stone-Campbell leaders began over four hundred colleges, academies, and institutes of various academic levels, most of which have not survived. This study examines the founding stories of twelve of the twenty surviving colleges that Stone-Campbell leaders founded between 1900 and 1940. The Disciples schools are Lynchburg, Barton, and Jarvis Colleges; Brite Divinity School; and Chapman University. Abilene Christian, Harding, and Pepperdine Universities are Churches of Christ schools. Kentucky Christian, Crossroads, Atlanta Christian Colleges, and Cincinnati Bible College and Seminary are Christian Church schools.

Weber, Christy A. *They Came Before Us: A Story of Women at Michigan State University, 1870–1895*. Michigan State University, Ph.D., 2004, 253 pp.

Order No. 3129558

There are those that stand at the forefront of any movement who intentionally or unintentionally lead the way for others and this is evident in the changing patterns of American education. Prior to the late eighteenth century, education beyond rudimentary levels provided in the home was exclusively for men in early colonial colleges. The pattern of education changed slowly as women began attending female seminaries in the eighteenth century. From this time through the nineteenth century, men and women contributed to this changing pattern by sharing perspectives both affirming and discounting female education through various modes such as books, articles, public speaking, and personal correspondence. Some institutional trustee boards and state boards of education wrestled with and began to change admissions policies, opening the doors of private and state colleges to women. In addition, parents began allowing their daughters to enroll in all-women or coeducational institutions. State colleges and universities initially were open exclusively to men. This was the case in the histories of land-grant institutions such as Michigan State University (1855). This research presentation highlights the early years of women's enrollment at Michigan State University from 1870–1895. These "first" women lived in relationship to families and people in their community, college, state, and country; these relationships influenced their decisions to attend college at a time when most women did not.

Whittenburg, Carolyn Lamb Sparks. *President J. A. C. Chandler and the First Women Faculty at the College of William and Mary*. The College of William and Mary, Ed.D., 2004, 405 pp.

Order No. 3122336

This study examines the progressive leadership of President J. A. C. Chandler in hiring the first women faculty at the College of William and Mary and explains the relationship between his presidency and his twenty-year career in education prior to 1919. During the early heyday of hiring women faculty in higher education, Chandler employed women educators at levels equal to national rates and surpassing regional standards. He did so in conjunction with his efforts to establish full coeducation at William and Mary. Chandler led a crusade to transform the College from a tiny, mostly male college into a vibrant coeducational state college. He expanded the student body by more than tenfold, made the student body gender equal, built a new campus, and created a utilitarian curriculum for vocational training. Chandler also took dynamic steps to hire women faculty at a time when most southern women educators taught in women's colleges. He hired women to teach in a wide range of disciplines, sought them nationally, and treated them equitably. His willingness to hire women came from twenty years of experience working with women teachers in Richmond. Chandler made the College a model in the employment of women faculty. Through his dream to transform the College, Chandler opened the College's doors to women faculty as well as to women students.

Williams, Christopher James. *An Historical Analysis of the Public Policy Affecting the Establishment of the Community and Technical College System in the State of Louisiana, 1972–2000.* Union Institute and University, Ph.D., 2004, 252 pp.

Order No. 3122851

This study chronicles the establishment of the Community and Technical College System in the State of Louisiana. The study provides a comprehensive history of the development of the Louisiana Community and Technical College System, and reveals the difficulties and dynamics encountered with the creation of a new system from an old system. The four conclusions are as follows: (1) The legislation that created the Louisiana Community and Technical College System arose from education and legislative forces. Other groups offered assistance after it was concluded Louisiana would have a system. (2) The Louisiana Community and Technical College System was expedited as more four-year institutions in the state moved toward selective admission. As selective admissions became a reality, community and technical colleges within the state grew. (3) Several people played a major role in establishing the Louisiana Community and Technical College System. They included Joseph E. Savoie, Commissioner of Higher Education; Governor Mike Foster; Acadiana legislators; James Caillier, former President of the University of Louisiana System; and William Perry, Governor Foster's Chief of Staff. (4) Opposition to the establishment of a new community and technical college system was minimized when established community colleges and technical colleges were brought together to work out disagreements that are a natural outgrowth of the development of a new and different system.

Wolfe, Kevin DeWayne. *Four Decades of Change at Southern Wesleyan: A Case Study of a Christian Liberal Arts College.* University of South Carolina, Ph.D., 2004, 183 pp.

Order No. 3130503

Southern Wesleyan University, an evangelical liberal arts college in upstate South Carolina, grew from two hundred students at midcentury to over two thousand by the end of the century while still striving to maintain its Christian mission. This historical case study identifies a number of changes that caused growth at Southern Wesleyan University between 1959 and 1999. The research determines, however, that the adult distance program (called LEAP) was the most significant change that led to this large increase in enrollment. The study also identifies numerous reasons for the changes at Southern Wesleyan University including: the energetic leadership of several chief executives, the desire to achieve financial viability, and the interest in securing a unique product or "niche" for the surrounding community. The research indicates that financial concerns and presidential leadership actually drove much of the change. The changes slightly affected the mission of the college but did not significantly alter it. For the traditional day students, no change in mission seemed to occur. For the large number of new adult students, however, the mission became Christian outreach as much as Christian growth. Southern Wesleyan University was chosen as a model because it achieved noticeable growth over the past forty years. Many colleges struggle with the inability to preserve their mission when faced with significant changes. Thus, the relationship between change and mission at Southern Wesleyan University also has significance at other institutions.

Contributors

Daniel A. Clark is an assistant professor in the Department of History at Indiana State University. Clark specializes in American intellectual and cultural history with a particular interest in the history of higher education. He is currently in the final stages of preparing his book manuscript, *Creating the College Man: American Mass Magazines, Masculinity, and the Corporate Middle Class, 1890–1916.*

Michael David Cohen is a doctoral candidate in history at Harvard University. He specializes in the history of higher education and of women and gender in the United States, and is currently writing a dissertation on the impact of the Civil War on American higher education. For their helpful comments on this paper, the author thanks Afseneh Najmabadi, the members of her graduate seminar in Feminist Theory and Historiography, Nancy Cott, Julie Reuben, Martin Trow, Eleanor Hannah, Katherine Chaddock, Roger Geiger, and the anonymous readers of the *History of Higher Education Annual*. For their help in locating sources, he thanks archivists Eric Hillemann at Carleton and Gary DeKrey at St. Olaf. Versions of parts of this paper were presented at the Northern Great Plains History Conference, Bismarck, North Dakota, 27–30 October 2004, and at the conference of the History of Education Society, Kansas City, Missouri, 5–7 November 2004.

Edward Epstein is a faculty member in the School of Art and Design at the University of Pennsylvania and *Marybeth Gasman* is an assistant professor in the Graduate School of Education at the University of Pennsylvania. They have published several articles together, including "Creating an Image for Black Colleges: A Visual Examination of the United Negro College Fund's Publicity, 1944–1960" in *Educational Foundations*; "Modern Art in the Old South: The Role of the Arts in Fisk University's Campus Curriculum" in *Educational Researcher*; and "Doorways to the Academy: Visual Self-Expression among Faculty in Academic Departments" in the *International Journal of Education and the Arts*. The authors would like to thank the following individuals for their insightful comments on previous drafts of this article: Roger Geiger, Kate Sedgwick, Noah Drezner, Chris Tudico, Ron Butchart, and the anonymous reviewers of the *History of Higher Education Annual*. In addition, we are grateful to Susan Pevar at the Lincoln University archives for her assistance with our research.

Susan R. Richardson recently completed her Ph.D. at Penn State. Her dissertation is entitled *Oil, Power, and Universities: Political Struggle and Academic Advancement at the University of Texas and Texas A&M University, 1876-1965*. The author thanks David Adams, Nancy Diamond, Philo Hutcheson, and Philip Jenkins for their comments on earlier versions of this paper and Roger Geiger for his assistance with the final copy.

Jane Robbins recently completed her Ph.D. in higher education management at the University of Pennsylvania. She has broad interests in the related areas of university-industry-government relations, public and institutional policies that shape the direction and availability of education and the fruits of academic research, and organizational behavior and ethical decision-making in universities. Most of her research is in the history of academic patenting and conflict of interest, and the history and reform of professional education. Her entries on gifted student programs and college preparation will appear in the forthcoming *Encyclopedia of the American High School*. The author appreciates the useful comments on an earlier version of this paper from Roger Geiger, Marybeth Gasman, and two anonymous reviewers. This paper was also presented at History of Education Society Annual Meeting, Kansas City, Missouri, November 3–7, 2004.

Perspectives
The current issue of *Perspectives* is available at $29.95 plus $5.50 shipping/handling. Orders should be prepaid in U.S. funds payable to: Transaction Publishers, 390 Campus Drive, Somerset, NJ 08873. Standing Order plans are available; please contact Transaction Order Dept. for details at address above or telephone 732-445-1245 or e-mail orders@transactionpub.com.

Back Issues and Sets of the History of Higher Education Annual
Single copies of Vol. 1 through 22 are available at $24.95 per volume plus $5.50 shipping/handling. Full sets (V1-V22) available for $274.45, shipping/handling additional. Send orders to above address.

Manuscripts
Perspectives on the History of Higher Education welcomes manuscript contributions for consideration in future volumes. Manuscripts should be submitted in triplicate, typed double-spaced (including quotations and endnotes) on 8 1/2 x 11 paper, with ample margins. Authors should follow the *Chicago Manual of Style*, 15th edition. The author's name, affiliation, telephone number, and E-mail address should appear on a separate cover page to insure anonymity in the reviewing process. Manuscripts should be submitted to Roger Geiger, Editor, *Perspectives on the History of Higher Education*, Higher Education Program, The Pennsylvania State University, 400 Rackley Building, University Park, PA 16802-3201. Inquiries regarding contributions are welcome and should be directed to the Editor via mail, telephone, or electronic mail. Telephone: (814) 863-3784; E-mail: rlg9@psu.edu

Web Address
http://www.ed.psu.edu/hied/annual/default.htm
http://www.transactionpub.com (editorial office)

For Product Safety Concerns and Information please contact our EU
representative GPSR@taylorandfrancis.com
Taylor & Francis Verlag GmbH, Kaufingerstraße 24, 80331 München, Germany

www.ingramcontent.com/pod-product-compliance
Lightning Source LLC
Chambersburg PA
CBHW062227300426
44115CB00012BA/2242